T0354286

Behind the Ether Screen

Memoirs of an Anesthesiologist

Gabriele F. Roden, MD

iUniverse, Inc.
New York   Bloomington

Behind the Ether Screen
Memoirs of an Anesthesiologist

Copyright © 2009 Gabriele F. Roden, MD

All rights reserved. No part of this book may be used or reproduced by any means,
graphic, electronic, or mechanical, including photocopying, recording, taping or by
any information storage retrieval system without the written permission of the publisher
except in the case of brief quotations embodied in critical articles and reviews.

iUniverse books may be ordered through booksellers or by contacting:

iUniverse
1663 Liberty Drive
Bloomington, IN 47403
www.iuniverse.com
1-800-Authors (1-800-288-4677)

Because of the dynamic nature of the Internet, any Web addresses or links contained in this
book may have changed since publication and may no longer be valid. The views expressed
in this work are solely those of the author and do not necessarily reflect the views of the
publisher, and the publisher hereby disclaims any responsibility for them.

ISBN: 978-1-4401-5063-0 (pbk)
ISBN: 978-1-4401-5066-1 (cloth)
ISBN: 978-1-4401-5065-4 (ebook)

Library of Congress Control Number: 2009932493

Printed in the United States of America

iUniverse rev. date: 12/1/09

In loving memory of my mother, Felicitas,
who never asked for anything.

Contents

Acknowledgments

I first wish to thank those who unconditionally supported me with never-failing empathy throughout the difficult challenges of my life. Family and friends made me believe in my inherent strength to overcome my own demons. Together they offered more encouragement and acts of kindness than I could ever write about in my lifetime.

I want to acknowledge and express my deep gratitude to my most eminent teacher, without whom this book would never have been started, much less completed. Kathryn Deputat's workshop "Releasing the Writer Within" unleashed the stream of my memoirs and kept my pen moving for ten years. She taught me to focus and gave me a voice on the page. Her thoughtful pauses provided a safe place for me to fill the gaps. Never making judgments about good or bad, just "tell me more," was all she would say. She made me empty the contents of my pockets of long-forgotten memories and bring them back not only to life but also into a new light. She had a unique talent to hear what I didn't dare to say long before I wrote it.

I believe that we can do and endure all things when we feel loved. I am deeply grateful to my husband, Bob, who for twenty years has unselfishly devoted his energy and generous spirit to my wellbeing. Knowing that I have operated from my left brain for most of my work, Bob has encouraged, supported, and inspired my atrophied creativity in many ways. I am most indebted to him for allowing me quiet time to write and creating a serene environment. The quiet light that washed over his colorful fine art paintings not only inspired me but also thawed out my deep freeze after long days in the OR. I most appreciated his loving support the days I came home without a smile. When the time came to think about the cover design for this book, he put his talents as a graphic designer to work and spontaneously created a concept.

Even though it has been years since she passed away, I still miss my mother's enthusiasm about my personal goals. I remember the afternoon tea when I told her about my intention to write a book. She always took great pleasure in my early writings and poems, especially my handwritten birthday wishes, when we were separated by an ocean, though never in our hearts. I will never forget her quiet tears, disguised with yet another smile, when I told her that I would dedicate this book to her. When I bring her graciousness to patients' bedsides, patients remember me.

My father was a dominant and difficult force in my life who loomed large in my childhood. I am grateful for his insistence on discipline and excellence that has made me successful in my endeavors, both professional and personal. I am also indebted to my father's infinite passion for the written word, which he passed on to me.

My older brother, Axel, remains the closest eyewitness of my childhood and professional development. His kind manuscript review of our early years revealed a fascinating coincidence in our immediate neighborhood. Though I was too young to appreciate its complexity then, this historic detail lent new insight to my story.

It was Axel's devotion and care of my failing mother over the ten years of her decline that allowed me to continue my work without interruption here in the United States. I am immensely grateful to Axel, who compensated for my mother's illness by his offer to take charge. It was at Axel's insistence that I brought this manuscript to print.

My younger sister, Cita, has also contributed greatly to my courage to write. She provided a most loving, yet intelligent and fair-minded, sounding board, while acknowledging my writing efforts with the keen skill of a language teacher and a literary scholar. Earlier drafts of this book gave my sister opportunity to voice similar childhood experiences that lay dormant. This sharing brought us closer than ever, and we have come to embrace each other as our greatest supporters. Perhaps most importantly, my recall of our childhood memories in these pages has created a special bond between my brother, my sister, and me, irrespective of our different lifestyles and geographic distances. Our irrevocable tie further inspired me to document the snapshots of our childhood.

Oh yes, and then there is my providential family of friends, Lucy, Phyllis, Emilie, Lily,

Calypso, and Shannon, for whom I would do anything. I would go to any length to say thank you for the years they have carried me on their wings of experience, fortitude, or just good common sense that sustained me through periods of fear and doubt. Two friends and teachers, Christian and Irene, and also my uncle Felix, deserve my deep gratitude for their inspiration and encouragement with this project. I greatly appreciate their gift of keeping my old European traditions and heritage alive.

Ultimately this book is a tribute to all who have witnessed and contributed to my grand yet humble journey inside and outside the operating room.

*It's not the answer that enlightens,
but the question.*

Eugene Ionesco

Prologue

The writing of this memoir began with a question.

"What do you think about when you sit hour after hour with a patient who is anesthetized?"

I don't remember who asked, but to me it was a pivotal moment.

This question not only intrigued me but also begged for an introspective answer. From that moment, while the steady heartbeat of my patients marched across the monitor, I began to pay more attention to my thought process. I explored my relationship with the patient beyond the mechanical delivery of a mixture of anesthetic gases. On the subway ride home each night, I recorded impressions, stories, and memories of those incidents that somehow struck an inner chord.

For most of my career my encounters with patients were fleeting. Sometimes I wanted to linger with them longer than the allocated time. Even though it often appeared a unilateral relationship, with all the action on my part, there was a unique essence of each patient that adhered to me like a post-it note. Certain patients remained on my mind by way of thank you notes, a word of advice, homemade cookies, or a good scare.

I weaved their stories along with mine to give gravity to the ethereal nature of our interactions and to make them last. I am deeply grateful to all of my patients who collectively transformed me into the person I have become.

Somewhere I still have bundled some old letters and poems, written in the 1930s, now discolored with age. They are authored by the father of a dear friend and business associate of my father. These poems bear witness of a deep soul speckled with suffering and hope. Here, on a brittle page, stood a noble man whom I never met, yet whom I came to know intimately through his written collection of personal tragedy and triumphs. Through my telling, I invite the reader to get to know me beyond a faded photograph. Also, since I do not have any children of my own, I would like to leave behind some kind of legacy that gives voice to the heart of my life energy.

During the process of taking notes of anesthesia events that followed me like shadows, another question popped into my mind.

Of all the medical specialties, what made me intuitively choose anesthesia without hesitation?

While I reflected on this matter, a connection to my childhood became apparent. I recognized a progression from the bleak gray post-war German environment to the stark walls of the operating room (OR) and the need in both places to diminish the pain of injuries and trauma. The experience of these turbulent times in my early years developed the urge and ability to restore physical and emotional balance and thus become a quiet caretaker of the immediate circumstances.

These questions were the catalysts that unraveled the intertwined fabric of my life, only to reorganize it in the chapters that follow.

Chapter One

From Silver Spoon to Stethoscope

In Praise of Air

Air waiting outside the womb,
To funnel a first breath
That lets us begin to be here,
Each moment drawn from its invisible stock.

John O' Donohue[1]

Oxygen

Sometimes I wonder if I received sufficient oxygen as my head was manipulated out of the birth canal. The night nurses had pushed my mother's gurney hurriedly to the delivery room. The obstetrician had detected a decelerated heart rate with his fetal stethoscope. While my mother's screams faded from exhaustion, the nurses shouted for "Sauerstoff!" Another nurse grabbed the black rubber mask off her anesthesia machine on wheels and turned up the green flow meter.

According to my mother, my birth was severely obstructed by a complicated breech presentation, which endangered both our lives. My arrival became an emergency at midnight on June 14, 1946, in Frankfurt, Germany. It was the first of countless medical emergencies at which I was present, even though I was not aware of this one.

Nowadays doctors don't hesitate to deliver breech babies by Cesarean section, an option not available when I was born. Resuscitative equipment at that time was probably primitive by today's standards. Most likely a few whiffs of oxygen, followed by some vigorous slaps on the buttocks, reversed my flaccid state of blue. Little did I know that someday I would become an expert in the skills of resuscitation.

The immediate environment I was born into consisted of a tunnel-like bunker below ground level. It had served as a makeshift obstetrical ward, where women in labor were assured temporary shelter from

---

1   From TO BLESS THE SPACE BETWEEN US: A BOOK OF BLESSINGS by John O'Donohue, p 37 © 2008 by John O'Donohue. Used by permission of Doubleday, a division of Random House, Inc.

the bomb attacks during the last phase of the war. How ironic that I was surrounded by gray tile walls of sterile delivery rooms without windows, not unlike most operating rooms that would become the background for my work as a doctor in the specialty of anesthesia.

As I learned later during my rotation in obstetrical anesthesia, there was never enough time to really put women in labor out of their misery with just a gas mask, nor was it safe to do so. Their cries of agony were more or less muffled with ether-soaked cotton, stretched tightly over a wire frame in the shape of a cone. This device would fit snugly over the nose and mouth of the patient. The constant drip from the wick of the cold canister of liquid ether silenced the most piercing cries.

It was the anesthetic of choice in the 1940s, usually administered by nurses. There was much opportunity for further development of anesthetic agents that would be safer and provide more comfort. What a coincidence that I would later choose this specialty for my own career and would observe the historic transition from an ether mask to the short-acting anesthetic agents of modern anesthesia. It was a gradual evolution over decades from the "art" of anesthesia to the precise and predictable science of today.

But there is more to say about my perilous birth. I was told that I stepped into this world with my left foot first, while the rest of me clung to the safety of my mother's womb.

Perhaps I was as frightened as my mother was during the war, which ended in May 1945. She had witnessed many of the ear-splitting sirens that screamed through the stillness of the night to announce oncoming air raids.

It was an ominous time, when cars drove around in the neighborhood with their headlights painted black. Some nights all the tenants who lived under one roof huddled together for shelter in the basement, until a second siren signaled the "all clear" of an air strike. Thanks to my father's foresight, my parents were out of the country at a time that would later prove critical for their survival.

It is my guess that I was also hungry and cold from the time I was born. At least, it was often the way I reacted physically after a long and labor-intensive case in the operating room. Countless times I reached the patient's recovery room shivering to the bone, with my fingers and lips blue, starving for warmth and food. There were no recovery rooms for surgeons who operated for hours in chilly rooms without any sustenance. It was a privilege to be a member of their team.

"Mammi" and me, a tender moment

It took a long time to comprehend a perplexing quirk of fate. Oxygen brushed me with the first kiss of life when I was born; perhaps it saved my life. Little did I know that I would dispense the same magic medicine day after day in my chosen career as anesthesiologist.

Paul Ehrlich Street—My First Address

My father, who was stationed in Russia at the end of the war, was unable to be with my mother when I was born. Instead, he received two telegrams. The first one announced that my mother and I were in critical condition, followed by a second one with the good news that mother and daughter had both survived. My mother tells me that he was jumping up and down, crazed with joy, about his newborn daughter. He already had a son, my brother Axel, who was two-and-a-half years older than me.

When my mother had regained some strength, it was decided that the most comforting place to start our lives together was at her mother's apartment. My father drove home from Russia every few weeks or months on roads peppered with Partisan landmines, to oversee the construction of a substantial log cabin for our next family dwelling.

The log cabin would be our interim home until it could be determined if and when the original residence in Frankfurt might be restored. Since the latter was ruined and building supplies and resources were unavailable in the aftermath of the massive bombing that had leveled the entire city, any restoration was assumed to take years. My father had survived the war without a mental or physical scrape. He would see to it that his family would soon reunite in a proper home.

The building site for the log cabin was in a wooded lot near the Frankfurt-Main airport. My father had some American friends who lived off base. They were kind enough to assist us with a supply of lumber and other essential building necessities. It took about a year before we could move into the log cabin. It was my first encounter with the charitable and generous spirit of Americans.

Meanwhile, after my birth I was safe and content to stay with my mother at my grandmother's apartment. My brother stayed with Dedda, my parents' elderly housekeeper, who lived in the country. I still remember how she held a huge, fresh, homemade loaf of bread against her large bosom to cut a slice for my skinny brother and smothered it with lard, roasted onions, and salt. In the same soft pillow of her bosom she embraced my brother with no less affection than his own grandmother.

I remember my grandmother's apartment from later years, when my mother and I would visit her once or twice a week. It consisted of one room and a balcony in an old baroque house, formerly a private villa, located on Paul Ehrlich Strasse. The balcony window was framed with heavy horizontal wooden slats that were rolled up or down with an encased canvas strap next to the balcony door. There was a massive mahogany bed that faced the window, an antique writing desk with lots of secret compartments stuffed with letters, and a reading chair with a floor lamp near the window. The bathroom was a long way down the hall, cold and drafty with faded blue tile, to be shared with other occupants. I remember that the white china bowl on my grandmother's nightstand was always clean.

The kitchen was also shared with other people. My grandmother wrinkled her delicate nose in contempt when someone else chose to cook cabbage. She fled back to her room, closed the door, opened the window, and retreated to her corner chair with embroidery or her prayer book instead of a meal. Amongst her reading was a daily spiritual lesson from *The Imitation of Christ*. The small, leather-bound volume with delicate engravings was a French translation, given to her at school by the nuns of the Sacre Coeur (Sacred Heart) order. This was also the place where she was taught the daintiest embroidery. She was accustomed to the finest of everything, an unquestionable birthright of Hungarian aristocracy.

My father had taken great care to make our small new dwelling as cheerful as possible. The great woodstove in the living room was surrounded by three walls of shiny green tile, the color of moss, which reached to the ceiling. It even had a tiled bench all around where you could sit and warm your back against it. Little did I know that this snug corner bench would become a fond memory for which I longed during the longevity of my career in cold ORs, devoid of any color or warmth.

Next to my mother's bed there was a built-in linen closet with neatly stacked sheets, freshly laundered and ironed. On occasion my mother would find me sitting in the middle of the bed in a great white cloud of sheets, which I had pulled one by one from the closet. I still try to make up for this innocent game by keeping my linen closet stacked with an orderly pile of white towels.

One night, within a year of moving in, my father needed to attend a business meeting at night and invited my mother to join him for a drink at their favorite piano bar in Frankfurt. My mother hesitated but decided to stay home with the children. She had fallen asleep on the sofa, when she woke up to a crackling sound from the ceiling and was startled by smoke all around her. There was barely enough time to make it to the bedroom, snatch us out of our sleep, one under each arm, and run out to the front lawn. Within minutes the entire log cabin was licked by flames shooting into the night sky before it collapsed like a box of matches, lit all at once.

My father, who had the ability to stay calm and unflappable in any crisis, happily scooped us up from the pile of ashes. He did dismiss my mother's housekeeper, who had left the iron plugged in and unattended. He then proceeded, with even greater determination, to accelerate the restoration of our original house in Frankfurt, destroyed in April 1944.

The only residue of the fire in my mind is a red, hot fear of fires. As a doctor I found it extremely rewarding to provide anesthesia for any burn victims. They struck a personal note that also sang of survival.

Pneumonia

My mother was just seventeen when she married, the same age at which I entered medical school.

At the start of my second semester of physiology, I became fascinated with the structure and the function of the lung. I was not even aware of the significance of pneumonia in our family history. I did not realize until recently that my mother's entire existence had hinged on a tragic bout of pneumonia that took the young life of my great-grandmother. This fatal pneumonia brought about the unconventional marriage of my grandparents, who raised six children, including my mother.

It was last Christmas when I missed my mother the most in recent times. I remembered her smile, as wide as her open arms that embraced me in a cloud of Chanel No 5. I phoned my last but favorite uncle, who knew my mother as a young girl and who told me the story from the old world that I only knew from faded photographs.

Uncle Felix remembered the painted carriage with the Hungarian family crest that rattled along the unpaved country road. The driver, who had tired of waiting for my great-grandmother, the countess, while she and her husband shopped in town, was not in the mood for anymore stops on the way home.

There was a loud conversation going on in the cabin between husband and wife. Their raised voices made the driver most uncomfortable. He cracked the whip on the horse just to get away from this private quarrel. The husband banged on the floor with his walking stick. The countess ordered the driver to stop the carriage. The carriage door flew open with the wind and the pelting rain. The countess insisted on walking home. She was not dressed for such bad weather, with just a light cape around her shoulders and indoor shoes. Her bonnet, tied loosely under her chin, turned inside out with the next gust of wind. Her husband and driver both knew that she was beyond reason, and nobody could convince her to get back in the carriage.

Castle Ecka

Castle Ecka was built by Agoston Lazar in 1820 on the left bank of the river Begej in the village of Ecka, now in Serbia. My grandmother's father, Count Felix d'Harnoncourt, married into the Lazar family. My grandmother was born in Ecka on December 3, 1888.

Since the 1990s the castle has been under the protection of the Institute for Cultural Monuments. The hunting lodge is fully restored as a hotel.

www.kastelecka.com/history.html

While her husband, Count Harnoncourt, was a proud man, his wife, Marianne Lazar, an Austrian-Hungarian heiress of great wealth, always held the trump card in the end. He cursed underneath his curled moustache and told the driver to move along. After all, it was less than a mile to the entrance gate of the estate. Surely it would not kill her to have her way.

By the time she arrived at the house, she was drenched to the skin but felt much better about having made her point. That night, however, she could not get warm while she shivered with an alarming rise of temperature.

The country doctor was summoned promptly. He looked worried when he listened to her chest and found her coughing violently. Her breathing got more labored with each day, almost by the hour, while her color turned a sickly mottled blue. The fresh air from the window while she was wrapped up in blankets did nothing to reverse this galloping illness or her color. The countess was besieged with a fulminating pneumonia and died within two weeks in the year of 1893, at age twenty-six..

As much as I wish someone could have been there at the bedside to rescue my great-grandmother with penicillin and oxygen, the inevitable turn of events was in my favor, for I might never have been born otherwise.

The countess left behind three children, aged two through five, namely my grandmother Marie-Louise, Felix and Alice.

The household turned dark after the death of the countess. The huge silk draperies hung limp and drawn across the French doors overlooking the sculptured rose garden. My great-grandfather hired nannies from England and Vienna to take care of the children while he went on extended safaris to Africa and India. Game hunting became his passion.

The children became rather spoiled by the nannies, the cooks, the gardeners, and their father during his brief visits home. When at home, their father paid the most attention to Felix and trained him in horseback riding and competition jumping at an early age. One day the hurdle was too high. Felix, by now in his teens, missed the bar. Horse and rider tumbled badly, leaving Felix motionless on the ground with a broken back, handicapped for life.

*My grandmother, Marie- Louise
d'Harnoncourt, as young girl*

My grandmother at approximately age 18

My grandmother as a young woman at Ecka

Once Felix was stabilized from the acute injury of the accident, he was rehabilitated at home. A special companion by the name of Carl von Carstenn was engaged to assist with his physical recovery and to keep him intellectually involved with current affairs inside and outside the household.

Carl von Carstenn was prodigy of an aristocrat Johann Wilhelm von Carstenn, (1882-1896), credited for developing a residential area of Berlin, named Lichterfelde. During his extended stay with Felix, he found adequate leisure time to also take an interest in my grandmother, then seventeen years old. They shared the intimacy of the keyboard at the piano. Under the disguise of formal piano lessons, their fingers intertwined.

Their whispers went unnoticed until one day when they eloped together. Old Count Harnoncourt was notified and abruptly returned from a safari. He roared through the house like a lion filled with rage and revenge. He made his discontent irrevocably clear by disinheriting my grandmother immediately.

Despite the scandal, my grandmother was already married to von Carstenn. They had four daughters, including my mother, and two sons, Carl and Louis. Her favorite son, Louis, a handsome Prussian military officer, was killed instantly in a riding accident at age twenty-two. Within the same year, my grandmother, although divorced by now, also lost her former husband who, oddly, died of pneumonia.

She was left with modest resources, no inheritance, and five remaining children to raise on her own. To sustain herself financially, she did remarry an older gentleman of means who had no outstanding qualities other than providing a decent home for her and her children in a privileged neighborhood of Frankfurt, Germany. My grandmother did not volunteer any information on this subject. My mother indicated that old Katzenstein was the cranky type who shuffled around the house in a silk morning gown and slippers. What she liked best about him was his parrot, Coco, who was more talkative and loved grapes. At that time my mother also had a turtle, Regina. She and her best friend, Mary, attempted to hitch up an empty matchbox with some fine twine wrapped around the turtle's hind flippers. When finally the turtle diligently pulled her wagon across the parquet floor, they cheered and clapped their hands.

It was in his house that my mother, at age twelve, let my father into the salon to discuss some business with my grandmother. He was so enchanted with the social skills of the chatty young daughter that he married her as soon as she turned seventeen, while he was twice her age.

My mother Felicitas Marianne von Carstenn, born 1923. A young portrait

My mother's wedding present 1940

My parents on Bahnhofstrasse,
Zurich, 1950

None of these details were known to me when, in my second year of medical school, I developed a strong interest in respiratory physiology. At the time I studied the lung, I was much more concerned about my father being a chain smoker and his many unsuccessful attempts to give it up. He made all kinds of bets and bargains with me or other family members. He secretly swore to me he would never light one again and gave me his boxes of matches ceremoniously, while he used a lighter to finish the rest of the pack of cigarettes. For a few days he seemed content with some dark chocolates by his bedside to fight the craving. Once the chocolates were gone, it did not take long for the cigarettes to find their way back. As an incentive, I even showed him colored plates from an atlas of pathology with diseased lungs that resembled black mushrooms compared to healthy pink spongy tissue.

It was predictable that my mother might eventually succumb to pneumonia after a long struggle with Alzheimer's, which kept her bedridden for her last two years. Equipped with all the knowledge I have gained as a doctor and having provided life-sustaining oxygen to my patients over three decades, I knew that I would not be able to save my own mother form the inevitable end. She survived a first bout of pneumonia with a course of antibiotics.

Near the end when the flame of her spirit barely flickered, I knew it was only right to allow her to die with dignity. This was not the time to intervene with heroic skills; rather, I would stand back and lean on the wisdom that it is not possible or desirable to question destiny, which often has a different trajectory than we might wish. At some point even a doctor has to recognize and accept that despite all efforts, a divine twist of fate has its own merits. Life would choose its course back on a stormy day in Hungary as well as in my mother's nursing home. It would dictate the end, before and after I became a doctor.

Boat ride from Hilton Head to Daufuskie Island SC, age 72

My Mother—Homeless Now and Then

After my father died at age seventy-seven, my mother left rural Ireland, where we had moved under some duress during my father's midlife crisis. She returned to Germany to be near her relatives. She settled in Frankfurt, where she immersed herself in the memories of the past in the same cosmopolitan city where I grew up. She cherished her vivid memories of exclusive stores, lavish jewelry, and a whirlwind of extravagant parties in our grandiose home. But the walls of her modest apartment soon turned gray from six cigarettes a day and the rising heat of old, hissing radiators. Her world closed in as she slipped at a distressing rate into a mental world of her own, where I often could not reach her.

At the age of seventy-four, many years after my father had passed away, my mother could not comprehend anymore where she lived or how to open the front door to her apartment. Her transfer to the nursing home for round-the-clock personal care was imminent. We knew that our soft explanations would not bridge the gap of the severed synapses of her brain, which rendered her as helpless and innocent as a child by the relentless cerebral progression of Alzheimer's.

She was delighted that all three children had gathered for the day to help her sort out her drawers and shoeboxes filled with old photographs, old letters, birth certificates, expired passports, and important announcements. So many cards said, "Thank you" and "We miss you." It was a gray day, and soon after we arrived, the rain came down in transparent sheets of water that kept us walled in, holding up the past together.

We knew it would probably be the last time she was in her own living room of her apartment, just a few blocks from my brother. The rain seemed to shield us from stepping out to the next destination, the nursing home, at least for the afternoon.

My mother's last apartment in Bad Wimpfen, Germany 2000

My mother travelling around the world, Egypt 1955

From then on we would wander in and out a few more times to pick up various pieces designated to go to our respective homes. The walnut corner cabinet with the sticky drawer and glass doors would fit best in my brother's dining room. The Dutch oil paintings of a sunset sail and the old fisherman's wife mending the net were best suited for my sister, while I carefully wrapped a delicate set of Meissen china in bubble-wrap to take with me to New England. It didn't matter that the hand-painted orange and gold dragons didn't match my simple beach cottage in blues and yellows. It would remind me of my parents' lavish dinner parties that always ended with a flamboyant dessert and the fragrance of espresso to send their guest s on their way home.

We had lit some candles on that rainy afternoon. It was a happy day for my mother to be surrounded by our laughter, and I knew we could make the violins sing like birds in Vivaldi's "Four Seasons" as long as we needed them. We pored over photographs scattered all over the rug, bundled in decades. There were the ski vacations in Switzerland, my rebuilt childhood home in Frankfurt, and our last home in Ireland, with the lush entrance of massive rhododendrons that stood like sentinels all the way up the long avenue. In one photograph my mother's big smile came face-to-face with a camel in Africa. This old camel lit up her faded memory in a flash of recognition of a life of rich adventure and three good children who survived it all successfully.

My father, who had taken some of the pictures, was strangely absent from our tight circle, like an observer waiting for the invitation. My mother gently reminded us how he too would have loved to help us piece together the fragments of our family collage. We acknowledged his passion for our family.

At times my mother still had her moments of clarity, and so she was in full knowledge and intention when she handed me a brittle faded envelope. She said, "I want you to have this. I know you will take good care of this, and I know that it will mean a lot to you."

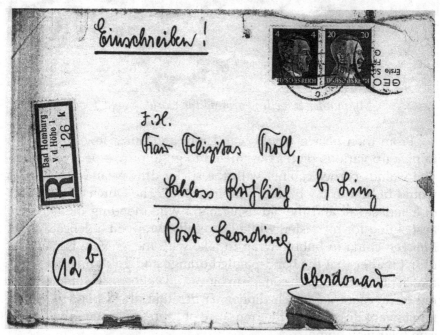

Original letter envelope dated April 1944

It contained an eyewitness account of the bomb attack on my parents' home in Frankfurt, written by my father's secretary, who had become a loyal friend. She sent this letter to my mother, who for the time being lived in Austria with my brother, then six months old. It was my father's plan to keep both of them out of danger.

Although I heard the story from my parents many times, when I took the letter to a quiet corner of the room and sat on a pillow to read it, I was suddenly there, many months before I was born, and I cried myself back into my mother's womb.

Liebe Felicitas,   *April 18, 1944*

I just returned from the post, where I picked up your gracious letter. Many thanks for your kind note, which brought tears to my eyes. What I presumed with great angst has actually occurred. Apparently, you did not receive my previous letter of the twenty-fourth of March. Since the entire regional mail was destroyed by an air attack last Friday, it will never be delivered into your hands. Unfortunately, I must recount the entire tragedy for you, which was so painful to write the first time, especially to you—something so horrific. In my opinion, you were solely created to be surrounded by grace.

Liebe Felicitas, as of the twenty-second of March, when the very worst air attack that has ever hit a city descended on Frankfurt, not one house remained standing in the Senckenberg-Anlage [Avenue]! Here is a brief account of the events that took place.

On Saturday the eighteenth of March, we already had a frightful attack. That evening I was all by myself in your house and took refuge in your Bomben shelter in the basement. I was hurled against the wall with great force and thought that everything would be in flames as I surfaced. Instead the University buildings stood in flames across the street. Most of the windows in your house were still intact, even the large sliders.

That evening I resolved never to go to into the Bomben shelter again by myself. When the first sirens went off to herald a precautionary alarm, I got fully dressed and brought my suitcase with essential underwear and clothes into the foyer of your house. I then went next door to the research institute, where four of us descended to the basement. There had not been sufficient time to even blast off the main alarm, and all the lights went out in an instant. All we could hear was the screaming and hissing of bombs dropping everywhere and a fantastic cacophony of artillery all around us. I could hear the screech of a Luftmine [air raid] crashing down in the immediate vicinity. It was immediately followed by terrible crashing sounds upstairs, shattering of glass, and a scorched smell that quickly became penetrating. It sounded as if the entire house had collapsed in a few minutes. The upper floor with the marble pillars came crashing down with a torrential noise. Felicitas, I thought I would never see the sun again!

The bite of the scorched smell got worse and worse. When the noise calmed down a little and the forceful blasts diminished, we attempted to find an exit. Everything around us was demolished. You remember the entrance with the massive stones and sculptured figurines, huge doors, and iron chandeliers: they had all tumbled down in a pile of rubble. We were able to get out through a narrow emergency exit in the side-wall and stood in the street, fire all around us. It was die Hoelle [hell]!

My first glance went to your house. Like all other houses in the entire Senckenberg-Anlage, it stood engulfed in flames from top to bottom! The entrance, stairwell, and basement were like a furnace—I had no access to get inside. Dr. Emmerich's house was also on fire. We had to walk as far as Bismarck-Allee, where we were informed that no fire engines were available, and if they were, they would only be used for public buildings. No water was left in the pond held in reserve for the sole purpose of extinguishing fires. There, at least I was able to thoroughly wet down my coat—and proceeded through the showers of sparks with a sponge tied around my mouth and a pair of sunglasses. Unmenschlich [inhumane]how many phosphor and sulphur explosive bombs they dumped on our part of town. Toward the morning I carefully scraped the phosphor deposit off my only pair of shoes. After that I had only one thought: get out, get out, get out … out of Frankfurt.

So here I am in the vicinity of Stierstadt, where an old colleague accommodated me in a small room of her attic. The first few days I was in a paralyzed state of shock and just took care of the most urgent mail. After four days I went with my friend's parents back to Frankfurt. At that time I noticed that even though all houses were burnt to the ground, your basement shelter had outlasted the impact. Monday morning, very early, I went to my boss and begged him for an opportunity to take his truck, before the permission to re-enter Frankfurt with a vehicle was released, to allow me to salvage the remains of the basement for my friends. Felicitas, please pass this on to Albert. Here is what I retrieved from your Bomben shelter:

Four mattresses, two blankets, two pillows, two oil paintings, odd dishes, one suitcase with shoes. Various preserves, homemade lard, two small tables, three upholstered chairs, one lamp.

In the house where I am staying, I have access to a kitchen. For now, this is where I brought all your belongings. Unfortunately, I came to the sad realization that various items that I had seen the day before scattered amongst the rubble had been stolen by the next day.

All the other hideous atrocities I witnessed I don't want to mention now. Maybe I will tell you and Albert when I see you again.

While indeed I was devastated, my first thought when I saw these terrible sights was some kind of relief, if that is possible, that you did not have to experience this. My eyes are slow to let go of these images; it is as if a burning mark has scarred my soul.

I will never forget this night and these sights. Over and over again, whenever I think about it, I find myself caught back in the aftermath of this terrible experience. Maybe it would have been better if I had taken the train and would have come straight to visit you and little Axel. Already I am fond of him, just by looking at the cute pictures Albert proudly showed me in January at four months old. All my girlfriends admired the adorable clothes I had knit for little Axel.

Also I try not to claim a past anymore, just the present—and a future! Hopefully there will be a future for all of us.

On Friday the fourteenth of April I was supplied from a first aid vehicle chartered by Dr. G. I received underwear, one pair of stockings, one dress, one coat, and three handkerchiefs, as I had nothing to change into. Now I have something to wear.

Though I feel healthy and have recovered physically, inside I am totally deranged. The one thought that gives me inner peace and serenity is that I still have you and Albert as friends.

Hopefully we will all meet again in good health. To you and little Axel, my most loving regards.

Yours
Emeli

P.S. Please remember me to your dear mother and wish her "Alles Gute."

My parents' Senckenberg Residence 1940

Senckenberg Residence restored 1948

My Father's Somersaults

My father was always one step ahead of new political and catastrophic developments in Germany, with the utmost confidence of a clairvoyant. None of the women in his life ever questioned his predictions—not his wife, his mother, or his secretaries. In his heyday he made sound business decisions on the wings of intuition with such power of conviction that there was no debate. It was like a weather front that passed through, and there was little point to question its purpose or direction. It was the natural order of the day.

The house that became my childhood home after it was rebuilt had been acquired in 1940 as the first residence for my father's young bride, seventeen years his junior. My father furnished their home with exquisite antiques, oriental rugs, and some significant Dutch oil paintings. My mother could still describe to me the intricate pattern of the parquet floor with inlaid rosewood. She loved the light as it reflected on the floor through the French doors. The silver, the crystal, and the chandeliers were carefully chosen for a lifetime and a family together. My mother's joy in establishing herself as a homemaker was short-lived. When my father thought it would be wise to join her mother in Austria to be out of danger while she expected her first child, she packed her bags and followed. Without an immediate threat, she found it difficult to leave everything behind but had no argument with the decision. The temporary move to Austria may well have saved her life.

Up until his marriage, my father was a handsome, well-to-do bachelor. At the age of thirty-four, when he married my mother, he was already a successful self-made businessman who dealt with the export and import of commodities across the globe. He would negotiate trades with tons of coal from South America or textiles and skeins of wool in blue paper sleeves from China. He had a knack and a vision to know which commodity was most needed where and then find the resources and the clients. He would find a way to deliver.

His attributes were a rare combination of charm, intelligence, and integrity that made him a very skillful negotiator. He was bold enough to reach for unconventional deals and made them happen. Dressed in impeccable pin-striped wool suits, his Clark Gable smile, brimming with confidence, could sweep anyone off his or her feet, the toughest businessmen and the crustiest bureaucrats alike. He was magical and magnificent.

My father, an early portrait

My parents' passport photos

In his office he took time to listen to the domestic dilemmas of his assistants, sometimes helped them out, and always gave them hope. It was at that time, in the late 1930s, when my father helped several Jewish business friends to find safe hideaways and some to escape. He took the bull by the horns and claimed to be invincible.

Women adored him. His office staff respected his principles and feared his attention to detail. There was no typo that escaped his keen eye. His dictatorial tyranny spilled well beyond the margin of the steno pad. With a broad smile, though, all was forgiven, and the ladies kept typing with a blind loyalty. His endearing charm, well developed in his office, would later pave the way for frequent flirtations and advances to high society ladies at the country club.

He could afford to bring a tiger cub from his travels to South America and kept her as a pet in his bachelor apartment. The housekeeper who came up from the country kept shaking her head as she bottle-fed tiger Luxi. As recounted to me, she prepared a meatless diet so that the wild cat would not become overly aggressive with visitors. It did not take long to notice my father driving an open convertible through town with Luxi the tiger sitting up tall in the passenger seat.

Shortly thereafter the director of the Frankfurt Zoo paid a visit to my father. He proposed on his first visit, and insisted on his second and third visits, that the animal be moved to a more proper environment in the zoo. After much debate, my father consented to bring Luxi to the zoo before he left town for his next business trip. Once in the cage, Luxi cried like a baby each time my father turned his back to leave. He finally calmed her down with his promise to pick her up and bring her home on Thursday. His return was delayed until the weekend. He received a phone call within twenty-four hours of the promised pick-up time that Luxi had died in the cage. He was convinced for the rest of his life that she died of a broken heart.

Another thrill was the perfect execution of acrobatic loops and rolls in his own bi-plane in formation with his barnstorming friends, who thought nothing of a low fly-by underneath the London Bridge or flying to northern Germany for a special brand of beer. My father's entire life was a series of somersaults that embraced all elements and reached across the ocean and the sky.

The last decade of his life, in his seventies, he spent almost solely on his thirty-two-foot sailboat, *Sunset*, crossing the Atlantic twice from Ireland to Antigua. It was on the ocean where he found lasting peace of mind.

Only much later in life could I appreciate my father's own sense of spirituality, which he found in the rough tumble of the waves and the endless horizon. It was a long search for the God that had melted on my tongue as a sticky wafer during my first Communion to be reinvented as a God of my own understanding.

Senckenberg Avenue
—My Childhood Home

Our house was rebuilt in 1947 after its destruction by the massive bomb attack of 1944. By 1948 the extensive structural renovations were adequate to allow our family to move in upstairs, while my father opened his office on the ground floor. A large bronze plate with black lettering attached to the left corner of the house announced Albert J. Troll, Export-Import. The ornate, sculptured baroque façade, carved in stone, was fairly intact except for two corner steeples. In my own mind this façade carved in stone represented a symbolic foreshadowing of my father's lifelong efforts to keep our family image intact, no matter what challenges befell us.

The back wall of the house also remained partially upright. During my entire childhood, our house still felt disfigured and patched up from the aftershock of the war. It had a temporary, transient feel and lacked a sense of permanent security. There were no trees on our modest patch of front lawn. It never looked groomed. The rough grass and the prickly hedge of evergreens were rarely cut by my grandfather, who lived on the third floor at night and in the basement during the day in his workshop. He also maintained the huge furnace and took care of receiving large deliveries of coal.

At the back of the house, a closed veranda on the second floor served as my bedroom. It overlooked a haunting skeleton of remnant walls of a house bombed out and left unclaimed. Mounds of rubble with weeds covered the ground inside the four shattered walls. At night, the tall, glassless rectangular windows scattered with broken bricks stared back at me in black. I was sure I saw owls perched on the broken sills and bats flapping about in circles. I remember rusty iron girders, which stuck out from half-broken floors like lost limbs. On one of the floors, I detected an old, faded, striped mattress that left me wondering if whoever slept on it was alive or dead.

Entrance door at Senckenberg

Axel at Senckenberg, doing diligent homework

These questions were beyond my grasp as a seven- or eight-year-old child, but I remember feeling disturbed about the families that may have been catapulted out of their bedrooms and out of their homes in their sleep. Their likely injuries bothered me. I was hoping that someone came to their rescue. I envisioned broken arms and legs and imagined people crying for help. I felt drawn to be with them and in some way wanted to ease their suffering.

Of course, I never mentioned my angst to my parents, knowing that my father had more important things to think about. He made it clear that he could not be disturbed between two and three PM, when he came upstairs for a quick lunch and a twenty-minute nap while we all tiptoed about.

There was not much point in bringing my concerns to the dinner table either, where my father would just dismiss my childish fears with a wave of his hand as he switched subjects or asked me to pass the bread. As far as he was concerned, we were the lucky ones to have a roof over our heads, no shortage of food, and some promising deals in the export-import business on a new horizon. Opportunities to trade odd commodities, anything from coal to wool, kept him busy in the office and preoccupied at home and provided enough spending money for my mother, who often liked to shop in town.

Instead I looked forward to telling my grandmother when she would come to visit on Friday, fish day. She would patiently sit with me in my veranda when no one else was around. She always made me feel less lonely. She would let me snuggle into the folds of her silk dress and laugh or cry with me over nothing.

I seemed to spend large blocks of time alone. My brother was already in school, two years ahead of me, and dutifully did his homework. My mother was out a lot buying meat, potatoes, and vegetables and then busying herself preparing dinner. Meanwhile, I took care of myself in my own simple ways. Most of the time, I kept the windows shut and the shades down, to avoid looking at the ruin outside my window. Instead, I tried to look out the side window only, which overlooked a luscious quadrangle of lawn with a neatly kept gravel path around it and old chestnut trees. I liked to read a lot, since it did not disturb anyone.

The adjacent property was actually a university-owned museum of natural mineral stones and granite. I became chatty with the housekeeper, who regularly cut the lawn that separated our house from the back brick wall of Nadia's house, who later became my best friend at school. Luckily it was located diagonally across the lawn

Rear view of 2nd floor: our living quarters, kitchen window, and my "Veranda" bedroom

quadrangle. He would allow us to draw a hopscotch grid in the gravel with a stick and left it until it was erased by the rain.

The back of our house was a dark gray stucco finish studded with small stone pebbles that would not take on any paint. Instead there were large green patches of moldy moss from the lack of sun. When I was by myself and looked closely, I would find spongy colonies of round-capped mushrooms on the cracked wall that looked sadly neglected. I wondered if we were too poor to repair the cracked wall and paint the rusty gutters with fresh creamy paint like they did at my friend Nadia's house. Maybe I was beginning to see something I would not fully understand until much later—that my father put great effort into maintaining a respectable façade.

Elementary School

On my first day of school, at age six, I felt very grown up in my gray woolen sweater that matched my powder-blue tartan skirt. After all, I had already been walking to kindergarten mostly by myself, sometimes with a friend I remember as being as shy as myself. My small pouch that hung from a shoulder strap across my belly button was exchanged for a large brown leather case with a snappy metal buckle that was strapped against my back.

Inside rattled a few modest tools for a long journey of learning. There was a wooden pencil case with an eraser, a hardcover

My first day at school

notebook, and for my first attempt at writing, a wood-framed slate with a box of white chalk. It was not so much the contents of my case as an ominous sense of responsibility to excel that felt heavy against my back.

I was distracted by my excitement over the large traditional pink and purple paper cone filled with sweets between layers of crunchy tissue paper that every child receives from proud parents on the first day of school. It served its purpose—to take my mind off the flutters of anxiety about meeting the teacher and so many other children. That morning I needed my mother's help to untangle my shoelaces, which on any other day I had mastered perfectly. After my father took some photographs, my mother drove me to school. She stayed a while, until she had found my desk, my teacher, and enough courage on my face to leave with a clear conscience.

What I remember most was the long walk to and from school, which took close to half an hour. First I passed some elaborate administrative buildings of the renowned Frankfurt University, which loomed with some large-scale, omnipresent law. Just in passing, their imposing structure felt similar to my father's dominant authority at home. To me both appeared cast in stone, unyielding, unforgiving. There would be no use banging my head against either.

It seemed that my father's office, just downstairs from our living quarters, was filled with files of rules that, under the bright fluorescent light, would illuminate the truth faster than I could twist the story. I had to obey and tell the truth; there was no getting away. In our house each room was wallpapered with unwritten principles.

Next, I would take a residential side street that seemed to stretch forever. Eventually I reached a wide avenue called Hamburger-Allee that was lined with two rows of mature chestnut trees that branched over the brick wall of the schoolyard. In the shade of the chestnut trees, the kiosk just outside the schoolyard that sold penny candy, ice cream, and lemonade still had its shutters rolled down on my way to school. I looked forward to spending a few pennies there before I started on my way home.

Later on, when I received regular pocket money equivalent to fifty cents a week, I saved it for the stationery store next to the school. I spent a long time there and loved to pick out new pencils and notebooks. I also bought an array of glossy Victorian violet bouquets, printed on punched-out paper, to paste in albums or swap to win an occasional friendship. These friendships never seemed to last, as I felt ignorant about the games other children played. On a rainy day we would sometimes drop in at a playmate's house on our way home. The only part of playing doctor I liked was the toy stethoscope.

The lighthearted laughter of my classmates was as unfamiliar as a foreign language that I could not speak, and I shied away from feeding into the giggles of gossip. Most of the time I preferred to walk home by myself. I thought of my family. I daydreamed about finding some skill, some way to shine and excel beyond my father's critique and my brother's talent to play classical guitar. And yet I felt a dull, crushing loneliness in walking by myself, separated from the brassy, brazen students.

During class recess I never liked the noise of the shouting and yelling in the schoolyard and the way little groups and circles formed without inviting me. Besides, everyone else's lunch looked more interesting than my pink liverwurst sandwich that had turned into

Bonifatius Elementary School

a greasy glob of gray in the heat. But nobody seemed eager to share with me. I was relieved when the shrill bell called us back to order in the quiet classroom.

My dwarf-sized teacher for the first four years might as well have stepped out of a forgotten book of fairy tales with her wiry orange hair, her geographic wrinkled face, and the name Von Mecklenburg, better known as Mecki. She knew everything about children and could be strict at times. Sometimes after class she put one of her kinder arms around my shoulder to relieve my burning desire to be amongst the best while my grades were mostly average. But at the end of four years, she wrote the required recommendation that would allow my transfer to high school. In her comments, she noted that I would do well with literature and languages.

During the entire four years of elementary school, no particular event stood out in my memory as being as frightful as the first day, which ended badly. When I got home, my father took a rare break from the office to share my excitement. When he eagerly asked me about my first day at school, out of my mouth, which had felt dry like a bag of straw all day, came simply, "Good!" It seemed a fair and safe summary of the day but sent my father into a fit of rage. I did not yet know that "good" was never good enough.

Later school portraits of Axel and myself

Family Snapshots

Photographs were not a priority when I was born, at the end of the war. There are no baby pictures of me and my mother. A renowned professional photographer in Frankfurt took my earliest photograph at age three. It was a black- and- white study of a little girl in her best dress, eyes filled to the brim with so much worry, ready to give in the battle of holding back the tears at the drop of one harsh word. There are very few other pictures of my childhood that speak the silent truth that I remember.

Even though my mother, my brother, and my sister never mentioned it, we all lived in constant fear of my father. All childhood play and activities were censored by my father's approval or disapproval. It was safe to practice typing in his office at age four or piano scales when he came home. At best these exercises earned me some encouragement after he inevitably corrected any irregular timing up or down the scales. "Make it flow smoother, smoother. Try again," he would say. The tea party with my dolls was sometimes rudely interrupted, and reading cartoons was out of the question. There was an unspoken curfew of all activities while my father napped from 1:30 to 2:30 each afternoon. The only choice was a quiet one, such as a cross-stitch project or homework for school. It was not a good idea to run around the house, for fear that a creaky floor might wake him up with a startle or an anxiety attack and ruin a perfectly good afternoon.

Promptly at 2:30 PM my mother would wake him up gently and serve fresh coffee with a sweet treat. My brother and I were always expected to join this little ritual and say something profound. Revived by his nap, he felt adequately refreshed to resume his business in his office on the ground floor. As soon as he left, I finished the leftover pastries to comfort myself. To this day, no matter where I am or what I do, promptly on the dot of 2:30 PM, I feel a knot in my stomach that craves something sweet to relax it. This physical sinking feeling forces me to stand back and deal with my flutters until I figure out how to reset the panic button of early history. It transcends all east and west time zones when I travel and renders me fatigued and unfocused for a short while. Now they call it hypoglycemia.

When I was older, school provided a natural respite from the ominous presence of my father's explosive nature. Also, Saturdays gave me some space when my parents took up golfing at a fashionable country club and were gone most of the day. I felt much safer listening to the murder mystery *Lady in the Fog* with my brother. This was my favorite day of the week, especially if my mother prepared and left us a big bowl of rice pudding with whipped cream and cooked cherries, until my brother also took up golfing. I missed his company. Besides, he always gave me a good portion of his rice pudding. He preferred a slice of sourdough bread with salted lard and bits of bacon.

All in all, I would describe my childhood as a continuum of underrated stress. We endured together, with an unspoken pact to comfort each other as best we could. We quietly embraced each other, and our vague sense of undeserved censure would never be lifted in my father's lifetime.

During my later teenage years, I longed to move to a place far away from the almost daily blustering outbursts and my father's empty threats that easily gathered momentum. His menacing eyes looked fierce and out of control. Was it the meal that did not meet his expectation or something I said? My baffled face would often launch another flare-up. It electrified me like a second blitz before I understood the first one.

The Neighborhood

Our neighborhood was hardly a residential area. It was a broad avenue, divided by a median strip with large trees and formal gardens with benches. Every few blocks there was a circular concrete pond the size of a helicopter pad, remnants of the water reservoirs from the war. Later, in peaceful times, they became a frequent destination for my grandmother and me to feed the ducks. At the farthest one from our house, there was a kiosk, where my grandmother rewarded me with a sweet treat for my effort to walk such a distance.

Diagonally across the street from our house was the Senckenberg Museum of Anthropology. Architecturally it was by far the most elaborate. Its enormous, bi-fold wrought-iron gate was in keeping with the ornate façade of sculptured sandstone, the color of the desert at sunset. In the lobby stood mounted an entire skeleton of

Senckenberg Museum of Anthropolology

a dinosaur, which gave me my first perspective of antiquity. I was fascinated by the anatomy of its wavy spine. Even now, during my yoga practice, I sometimes think of the old dinosaur and aim to reproduce that curvature in my own spine.

Looking out the kitchen window, the house to our left was as close as the width of a Linden tree that reached tall above the brick wall on the other side of our driveway. This building was occupied by a silent population of rare stones and minerals of museum quality. It also had been destroyed and rebuilt after the war, with its massive stone façade still intact. The largest black rocks were displayed on white marble pedestals in the lobby and competed with the dinosaur for my attention. To me these amorphous slabs just looked like large lumps of coal. However, I was interested in the upper floors, where the smaller stones seemed more precious and colorful. On the top floor, they had turned into little heaps of stardust, and the housekeeper would occasionally allow me to look at them under their glass display.

There was concentrated knowledge and visible brainpower all around us. When I looked out our living room window to the right of our house, I could peer at eye level into a fluorescent yet mysterious conference room. Young men in white lab coats and horn-rimmed glasses with permanently rounded shoulders would bend over typewriters for hours. They seemed a quiet group who barely talked amongst each other, except during table discussions that seemed to last for hours. Once in a while on a sunny day I saw them venture out as far as the front steps to eat their sandwiches at noontime.

It was only recently that my older brother pointed out the significance of what I, as a child, had misconceived as just another institute in our neighborhood. I didn't know that it was the new location for the Frankfurt School, where brilliant social research took place simultaneously with, yet way ahead of, my own life experiences.

The Frankfurt School was the informal name designated to scholars of the Institute for Social Research of the University of Frankfurt in the 1930s. The main focus of famous sociologists and philosophers was to form a "critical theory" in opposition to Marxism, Nazism, and Communism. When Hitler came to power, the institute closed down. Most of the scholars regrouped themselves in New York and affiliated with Columbia and Princeton University. After the war the institute returned to Frankfurt in 1949 and took residence in a new building next to our home.

The Frankfurt School of "Critical Theory" contributed to the German intellectual revival after World War II.

Next- door "Frankfurt School" of Political Science and Philosophy

Amongst the most famous philosophers who emerged from the Frankfurt School are Theodur W. Adorno and Erich Fromm. Both are credited with a psychoanalytical focus and research on the "authoritarian character." In their discussions of individual emancipation, they struck a personal note. In Adorno's book *Authoritarian Personality*, published in 1950, two years before I entered elementary school, the author addresses complex analytical aspects of early childhood experiences and their internalization. In a subsequent publication in 1951[2] he states,"Love you will find only where you may show yourself weak without provoking strength" and "To say 'We' and mean 'I' is one of the most recondite insults." Little did I know that ten years later "We" would move to another country, which was solely my father's wish.

Today, at age sixty-two, I can't seem to escape the figment of my imagination that my father's shouting traveled out of our living room window and spilled across the narrow alley into the adjacent institute. I now imagine that the scholarly discussions I witnessed, may have been fueled by observing my father's forceful pace back and forth in our living room, arms swinging wildly. Did they silently witness him strike my brother or me across the cheek? Did an occasional lashing for yet another trivial lie I can't remember provide further food for theories of a liberated self?

Only from an old black-and-white photograph was I reminded of a different glimpse. Next to the same living room window, my childlike mother sat in a large, winged upholstered armchair. She held me close in her lap while I pointed to the white beam of light that fell on both of us through the window. Although her arms were not big, the winged arms of the chair were large enough to hold both of us. When I now look back on those times, this frightened child was enveloped in a white light and carried by the grace and dignity of the gentle spirit of my mother. No unwanted hand could gravely harm her.

Adorno's statement, also from *Authoritarian Personality*, "Intolerance of ambiguity is the mark of an authoritarian personality," was as relevant on my first day of school as it is to this day in my career as anesthesiologist.

With my vague verbal summary to my father of my first day of formal education I was jolted with a lasting whiplash of authority. Not only was "good" not good enough, but I also quickly understood

---

2 *Minima moralia, Reflections from damaged life p190-192*

that uncertainty was unacceptable. How ironic that in my chosen profession, there is no room for indecisiveness. Every hour at work I must take control and speak and act with authority, which is the cornerstone of survival for my patients.

Further down, along the same avenue that we lived on, I would notice the polished brass plates that belonged to doctors of various specialties. My attempts to pronounce or guess the meaning of gynecology or otolaryngology gave me lots to think about. Around the corner and adjacent to the dinosaur museum were mysterious libraries, accessible only to university students and professors. Sometimes I wondered what it would take to study medicine.

Nadia

The brass plates I was most familiar with were those of Nadia's house, my childhood friend. Side by side, her parents had their names engraved on two shiny brass plates as professors of ear, nose, and throat surgery.

I remember my sense of awe at the gnarled magnolia tree the day it burst into a canopy of pink and white blossoms in her front yard. I longed to bring a bouquet to my mother and inhaled the sweet fragrance to soothe my chronic sense of uneasiness when I thought of our own home. I cheerfully slipped through the formal scrolled wrought-iron gate and skipped across the smudged chalk lines I had drawn two days earlier with my friend. I went to visit her, her parents, her grandmother, and her dog several times a week.

The massive varnished oak front door of Nadia's house, with

Nadia's home

its intricate bell and speaker system, was slightly intimidating. The front entrance was mainly designated for patients who came to see her parents. On the days I was buzzed in by the receptionist as an extended family member, I felt particularly important and privileged.

Most of all, I admired Nadia's mother and had an early sense of wanting to emulate her elegant authority, her knowledge, and her wealth. I loved watching her in her starched, crisp white coat against her permanent tan, her jewelry, and her stethoscope. I felt intoxicated by the mild smell of disinfectant mixed with her expensive perfume that lingered outside the treatment room. I liked the shiny parquet floor and the white glass cabinets, as she was rushing from room to room to see the next patient. She was never too busy for a light-hearted twinkle in her eye or a word of encouragement as I passed through to find my friend upstairs. Somehow she always found time for a hug, and sometimes she let me look around in the treatment room.

On days when I was in a hurry to share some important news with my friend or make plans for a sleepover at her house, it was faster to cross the square patch of lawn next to my house and climb over the brick wall. It gave me great pleasure to remove loose pieces of mortar on our neighbor's side of the wall to create a better threshold to wedge my toes in. I hoped that no one was watching.

The red brick wall at the end of our neighbor's property was tall enough that I carefully considered my jump down the other side. I would sit on its edge as if on a diving board and ask for courage before I let myself go into a brief free fall and a hard landing. There was no real backyard at my best friend's house, just a lot of packed soil and clay with some weeds, a narrow lot that would accommodate two cars back to back. It seemed that there was a permanent heap of half-mixed concrete with murky puddles and a wheelbarrow left behind by the construction workers. It was an ongoing project to repair the back wall of the massive three-story stucco house built at the turn of the century.

I took the jump down Nadia's back wall and considered it a good landing when I didn't scrape my knees or my hands. I then quickly and light-heartedly entered her house by way of the back stairs. It was a tightly wound staircase with steep steps painted glossy gray. The staircase was framed by a black banister and bright white walls. It seemed like climbing a tower and would make me dizzy whenever

I went too fast. The stairs led directly to the old butler's pantry with mysterious drawers, just outside the kitchen on the second floor.

I was slightly apprehensive climbing the back stairs, as the family bulldog might tear down the stairs any moment with a fierce growl and knock me over by putting his paws on my shoulders and drooling all over my face. The only time he seemed obedient was during meal times in the dining room. Nadia's father, an imposing man of large stature and a voice as deep and powerful as the bark of their great dane, would pick up the silver sugar bowl and tap it lightly on the dog's head, saying, "Sit, Bruno, sit," to which he responded like a lamb and stretched out on all fours.

It didn't really matter to me if Nadia was home or not; if not today, I would see her tomorrow. Someone of the family was always home, most likely her grandmother, whom I loved as much as my own. Her small apartment was up on the top floor. She was a tall, round, robust woman with a Lithuanian accent and pudgy arms that would always be open for hugs. Her tiny gray eyes were almost lost between her fleshy cheeks, but I could always find that smile. She kept a close friendship with my own grandmother, who paid her a regular weekly visit for mutual support and respect. Both of them had to leave their old countries, Lithuania and Hungary, under political duress and shared their memories and their concerns for their daughters and granddaughters over tea and biscuits, sometimes in Russian.

Twice a week for five years, from age ten to fifteen, my friend Nadia and I took ballet lessons together. One of my expectations was that if I followed faithfully, I would eventually look like Nadia.

She was tall and willowy. Her long legs and strong feet gave her the natural grace of a racehorse. Her smooth skin was like whipped cappuccino, even between her toes. Her long brown hair flowed like a silk scarf around her skinny shoulders when she danced. She slid into a split on the floor without any signs of discomfort, stretched legs pointing to opposite walls. She could also lift her legs from a sitting position and curl them around the back of her head, as pliable as strands of dough. From the window-frame of her twisted legs, she would look out with a smile and remind me about summer vacation. "Make sure your parents call mine so we can meet in Timmendorf."

Sometimes I would be so envious of her double-jointed agility that I had to fight back the tears. The wiry dance master invariably picked her from the circle of students still assembled on the floor to take the lead position at the bar. I usually ended up in the last third of the row. Neither did I move up to the lead position when we turned around to the other side, away from the mirror for more mandatory plies and warm-up drills. However, as soon as our regular pianist started to count and played the familiar etudes by Chopin, I forgot my underprivileged status at the bar.

After class we massaged our wounded toes. It was an easy downhill road that took us back to our neighborhood. It seemed short while I happily chatted my way home with Nadia.

When she was not with me, the walk home was much longer. I stopped at the candy store. I bought large chunks of pink-and-white striped peppermint to fill the absence of my friend. I always had enough pocket change for something sweet, which, I acknowledge was a poor choice to ward off my hunger.

Later, in our early teens, she was the chosen one I could confide in about my crush on one of my brother's tall classmates. His name was Michael. His horn-rimmed glasses were refined and experienced, I thought. I had seen him a few times at church on a Saturday afternoon, which seemed an odd time for a young man to go to church. He had come by himself.

"Do you think he showed up to see me?" I asked her.

I didn't really want to know the answer, while Nadia shrugged her shoulders.

"Keep showing up yourself," was her somewhat disappointing but practical advice.

We changed the subject.

"Where did you get the white top with the sparkles?" I asked instead.

"On sale at Schneider's; you want to go and check it out?"

I waved off, disappointed. "I don't have money!"

Sometime later Michael and I did get to the talking stage, and he invited me to his home after church for tea and cookies. No one else seemed to be home. We stayed in the living room the whole time and sat on opposite sofas. We talked about the theater. No invitation followed. That was the extent of the relationship. I went back to Sunday-morning mass.

Nadia had much more freedom to date than I ever had. Her father took care of a waiting room filled with patients. My father watched closely with whom I spent every hour of the day. Indeed, Nadia's father allowed her to hold party after party at her formidable house. She invited mostly friends from her private school, while I attended public school.

The one party I really remember took place on the ground floor

Nadia, my childhood friend

in the library. Its leaded stained glass windows, reaching from floor to ceiling, overlooked the front yard. Looking through the wavy glass, the canopies of the magnolia trees ballooned to twice their size. Besides the dark oak-paneled walls, there was an intricate inlaid design on the parquet floor. There we fluttered and flirted into a slow shuffle as the night went on. The lights were dim while I tried to understand why Nadia was always in somebody's arms, whereas I could not connect with anybody. I just stood and stared at the couples without knowing what to do. I detested wallflowers and had no respect for them. But more often than not, I became one. I longed for Nadia to tell me her secret of how to be popular and more attractive. Should I change my hair, my dress, my body, my words, or the entire me? Sometimes I wondered if there was anything right about me. I had been excited about the party but felt most uneasy and was relieved to go home empty-handed and not kissed after midnight.

I believe it was at one of her parties when Nadia met her husband to be, a dashing but sinister-looking, wealthy young man from Colombia, who seemed to know the way of the world.

My Early World of Medicine

I was introduced to the world of medicine by default. My four years of elementary school from ages six to ten felt like a continuous effort to straighten me out. It seemed a never-ending task to correct the squint in my eyes. There were other appointments with an orthopedic doctor to examine my all-too-flexible bowed legs and align the tilt in my posture due to a mildly S-shaped spine. Finally, my permanent incisors overcrowded my narrow jaw and began to overlap like rabbit's teeth. My parents insisted on braces.

There were multiple office visits with the stern eye doctor. The intricate equipment fascinated me but even more so, the brains required to operate it. With each click on the big black wheel with more windows than I could count, my vision would change in an instant. The doctor became even sterner after my father refused to consent to an operation he recommended.

The doctor predicted that I would wear glasses by the time I would go to my first dance. Instead of the operation, he gave me regular appointments with his nurse, who was to exercise my eye muscles. She coached me to focus on vertical copper rods, which she passed rapidly at arm's length from one side of her body to the other. Between appointments, my father reminded me harshly to look straight, while my eyes rolled hopelessly out of control.

It took me more than forty years to reconsider the possibility of having the operation, which was done successfully at the age of fifty-one.

The orthopedic appointments for my bowed legs bored me at best. My mother sat patiently with me in the waiting rooms. Together we read about unruly "Struwelpeter" and "Pipi Langstrumpf," a brazen girl my age with pigtails the color of carrots and long legs in red-and-white striped leggings. There was nothing I liked about these appointments. The special insoles I had to wear in my shoes felt strangely uncomfortable. I don't remember any outstanding features about the doctor except when he would squeeze my feet into various shoes. The worst part was the frequent home assignments, where my father would have me walk up and down the length of the living room with my spine as straight as the demonstrated broomstick. Over and over I was told to hold my head up high above average so I would stand out from a crowd and rise above the rest of the world. It was at this point that my mother signed me up for my beloved ballet lessons.

For the most part, I found that all the doctors were very kind to me. Generally, I felt more at ease with the lady doctors. There was a female pediatric doctor with large, owl-like glasses and the name of Dr. Habicht, which means "hawk."

She had the unpleasant task of giving immunization shots to my brother and me. I didn't really understand why I needed a shot when I wasn't sick, but I did not mind them too much, as she always rewarded my tearless stillness with a honey-flavored cough drop.

When she knelt down right next to my face, she looked even more like an owl, especially when she came at me with a wooden tongue depressor, which resembled the beak of a large bird. She pressed on my tongue with the dry wooden stick while I tried to say, "Ahh." It made me gag while she looked around with a bright flashlight. She took my mother aside and whispered something that felt like a secret I was not supposed to hear. I don't recall being told that I needed an operation for my tonsils.

All I remember is being in a ward with other children. I cried a lot when my mother was waving and smiling through a large glass window before she turned and walked away. The tiny chocolate trains, which she had brought for me in a long, flat, green box with pictures of mountains and cows, melted in my hot little hand, mixed with tears.

The most impressive doctor during my childhood, besides Nadia's mother, was the female professor of orthodontics at the University Medical Center. To be a patient of hers was considered a great privilege. At that time, only families that were well-off could afford her private fees. Other patients even came from as far as Switzerland for her renowned expertise in this new specialty.

With her extraordinary height and stature, she made a grand appearance and immediately instilled confidence and knowledge. The waiting room was always packed with mothers and their children, scattered toys, and grown-up magazines. I loved the clicking sound of her high heels on the parquet floors as she moved back and forth from the waiting room to the treatment room. She was a moving portrait in black and white, with her immaculately starched white coat and the black luster of her long, wavy hair. Her smiling row of perfect white teeth matched the string of pearls against her olive skin.

The first few times in her treatment room, she spent time showing me rows and rows of cast plaster molds of the most grotesque-looking teeth with a normal looking set next to them—before and after her treatment. They were all neatly stacked in white glass cabinets. There was nothing as grotesque about my teeth, and I was wondering why I was there, until she explained that my mouth was too small and would cause a crowded overlap of my permanent teeth. Once I was in her green-and-white dental chair, I gladly endured the chalky taste of so many impressions to fit me for braces. I wished that someday I would acquire her knowledge, but most of all her power. Throughout my lifetime my teeth and my memories of her have remained assets I cherish.

All the doctors I visited in my childhood possessed two attributes that I desperately wanted: an enviable amount of knowledge and the right to a magic confidence and control, both of which I lacked at home.

Lessons

Sometimes it seemed that I had to do everything twice before I got it right. I remember my frightful performance anxiety when playing whatever piece of music I had practiced all week on the piano for my father. He was the musical expert in the house and played the piano and violin remarkably well without any lessons ever. My fingers invariably tripped in the opening bar, and I knew that the second time around was my last chance to avoid serious criticism. I could never make the scales sound as smooth as a zipper. Maybe it was just the grand piano that intimidated me, as my father had it custom made in an unusual honey-colored rosewood just after the war. To this day, I still start my piano practice with a tenacious repetition of the opening line.

My initial desire to study piano when I was a child was denied several times on the grounds that I did not have the discipline or perseverance required to make the investment of time and money worthwhile. My brother was already quite successful with the classical guitar and performed well for guests and family, which left me in a corner, filled with pangs of jealousy mixed with pride. Finally, at the age of twelve I was allowed to start scales with a straight-laced lady teacher and her upright piano. I liked her best around Christmas time. Fraulein Mettinger softened a bit around that time, and her one-room apartment would embrace me with the aroma of gingerbread cookies and tangerines, all laid out on a plate with pine branches and walnuts to fill the gaps.

Sometimes I wonder why I chose such a demanding and frequently crisis-oriented specialty. At the time my decision was made partly by default. Almost from the beginning of medical school, I was attracted to the surgical environment rather than the discipline of medicine, one reason being that I liked action and the use of my hands. I did not think I had the patience to watch patients on a medical floor, recovering invisibly slowly, often by just being removed from their self-defeating habits into the wards of doctors who seemingly scratched their heads from round to round, while the natural healing process gained the advantage.

I would have preferred to be a surgeon myself but realized that my given manual dexterity and optical depth perception would not win me a national reputation. My visual defect was rudely pointed out to me when I first rode a bicycle. Soon out of control on the merry-go-round of a circular gravel driveway outside the front door of at a hotel in Holland, I landed on top of a bumper of a guest car. Also, when I took driving lessons with my father, it was clear that I did not visually negotiate the winding country roads in Ireland the way my father intended me to.

A basic lack of manual dexterity for small stitches in sewing class at age ten caught my parents and me by surprise. We had just come off the ski slope on a Christmas vacation in Switzerland and were settling into the armchairs of the hotel lounge for afternoon tea with live, old-fashioned music to dance to. My father arrived with a bundle of mail, mostly business, forwarded from Germany. I remember a blue thin envelope that obviously contained bad news, judging by my father's stern expression. I could see thunder behind his brow directed toward me. The music made me dizzy. It was juxtaposed with the clash of his fist on the small, round, glass-covered table that made the teacups jump and rattled the silver spoons on saucers. A note from the teacher who taught handicraft and sewing announced that I had failed in her class. I was unable to eat for the next two days.

What I did not realize at the time of my early pull to the surgical environment was that the specialty of anesthesiology was a natural step into an environment that was most familiar to me. Constant vigilance of my father's next outburst of temper kept me ever alert to deal with unexpected emergencies. I learned early to adapt by staying calm and speechless until the worst was over. I had developed a natural survival skill by becoming a quiet caretaker of others.

A more obvious advantage of the specialty was the elusive promise that it would allow me to enjoy a prospering family life and selectively choose my work schedule, neither of which became a reality. I had visions of entering the operating room in a white-starched coat and high heels. I wanted to look like a lady, much like the mother of my best childhood friend, who held tenure as a professor at the university and shared her office with her equally famous husband.

Little did I know that my daily uniform would consist of wrinkled scrubs in blue or green. Tied at the waist with a cotton string, the pants sometimes had holes glued together with surgical tape that had been cycled through the laundry many times. But there was no time to change. Surgeons don't wait. There was no way out of scrub pants that absorbed warm blood from a patient until it stuck to my thigh during a procedure. I remember the warm urine that sometimes spilled from a leaky valve of the catheter bag and soaked my pants while I took an hourly output measurement. I would just have to stand there, holding it off my leg until it dried. The relief of a shower would have to wait until the end of the day.

Although my early impressions of medical miracle workers may have played a part in my choice to become a physician, I recently became aware that an unconscious undercurrent may have been a stronger catalyst in my decision.

The idea may have been born by the need to gain control in my life. The profession would finally unchain me from the constant reminder to rise above mediocrity, despite grades that, in my later years of school, exceeded my father's unacceptable average. There would hardly be anything as powerful as the feel of a syringe in my hand, loaded with a potent yellow liquid that would send any patient into a deep ocean of unconsciousness.

Typing lesson in my father's office

Buchschlag

In 1960 we were evicted by eminent domain by the University of Frankfurt from Senckenberg Avenue. Our new home was located in an established and prestigious suburb of Frankfurt. My father, being a resourceful and well-to-do businessman at that time, had earmarked this very formal home, built in 1914, with the grace and elegance of a mansion.

It had been on the market for some time but did not stir much interest for the average buyer. It contained twenty-two rooms in all, if you counted the dressing room off the master bedroom. With its formal garden and sculptured hedges, it required a steady staff for maintenance of the house. While my father deliberated on the purchase, another buyer appeared. Both competed equally fiercely for the bid. My father took his offer to a courageous height but eventually reached his ceiling. The other buyer had the financial advantage. He closed the bid beyond our means. However, he was not seriously interested in living there, just the acquisition as an investment. My father negotiated a five-year rental lease for our family, and we moved in.

By now my baby sister had been born in Lugano, a chic and charming town in the south of Switzerland. It was located close enough to the Italian border for nocturnal smugglers to cross the mountainous terrain along the perimeter of the lake by foot. The spoken language was Italian, and I still remember how to buy "cento grame de prosciutto" at the local market.

My newborn sister, Cita, the shortened Italian version for Felicita, spent her first year of life in the sunny backyard of a vacation home, which my father had rented for five years. There she was nurtured by my mother in the garden, while being bathed, fed, and changed on a military schedule by a highly structured and disciplined nanny in a white uniform named Dedda. While Dedda pureed carrots and spinach in the kitchen, it was off limits to everyone else. I looked forward to having my mother, my new baby sister, and the nanny join us back in Frankfurt in this old formidable house, Buchschlag.

I wanted to play with my baby sister, only to find out that she already had a mind of her own. She could not be persuaded to share her snacks or her toys. More often, the nanny snatched her away for yet another bath.

Buchschlag, which I experienced from fourteen to seventeen and my sister from one to four years old, was the epitome of my exposure to sophisticated living. Five huge French doors lined the façade along a front terrace with curved stone steps into a scupltured garden. The doors opened to Frankfurt's elite society, with music, dinner, and garden parties.

My sister Felicitas, called "Cita", age 4 at Buchschlag

The formal elegance of the house made up for my social shyness and personal embarrassment at the time. I was already rather chubby then. I remember a stylish party my brother and I were allowed to host for our teenage friends. I danced all night in the Steinhalle (stone foyer) in a blue dress with a great big white embroidered collar. The dress was quite flattering. I thought this was my chance to really impress Michael, the sophisticate from the Goethe Gymnasium, on whom I still had a hopeless crush. But he only danced with me once and after the party never asked me for a date.

I was allowed to select my own furniture for my new bedroom in the front wing of the house with a generous but shady balcony. I chose a contemporary Scandinavian design in teakwood. The custom-made drapes in a vibrant blue with accents of purple and a large carpet in icy blue only added to the sense of cold I always felt in this part of the house, with its northern exposure. I thought the furniture looked more interesting in the store than when it arrived in my room. I surrounded myself with lots of books and artwork on the walls to create a sense of coziness.

Buchschlag – front of house, my room left upper balcony

Sometimes I felt a bit isolated in my drafty blue corner room. I gravitated more to the back of the house where nurturing was tangible. I loved to visit my mother in her bedroom while she was sorting out her wardrobe. She often had a new dress to show me and would let me try on her jewelry.

I also spent much time in my baby sister's nursery. It was also located toward the back of the house that overlooked the garden and featured an adjacent room for the nanny. It was the sunniest part of the house. Dedda spent most evenings lathering luxurious lotions all over her tan arms and legs in her crisp uniform. I used to love the smell of baby powder that followed her. She moved with clinical precision.

My brother Axel was studying or practicing his classical guitar in his front bedroom, or else he jammed with his school friends, who drummed up a band on the third floor. I did not feel welcome beyond the door that carried an invisible sign to "Keep Out." Besides, I had to practice my own scales and short pieces on the piano in the great hall to demonstrate some progress when my father came home in the evening after his daytime business in Frankfurt.

The dinners we had together in the dining room were often cold by the time the maid carried them from the front kitchen through the Steinhalle. I particularly disliked limp vegetables or anything smothered with a sauce that had turned lukewarm and lumpy. I would not eat much of it at the table but would find something to my liking in the kitchen later, usually a dessert.

My favorite days were when my grandmother took the train from Frankfurt to visit for the day. As soon as I came home from school, I hurried to find her in the sunny salon. There she would usually do some of her fine embroidery or would teach me some English or French. She would tell me stories about her own world of aristocracy and her significant estate in Hungary, left behind at the end of the First World War. Sitting next to her in the salon, I felt that all was not lost, and I was happy that Buchschlag brought back a glimpse of the old world for her. In that space, she had a radiance about her that I shall never forget.

I felt anxious when my father brooded for a long time behind the heavy sliding door of his study. One never knew in what kind of mood he might surface for his evening cognac by the fireplace. Whenever he called one of us into his study there could be trouble, or at least reason to be concerned, such as a bad grade or a cut in weekly allowance for something we forgot to do. Sometimes we used this room to play a round of family bridge or my father would settle down there for a lengthy game of chess with my brother. My brother was victorious when on occasion he could declare my father checkmated.

The Christmas tree had its traditional place in the living room, centered in one of the French doors next to the piano. We always used real candles to add to the glow of the fireplace. We dressed very formally on Christmas. My brother and I were encouraged to do our best with a brief musical Christmas recital with the guitar or on the piano before receiving any gifts.

For the few years I lived in Buchschlag, I was saddened by the fact that we did not own the house. The next move was predictable, although the destination was not. Even then I felt that our existence there was like a bright flame of my father's ambitious and exuberant, sometimes volatile, spirit. The time we lived there seemed much shorter than the three years we actually spent there. I thought I could still smell the fresh paint when my father announced his next bold move. At age fifty-seven, he felt the strain of it all and could not tolerate the idea of living under someone else's roof. Instead, he had purchased a seventy-five-acre country estate in Ireland for a reasonable sum. On this parcel of land sat a house, over one hundred years old, in a state of disrepair. But he could call it his own. He would fix it up and make it a habitable dwelling for my mother, my baby sister, and myself.

Glenbeg House as purchased by my father in 1960

He yearned for solitude and announced that "We," as a family, would move to Ireland in 1963. My older brother, who had already begun his studies, would remain Germany.

The announcement of our move caused a big gasp of surprise and good gossip amongst the circles of Frankfurt's elite society. Any concerns for the family were quickly drowned in the party of the decade. I remember my mother's long, sequined silk gown, the color of celery, and my father looking like Clark Gable in his tuxedo, with a cluster of women in line for the last of his infamous kisses. I only knew them too well, observing, receiving. My mother did not share my father's enthusiasm about the forthcoming move, but raised no serious objection.

There was no substantial argument when my father felt it was time for him to retire and sail into his sunset, which became his passion. *Sunset* became the name of his boat that he sailed from Ireland, via the Azores, to Antigua and back.

It was a sad day when they packed my blue room into an overseas container. It would be weeks or months before I would unpack my favorite books and my collection of tiny turtles and teacups and find a new home for them. I tried not to look back but forward to our next adventure, like my grandmother would, when I heard the front door shut for the last time.

At the time of our departure, I did not think that I would ever set foot in the house again. It was a brief privilege to live there for three years, one that left a distinct mark on the geographic map of my residential footholds. To possess it was a childish dream, but to have lived there was an experience that has remained with me throughout my life as a certain expectation to always create a quality home within my means. For the most part it became a memory I would always treasure in my heart.

During a recent trip to Germany I learned that Buchschlag had changed ownership. It was acquired by a young CEO and his family. Through an old family friend, my brother and I were introduced to the new owners. The couple promptly and graciously invited us for tea.

Here was an amazing, unexpected opportunity, thanks to the generous invitation of the present owners, to be able to retrace my steps one more time back into my childhood in the house I loved so much. Spending two hours in this house after thirty-eight years was a conscious walk back into my childhood. For two hours I was fourteen again. I was wrapped in the memories, like in an old dress found at the bottom of a steamer trunk that was shipped to our next destination in Ireland.

I have thought a lot about the delightful afternoon at the house. My nostalgia for the past was more than compensated for what I found in the present. The expansive house has turned into a home and haven for the family that I always dreamed of as a teenager. It is filled it with color, light, and life and the finest expression of a well-adjusted family. I must be careful not to compare how I felt about the house in the past with the magnificent transformation I met in the present. It is only fair to say that anyone who had visited us in 1961 would have been equally enchanted by the graciousness of my family.

Ireland, a Stepping Stone

When I was sixteen my father made the irrevocable decision to sell his business and retire to Ireland. He had developed a passion for sailing the open ocean.

I don't remember much of a preparatory time for our move to Ireland. The move was scheduled for early May, just one month before my seventeenth birthday. An initial sense of adventure turned into a sobering reality when all our furniture was unloaded from the boat in large wooden containers, each the size of a trailer. The furniture arrived; I left behind my friends. My brother had already begun his college courses in Germany and also remained apart from us. I missed Nadia. My arms were not long enough to reach out to her across the Irish Sea.

It was unlikely that I would catch up with Nadia anyway. She was what we then called a jet-setter. I never knew her whereabouts. She could be in Nice at the Cote d'Azur one day and in Spain the next. I imagined wherever she went there would be a party.

It was not long after we moved to Ireland that Nadia, at age eighteen, moved to Bogota. There she was to be married into the household of a large plantation. There was a permanent staff to care for her while her husband traveled around the world of business. What at the time seemed an enviable romance, compared to being stranded next to a tiny rural schoolhouse in Ireland, would turn out to be my opportunity and the beginning of Nadia's tragic destiny.

The same hands that wrapped passionately around Nadia's waist would later whip her into unconsciousness and drag her into a deep and dark underworld of drugs. We didn't know then that we would never see each other again. Nadia always signed her letters to me with one thousand kisses with large, round Os. Over time they became less frequent. While I was saddled with chocolate cravings, Nadia was consumed by a hopeless fight against a fatal addiction. While I stepped into her parents' footsteps and pursued a career in medicine, Nadia became more and more anesthetized by potent concoctions of drugs and alcohol. She quietly slipped away in her forties in Spain. By the time I recognized her serious distress, it was already too late. My few and feeble attempts to come to her rescue were in vain.

To this day I often think of my lost childhood friend. Since then, my fight for anyone in the clutches of an alcohol or drug addiction has a sharp edge and a tireless willingness to go to any length or distance to bring him or her back to reality. How peculiar that I lost part of myself anesthetizing others.

It was a well-conducted but complicated move from Buchschlag to Dungarvan, Ireland. It was also a time when I needed my mother the most. During our first few days in Dublin, my mother and I were in a state of disbelief about our new home. We laughed about the most unattractive display of shoes in a store window we had ever seen. They were so klutzy that they rolled off a stack of boxes and landed upside down. We laughed until we were in tears, not caring if these were tears of loss and longing or about the only joy of having each other to hold on to. We sat down, drank tea, and pushed away the soggy cucumber sandwiches.

Just like her mother being forced out of Hungary, my mother eventually found a way to accept her new way of life, so different from what she was accustomed to. And just like her mother, she rose above her personal challenges with grace and dignity.

We were barely established in Ireland when I turned to the obvious task of quickly adapting to the new language. I was enrolled in the School of Ursulines starting in September. This total immersion into the English language would be the surest way to develop my scanty vocabulary and finish my last year of high school at the same time.

During the first summer in Ireland, the few phrases of English I had learned at the Frankfurt high school were barely adequate to buy cupcakes or scones at the cake shop. The display of pink-and-yellow frosted concoctions was alluring in the gray square of the small town, three miles from the house. Once in a while my mother and I ventured into Dungarvan, but when we could not find whatever we were looking for, we turned to each other. Once a week, on Thursday, there was a cattle mart in the town square. It usually took a day or two to remove the green liquid mess left behind.

Everything was different in Ireland. Even the telephone seemed as antiquated as when it was first invented by Alexander Graham Bell in 1876. There were no numbers on the rotary disc. It moved in slow motion and only served to contact the operator. After a series of clicks came the brassy voice of the lady at the switchboard, mounted in the backroom of the post office. "Hello."

"Oh," she said, "you are the new family who moved to Glenbeg House." She coughed. I was sure she smoked a lot.

"I'd like to call Germany," I said impatiently.

"Yes, Miss, can you call me back in five minutes?" she wanted to know. "Or better, I'll call you when I have a free line."

"Thank you, but never mind," I said. By now my father was back in and out of the living room, stacking logs in the fireplace.

The view out the large, square picture window of the living room at Glenbeg House was full of promises. The window, braced by the massive stone walls, overlooked a wide ocean bay on the east shore. Rumor had it that the opening scenes of *Moby Dick* were captured on film from our front lawn, high up on a hill.

Glenbeg renovated as our family residence in 1963

At the far wall of the living room, the flames flickered high as they danced inside the black mantelpiece, which otherwise resembled a tombstone. The oil lamp on top of the mantelpiece was not lit because its etched glass dome had a serious crack. It could easily be damaged further if it was removed to be cleaned and put down on a hard surface. It was just as well to leave it unlit. Time on the brass carriage clock next to it had stood still for a long time.

The living room at Glenbeg House

At the left corner of the fireplace there was a commanding high wing chair, upholstered with petit point tapestry. In it my father looked distinguished in his gray lamb's wool cardigan that matched the color of his beard. Within an arm's reach from the chair was a curved inlaid chest of drawers that leaned against the long wall. On it a heavy brass tray carried a variety of bottled hard liquor, almost always down to the last quarter of their contents. Unscrewing their caps was the opening bar of homemade philosophy.

The wooden inlaid sofa table in front of the large chair was graceful with its curved legs. On it, crystal tumblers half-filled with scotch were set up to encourage in-depth conversations. These were usually conducted between five and seven in the evenings. Everyone at home was expected to be present.

My father often rubbed his hands over the carved lion head armrests when he contemplated his next move. They seemed to keep him calm, yet in times of crises provided something to hold on to when his hot temper threatened to lift him right out his chair. The wooden lion heads could take the blunted blow of his fist that was sometimes meant for me and not buckle. The chair held up well to him over the years.

Sometimes I would look in through the window from outside and wonder how the same space could look so different with just one pane of glass between me and the chair. The flames in the fireplace danced cheerfully while my father was dozing.

Convent Habits

I remember Mother Ambrose looming with her large frame behind the massive wooden double door of the Ursuline boarding school. The heavy brass knocker was polished with new vigor every day. My father was on his best behavior when he dropped me off under her wings. After all, she was the headmistress of the school. He tried hard to make a good impression. She received him with her most saintly smile. Her pudgy, pasty face showed evidence of too much bread and too little exercise. Her doughy hands were mostly tucked in the folds of her flowing black habit. It was always wrinkle-free. The white plastic collar around her neck was as rigid as a napkin ring.

Her authority was not negotiable. She boldly proposed that her hope for me was to matriculate from a two-year curriculum in just one year, despite the language hurdle. Apparently she had a keen eye for her students and made an accurate assessment, as I rose to the challenge.

Leaving the tensions of home outside the tall, mossy walls surrounding the school, I found relief at being embraced by halls and corridors filled with silence. My assigned dormitory smelled of beeswax that evaporated off the dark polished wooden floor. The aroma mingled pleasantly with that of laundered white sheets and neatly folded cotton blankets. I came to appreciate the uncluttered order and comforting simplicity. Surrounded by this hushed ambiance, I learned to study and to pray.

I felt safe in the intimate blue-and-white chapel. It was faithfully filled with fresh-cut daffodils next to candles that burned perpetually. Side by side, they seemed to deliver the essence of my prayers. With all the humility I could muster, I conversed with whatever spirit hovered in the chapel.

I yearned for reassurance that there was a greater purpose to my confinement in this new and strange environment. Where would I go from here? Maybe it was as simple as staying right here and becoming a nun. Sometimes I felt a sense of belonging as obvious as that of the

Gabriele F. Roden MD

silver chalice on the lacy linen that flowed across the altar. It would not take much to convince me. Being obedient was already as natural as placing one foot in front of the other, while I longed for stability outside our home. Entering the convent would certainly ensure a sheltered lifestyle. Besides, I liked whatever came out of the kitchen. I found bliss when the chunky Irish brown bread with marmalade was passed along the long rectory tables and purpose when I volunteered to clean it up. No one here made me feel ashamed or thick.

Another favorite niche was the library overlooking the rose garden. Heavy shelves of dark oak were stacked to the ceiling with inspirational books about saints and martyrs. Their bound pages were enriched by having absorbed the whispered secrets of students and novices for many seasons. It didn't matter which part of the country the novices came from. Once they had taken the vows of chastity, poverty, and obedience and settled into their daily routine behind the convent walls, they all had three things in common: their habits, their pale skin, and whatever world they left behind.

Their habits flowed and gushed with each step, like a puddle of water around their ankles. Sometimes it felt as if their black cloud would first envelop and then inhale you with a gasp if you argued. There was no point. All the nuns liked hiding their hands underneath the top layer in some deep pockets next to the safety of the rosary beads. Maybe idle hands could get into trouble and do shameful things. Perhaps they needed to control the urge to slap you across the face for being young and still having a chance at romance outside the high brick wall.

Their skin, rarely exposed to the sun or the elements, was the chronic color of milk. There was no radiance of passion, no red blotches from being kissed on the neck. I imagined it would feel cool to the touch like sculptured marble, chiseled to the conformity of convent rules. Their features, almost never off balance, were embalmed by the repetition of the same daily routine.

I often fantasized what personal distractions might render life as a nun bearable in the long run.

Up at dawn and on their knees. A splash of water on the face, under the arms, and on their private parts would do for now. They didn't waste time or money on make-up and hairdos. There were some benefits to a cloistered lifestyle that only revealed the eyes and the corners of the mouth.

I was up early one morning and on my way to the bathroom, with my toothbrush in hand and a towel over my shoulder. I met a sister in the hallway as she breezed by me without a smile of recognition. She seemed in a terrible hurry, almost running. It was her duty to prepare breakfast for the girls in the kitchen. The precise act of cutting the fresh loaves of bread into equal wedges and not eating the crusty crumbs before communion must have kept sister's mind off some other guilt written all over her face. What could possibly have happened before dawn?

I had idle time to imagine her back in her Spartan bedroom. I dreamed up that she became aware of a delicious temptation while she waited for the day. She would tell herself it was only natural and not a big deal, as she would gather the different parts of her robe to get dressed for the day.

Whatever it was, it made her close the door to the confessional ever so quietly behind her, just as I was the first to enter the chapel for morning mass. I knew enough to realize that if she received communion in a state of sin, she would have a bigger problem.

She slid out of the confessional more gracefully than she entered. She appeared at ease again, free of guilt to join the fellowship of sisters who were equally committed to the vows and equally human. They too had left a world behind, with brothers, sisters, and cousins. It was a messy world. When they entered the convent they seemed relieved to be unburdened of the constant clean-up job of relationships. They were eager to learn new relationship skills based on more spiritual principles, and so was I.

I was suspicious of those who had slowly but steadily gained weight underneath the forgiving habit. The weight had festered until the folds of their bellies, hips, and buttocks became one with the black cloth. I had my share of eating for reasons other than hunger. I often felt fearful and lacked confidence about my future. There was not much opportunity to talk about the power my father had over me. To get back to the books was a safer place.

There were other reasons to drop myself onto the kneeling bench. The narrow wooden board dug into my knees no matter how I shifted my weight. The slight discomfort brought me back from soft daydreams to a reality that was not solid yet. I stayed on the bench searching for direction. I wanted to be useful on earth and not succumb to a frivolous and fluffy lifestyle.

Around Christmas time one of my classmates, the daughter from our neighbor's farm, fell in love. Another prosperous farmer from our hometown pursued her in earnest. His intention to marry her was quickly obvious to all. He took her to the theater and other shows in Dublin on weekends. When she returned on Sunday evenings she cried a lot. For the next few days she lit up the classroom with her hearty laugh and a fresh and freckled glow. Her curly red hair bounced along the corridors as she shared her newfound love freely with all of us. She did not make it up either. Each month a huge bunch of long-stemmed red roses arrived reliably, along with more invitations to family gatherings and other outings. This was better than reading a novel. It was real, and I longed for it to happen in my life also. After all, I needed to return to the world outside these halls.

I felt a strong desire to establish myself in a profession that would sustain me and engage me on the long road ahead of me, irrespective of where my family or I lived. I wanted to be part of a community committed to healing. Put in plain words by the nuns, this place was about healing souls. The bounty was always uncertain, intangible, at best an act of blind faith. I concluded the art of healing bodies with medicine would be more perceptible, more corporeal. The more I thought about it, the more sense it made, and I quickly fell in love with the idea of becoming a doctor. I had read much about Dr. Albert Schweitzer (1875–1965), an Alsatian theologian, musician, and medical missionary, who was awarded the Nobel Peace Prize in 1952. I shared his passion for the ingenious and orderly composition of Bach, which had a medicinal effect on me at an early age.

My decision to study medicine had come to me during the quiet time in the chapel as a more worldly choice than entering the convent. It would allow me to make a humane contribution and qualify me as a capable citizen of the world, with a gift from the heart that would be welcome anywhere. My resolve rang true. I was excited to announce my new revelation to my family at the next break. Maybe my declaration of my intent to study medicine would also help compensate for the demerit of having gained an unsightly amount of weight from the delicious double desserts and Irish spuds (potatoes) I had consumed.

Both my parents were overjoyed after they listened to my sincere plea. It prevailed over any doubt about the strength of my conviction and such a brave and grave commitment at age seventeen. By the end of the next term, after I had demonstrated a concentrated effort with various teachers and a few more consultations with Mother Superior Ambrose, my father was adequately satisfied to approve and fund my enrollment in medical school. My parents remained extremely supportive throughout medical school, which turned out to be the most barren financial time for my father ever. While my parents lived on meals of cabbage with thin slices of corned beef to save money for my tuition, I received a lifetime ticket to an undiscovered world of my own.

The study of medicine enthralls me even to this day. The discipline required to practice medicine while living a moderate lifestyle and the compassion I have found for my patients have indeed become my home, no matter where I am now.

Lectures, Libraries, and Landlady

My entire existence during medical school in Cork was framed by two questions: How did I get here, and where do I go from here? These thoughts were my steady companions as I walked uphill and downhill each day from my digs to arrive at the historic campus quadrangle of University College Cork. Fifty miles from home was a safe distance to point my finger at my father for such an unconventional, incomprehensible move to Ireland. Mostly I felt sorry for my mother and myself. She too seemed displaced and confused these days.

Along my route, I could not connect with the architecture of the long stretch of dark gray rows of houses, as dull as the forever-overcast sky. Their walls seemed permanently damp, with a tinge of green. Tiny windows were squared off with glossy painted window frames in various shades of browns and blues. There was no sun to let in. Instead, their lace curtains seemed permanently drawn shut, no matter what time of day I passed by. I felt foreign and shut out from a community I didn't know. Between five and six in the evening, which was tea time, I could smell their fried rashers and sausages. The ceilings were so low that it was easier to imagine a man sitting down for his cup of tea than standing upright inside. In the morning there was no sign of life.

I did my best to fill this bleak emptiness with a thirst for knowledge, a desire to excel in my studies and a huge hunger for comfort foods, which added nothing but unsightly, burdensome weight to my obstacles. Besides a poor body image, a fierce competition contributed to my sense of isolation from my first-year classmates.

There were ten foreign students in pre-med, who rallied for only four places in med school that were designated for students from abroad. Pre-med consisted of the basic sciences of botany, biochemistry, physics, and zoology. Once or twice I took home a half-dissected rabbit and a dogfish to impress my family, but their curiosity was short-lived as they retreated from the pungent smell of formalin. I desperately wanted to be one of the selected four and studied day and night until my letter of acceptance from the dean of med school arrived.

My new class at med school consisted of forty-nine honor students who had been selected by merit out of a group of one hundred applicants during pre-med. This class integrated the four foreign students, including me. Two of them, male students who confidently carried large attaché briefcases, were from England and at least spoke the same language. One other female student was a nun from Nigeria, who was shyer than I was. Her multicolored headscarf, wrapped around her wiry braids, kept slipping out of place. She smiled a lot but said little. All the others seemed to know each other or their cousins' cousins. Amongst them were a red-haired twin brother and sister in our class and their country cousin.

My stack of books and the enormous, cathedral-like study hall provided a quiet hiding place. The huge, arched wooden ceiling rafters high above the stained glass windows of the nineteenth-century granite wing were as far out of reach as six years of intense study between my first year and graduation. It was better to keep my eyes on the page in front of me, which explained the molecular structure of the cycle of Krebs.

On occasion I gave myself permission to break away from the library and stroll downtown along St. Patrick Street for window shopping and a welcome relief from my heavy mood. I took shelter from the rain at Cash's department store. At least it was carpeted in dark red velour, holding up to its promise of class. Counters of sweet perfumes were manned by friendly retired sales ladies, who attended to customers at their own speed. Ladies' garments were up the wide stairs. I just wanted to look for a new outfit, something to make me feel lighter. The ones I liked best did not come in my size; there was not much choice. While trying things on, a sideways glance in the mirror made me feel worse and deflated my brief excitement in an instant. My choices were further limited by looking for items on sale, since my parents paid dearly for school and my landlady's rent, with a hushed restraint. It was not wise to spend my slim monthly allowance the first week, when times were hard at home. My father, always optimistic about the next spur-of-the-moment business move, more often than not was not as successful as he had hoped.

Often I felt like I was juggling three challenges at once: English, Irish customs, and the language of medicine. Even though I had mastered my basic English quite successfully during the past year, I still liked to sit in the front row of the old lecture halls in med school to take full advantage of the body language and facial expression of the teachers to help fill in the blanks. Besides, it would eliminate the distraction of being gawked at by the fellows, since there were only seven or eight female students in our class of forty-nine.

I tried to win some friends, but they did not come easily in the beginning. I could sense awkwardness on their part, feeling shy with my accent and my being unfamiliar with the local customs. Eventually I was admitted into the tighter circle of my class. With time the shyness fell away, and our camaraderie developed steadily with the need to travel across town to various hospitals. Some of the students had their own cars and were kind enough to offer me lifts instead of having to take the rickety bus. Young Sandra was the daughter of a prominent cardiac surgeon who loved to go shopping on the way to or from the clinics. She thought I had good taste, coming from Europe, and often consulted me on outfits I could hardly afford. With my father's precipitous retirement, we were left without any income, a huge, cold house to heat, and although moderate, my school expenses for a few years to come. I did not want to squander it on fashion, especially since by now I was considerably overweight. The best part of getting a ride was meeting for coffee at the Bridge Café after a long morning at clinic. Like jigsaw puzzles, we pieced together glimpses of the private lives of our professors and medical doctors and surgeons we met on the wards. Any piece of information was welcome and found a place in our shameless fantasies of what it would be like to be married to a doctor.

Our professor of anatomy might as well have stepped out of a painting of historic scholars that framed the walls of the cavernous study hall. In his pinstriped suit, penetrated by a permanent odor of formalin, he was a semi-alive version of a dusted copy of Grey's Anatomy. His lethargy was a blend of decades of teaching and spending most of his waking hours with corpses. I don't remember any smiles beneath his salt-and-pepper mustache except a brief advisory on etiquette—to treat the bodies sprawled on stone slabs with utmost respect. When the professor was elsewhere, bolder students often named the corpse at hand and carried on a conversation with him or her.

In the second year of medical school I became fascinated with the intricate function of the rabbit heart and lung. The professor of physiology should have been a football coach in his tweed coat, only missing a whistle, a no-nonsense kind of man. He drilled us with pneumonics that became as steady as a heart beat. I found myself in a state of hyper-vigilance with adrenaline pumping through my system. It was in his class that I first became aware of the specialty of anesthesiology as an option to apply this living physiology in a clinical setting.

The clinical rotations through several Cork hospitals began in our third year. The largest public hospital was named St. Finbarr's. It was located on top of Douglas Road and dominated a large territory, like a fortress out of a Jane Eyre novel. Already at that time it appeared old-fashioned, a sprawling gray, gloomy, granite campus that had served the poor and the sick for decades. Its rooftop spewed steam and smoke form the many kitchens and laundry rooms. The building never dried out from the frequently lashing rain. In the winter it was a dark place.

Inside were open wards with white, metal-framed beds covered with white sheets and blankets, lined up against long walls. Nurses with white hats and uniforms would dash about with medicines and covered bedpans. There was no TV. The patients seemed to get along all right and kept each other company with news, jokes, and family stories. They shared their bottles of yellow Lucozade and water biscuits. Any visitors would also chat with the patient in the bed next to their relative or friend. Chances were, they knew each other, anyway—or at least their cousins.

Our professor would lead our group of eight to ten students to the bedside of a jaundiced patient. Of course, the patient had given prior permission to the nurses to be the subject of discussion without giving away the diagnosis. This, like detectives, we had to arrive at ourselves, considering all the differential possibilities given the signs and symptoms. Each category of infectious, inflammatory, or tumor-related disease had its own peculiar idiosyncrasy. I was good at this and had to restrain myself from blurting it out from the back of the circle. I also liked to linger with the patient while my classmates moved on and offer the patient some encouragement, as simple as, "Thank you. I hope you feel better soon."

There were other teaching hospitals spread throughout different parts of town. The Mercy Hospital next to the Black River was a small, intimate hospital mostly for private patients, which required our best behavior. The North Infirmary was a hike to get to but stood out with the most prominent cardiovascular surgeon in town who, as already mentioned, was also the father of my classmate. He made us tremble with his authority, and we were awestruck with his dizzying setup of surgical instruments. This was my first encounter with life-or-death surgery. The Bon Secours Hospital was just a block away from our classrooms. Each time we assembled in the lobby, we were greeted by an oversized statue of Virgin Mary with rosary beads, while the nuns floated to and fro with hushed voices. The patients here were attended to with devoted care in private rooms and with better meals. The best tea and sandwiches, however, for the professors and their students, were served at the Erinville Maternity Hospital around the clock, before and after deliveries. It was there I witnessed the first birth I had ever seen. I was surprised by and never quite understood my lack of compassion for women who pushed without epidurals to get every ounce out of the next contraction. I was just a helpless bystander who had no clue about their experience. Could I possibly be envious or jealous? Any feelings of that sort I discarded with the bloody and messy sheets in the laundry hamper. But a burst of desire and loneliness seized me when the baby cried and was received into its mother's arms.

During the same third year of clinical rotations I had the opportunity as a visiting medical student at Charing Cross Hospital in London to observe my first open heart surgery.

The upper viewer's gallery was separated from the surgical field by an angled sheet of glass. I shared a wooden bench with other young staff members at Charing Cross Hospital in London. I hovered directly over a cavernous chest cavity held wide open with large metal retractors that pressed against the rib cage. The lungs inflated and retracted in unison like two pink sponges. The surgeons' heads seemed small next to the huge dome shaped lights. Together heads and lights zoomed in on this sick heart, which looked like a wriggly red ball of flesh. Gloved fingers felt and searched for new possibilities.

The anesthesiologist dialed various flow meters up and down on a complex machine to protect this life-sustaining organ in its total vulnerability. This was startlingly different from the rabbit heart suspended in a salt solution in the physiology lab.

All of a sudden there was an undeniable knowing that some day I would be a member of such a team and stand at the head of the patient to guard his or her life throughout any surgical intervention.

Back in Cork, my steadiest friend and closest advocate during my six years in med school, besides my mother, was my landlady, Mary D., inseparable from her old dog, Prince. Prince moved very slowly, like an overstuffed sausage on disproportionately short legs. He was followed by a foul smell, and as often as I tried to stay clear of him, he would come and nestle against my feet. He actually helped keep them warm while I studied in the unheated dining room with my chair pulled as close as possible to the firebox, which my landlady devotedly prepared every night just for me. I pulled the chair just close enough to prevent the varnish of the wooden legs from blistering, my own feet placed on the tiled hearth until my legs were covered with red blotches from the heat. The red blotches had actually turned brown on my landlady's legs from years of reading a book by the fireplace in the living room. It was a tiny house, with the living and dining rooms downstairs and a kitchen that would barely fit a small table and two chairs. Upstairs were a front and a back bedroom and a small bathroom. I was allowed to sleep in the front bedroom with the bay window and a vanity with a mirror that was always covered with frost from the cold dampness.

I remember the day my father arrived with an electric blanket to replace Mrs. D.'s slushy hot water bottle wrapped in a towel. No special occasion comes to mind when he also presented me with a new RPM record of the "New World Symphony" by Antonin Dvorak. I felt happy and warm while I listened to the passionate, *molto allegro* first movement and dreamed of America. Later I learned that many have proclaimed that the spirit of Dvorak's symphony is quintessentially American in harmony with the nature of America as a melting pot. Dvorak was interested in the Native American music and spirituals he heard in America. Upon his arrival in America he stated, "I am convinced that the future music of this country must be founded on what are called Negro melodies. These beautiful and varied themes are the product of the soil."[3]

I loved the days my mother came to visit me in Cork. For her it was an equally joyful outing and a rare opportunity to shop at the nicer stores. We usually met in the quiet lobby of the Hotel Victoria on St. Patrick Street, next to the department store. Other guests clustered around low glass tables, deep in their own hushed conversations. The only sound I remember was the clink of the teacups on the glass. We had missed each other and didn't care if the tea was lukewarm. Her life seemed dull compared to mine, with frequent trips to the butcher in town for dog food. Chanel, a frisky cocker spaniel puppy, kept her good company and still made her laugh when she dashed off to catch a mouse. At home my mother helped my father clean up the mess

---

3   Peter Gutmann, *Classical Classics*, Dvorak's New World Symphony, Classical Notes.

left over from homemade sausages, while he scaled fresh salmon that the poachers had dropped off at the house. I considered myself lucky to be able to study.

Arm in arm, we then descended upon the department store to look for bargains. She could sense my heartache when nothing seemed to fit. "You look beautiful," she insisted lovingly and would not leave until we found a new sweater or blouse that would help us to separate when it was time to kiss and hug goodbye. I would escort her to her little red Volkswagen and wave until she had to move forward with the next green light.

It was time to walk back to school in a drizzle for the afternoon lectures and then the library. I chose to walk through the under-cover indoor market to stay dry. The smell of sawdust on the ground mixed with that of slabs of raw beef, and the sight of entire butchered hindquarters hanging from the ceiling made me nauseous. Perhaps a green apple would make me feel better. It was affordable, non-fattening, and would keep my mind off the still-foreign surroundings for a few minutes.

The rain was a good enough excuse to take the bus back to school instead of walking all the way. I carried too many books to bother with an umbrella. Besides, I had no clue how to take care of myself. At home I was told that umbrellas were only for weaklings. A bit of rain would surely not cause a meltdown. But in Ireland a daily shower was the norm. My landlady seemed smarter. She never left the house without her umbrella.

Finally the right bus, Number 10, arrived. I could not read or pronounce their posted destinations in Gaelic to places I did not care to explore. They were all the same to me and meant nothing. Should I sit upstairs or downstairs? Upstairs had the advantage of being all by myself while I tried to sort things out. Sometimes I feared that the old bus would topple over as it was huffing and puffing up steep hills with narrow streets, negotiating tight corners. Downstairs were mostly animated housewives returning home from daily mass, with bags of groceries. They proudly announced other bargains around town. They always seemed cheerful and all seemed to know each other, calling each other "Love," while waving goodbyes getting off the bus. They exchanged news about cousins, weddings, and babies, usually in that order. I settled downstairs. At least there was a spirit of friendly fellowship, including the bus driver, eventually getting home for tea. My landlady's brother was a bus driver. At least it was company while the bus rattled out College Road.

It was Thursday already and time to make a decision about going home for the weekend. I missed my mother and felt guilty but safer staying in town with my books.

For me going home to Dungarvan was always riskier. It did not take much to traumatize my spirit. It was almost predictable and would make it harder to concentrate on next week's assignments. Good grades would compensate. Good grades were cumulative tickets to freedom, to find a place to live of my choice. Get away from home, get away from it all. Someday it would all make sense.

Graduation

My medical diploma from UCC, University College Cork, is still rolled up in its original cardboard cylinder, just the way I received it on that glorious day of June 1970. Unlike other medical specialties, I do not meet any of my patients in a typical office setting with framed certificates on the walls. My credentials have taken residence in my head, my hands, and my heart.

It seemed incomprehensible to me that the gradually acquired knowledge led to an abrupt shift in my status from medical student to a fledgling doctor on that day. I was about to be pushed out of my nest to carry the message of hope and healing to patients, who from now on I could call my own.

There would never be enough space between the lines of the document that I was about to receive to hold all I had learned. I had gained important diagnostic skills at the bedsides of many patients. I also realized that besides the scrolled Latin script, the sheet of parchment contained the essence of a different language. By now medical terminology had become second nature to me. In medical terms any condition with "itis" attached to its primary organ spells inflammation (e.g., appendicitis). Any "ectomy" refers to the surgical removal thereof (e.g., appendectomy). From this day on I could trust that the basic building blocks of medical knowledge were mine to stand on at any moment.

It was a bright and sunny day, which in Ireland typically and most reliably occurs in the month of June. The lawn of the campus center stage had been meticulously cut for the occasion. For once I did not worry about my appearance, knowing that the large black gown would adequately cover my size eighteen sleeveless dress with its formal black-and-white printed design. This would soon be exchanged for a white coat. My mother wore a royal blue silk coat with a rose-colored pillbox hat, also in silk. She looked regal.

My father was strangely quiet that morning. He suddenly felt overwhelmed by the accolades of the faculty who honored the graduates, as well as the solid scientific knowledge of his daughter, who now knew all about medicine. His antique book with lessons from Paracelsus about the therapeutic effect of water had been replaced. Even more likely, he was already nostalgic as he watched his daughter receive her ticket that would surely take her away from home to America, with an ocean in between. But when the roll call began and my name was called, he promptly rose to get closer and claim his contribution to my having reached this milestone.

There was one guest of honor I wished could have been present on the day of my graduation. I missed my grandmother. Since her eyesight was failing when we left Germany, she moved with us to Glenbeg House in 1963. She passed away in 1966, during my third year of medical school. I remembered the weekends I came home and would run upstairs to find her in her bedroom. She would sit by the window for the best possible light and tell me about her liver, which worried her. She never drank anything but a sip of sherry to keep my father company. I had learned that hot water with lemon was good for the liver, and she made it part of her morning routine. It did nothing, however, to stall her malignant metastases, which surfaced later. She had been my most supportive advocate throughout medical school and told me over and over again, "Once you are a doctor, no one can take it away from you for the rest of your life."

When I returned from the podium with a handshake from the dean and my diploma, my father, just for a second, appeared almost diminished and inconsequential. There was no stopping me. As I moved closer I saw no cloud in his face, no frown on his brow, but a quiet look of pride and approval. All the lessons from childhood were finally rolled up in this paper sleeve with my name and my new degree, which read BM, BS, BAO: Bachelor of Medicine, Bachelor of Surgery, Bachelor of Arts of Obstetrics.

My little sister, eleven years old, looked up at me in awe. My mother was speechless but radiant. After tear-filled hugs, my classmates scattered with their families for a celebration and lunch at the local hotels. Great expectations simmered down once we got in the car and headed home to a familiar home-cooked meal. Since it was a special occasion, my father had prepared and poached a fillet of fresh salmon. He had kept it in the freezer for this day, next to my mother's precious diamond ring and her long, double-stranded pearls. He considered it a clever hiding place for her jewelry when we locked up the house and went on a day trip. But today she wore both, and the salmon and the jewelry saw the light of day.

I clutched my diploma between my legs in the front seat. When we turned the corner somewhere between Youghal and Dungarvan, the bay opened wide and shimmered in the mid-day sun. I suddenly realized that after all that study, here I was holding a new kaleidoscope to view the world. While I still felt like I was in the womb of my family, my diploma was also my passport to America.

How could I leave them all? I imagined my mother would continue cooking her mother's Hungarian recipes, while my father would type letters in the dining room. Now that I was a doctor, I wanted to comfort my family members as if they were my first few patients. "Don't worry," I wanted to say, "I will not leave as a daughter or a sister, but I must carry out my work as a doctor now." I showered them with promises of letters and loyalty.

When my father handed me the dish with salmon, rice, and a green vegetable arranged in a circle, I was still his daughter. Nothing much had changed on the outside, and yet everything had changed inside of me. My diploma gave me unspoken permission to move on and follow my long-cherished dream.

Graduation day from Medical School, University College Cork, June 1970

Internship

Any medical graduates from UCC who had ambitions to pursue their specialty training in the United States were traditionally matched for their internship at St. Vincent Hospital in Worcester, Massachusetts. The hospital administrators welcomed their arrival, as they were known to be well trained and hardworking and to possess good bedside manner. The most recent graduate from our school had interned at St. Vincent's a year ahead of me and gave an equally favorable report about the hospital: a friendly staff, good food, and generous apartments that were provided for interns and fellows across the parking lot, just footsteps away from the main entrance. It sounded exciting.

After I landed in Boston, it was a short bus ride to Worcester. The taxi driver pointed out St. Vincent's from the freeway, a large, winged white building that reflected the afternoon sun from its commanding location on top of Vernon Hill. I could see huge arched windows, not unlike a clinical monastery. In fact, the thin vertical panels of pale blue accent color reminded me of the blue-and-white chapel at the Ursulines. This hospital was also run by the Catholic order of the Sisters of Providence and I knew I would quickly adapt to this institution. Best of all, I didn't have to elbow my way in. My clinical aptitude was recognized and appreciated before I ever engaged it.

My enthusiasm was a good social skill to easily make friends with the support staff, the ward secretaries, the nurses, and the respiratory therapists. They knew the routine, and I was not shy about asking for and relying on their suggestions of how to write proper orders or whom to call for help. I quickly learned the settings of any ventilator in the surgical ICU. This was of particular interest to me since it functioned not unlike an anesthesia machine, except that the patients were sedated by an intravenous injection and not anesthetized.

The hub of each ward was the nurse's station, loaded with charts, chitchat, and chocolates free for all. There was a local brand in a white box. A different-colored bow was printed on the lid, depending on the content. Gold was chewy with soft caramel, turquoise was crunchy with nuts, and red was dark chocolate, I had my favorites. Whenever my beeper went off for a new admission intake history, these open boxes invariably sat on the counter next to the secretary. One or two before and after I completed my assignment seemed a reasonable reward at first but then became a sneaky habit that would later take a disciplined effort to undo.

Whenever I interviewed a patient I made sure I was equipped with my own stethoscope, a name tag with a bold MD after my name, and my beeper. Since I had just turned twenty-four, my baby face raised some eyebrows. Some more alert patients would question me, "Are you really a doctor? You look like a kid out of high school." The next question was also predictable. "Where are you from? You have such an adorable accent. Are you French?" After I diligently explained my background in a nutshell, it was my turn to ask questions as I sat down next to the bedside. First I rearranged the pillows so my patient would be more comfortable but also so that I could listen better to the heart and lungs. It has been said that one intern in New York actually fell asleep with his head dropping on a lady's chest while he was lulled into slumber by the steady "lub-dub" of her heartbeat. This never happened to me, although sometimes I closed my eyes in search of a faint heart murmur, barely audible. But since it was recorded on the chart in another entry, I had to find it.

I remember one lady patient who was recovering from a bout of angina in the medical ICU. She didn't look as sick as the other patients and wore bright lipstick and lots of jewelry. She was the wife of a local town official in high esteem and was always surrounded by visitors and lots of flowers, an unusual occurrence in an ICU. She took pity on me, since I had just arrived from Ireland and knew no one. She introduced me to her lovely family, her kind husband, and two children my age.

I was invited to their home to share the holidays and many delicious Armenian meals. I had never heard of hummus or baba ganoush, a pureed eggplant dish. To this day I sprinkle cinnamon on my roasted chicken and toss a handful of pine nuts onto my rice in memory of my first family of friends. Life in America was good in the seventies, and I had arrived.

Throughout the entire year of my internship I learned about American hospitality. Every holiday—and there seemed many—I was invited to a family cookout and I had my first Thanksgiving dinner in the fall. I had never seen so much food spread out on one table, nor such a gigantic bird come out of an oven. It was hard to focus on any conversation with so many choices laid out before me. It was a feast. The loud noise of roaring football fans on the largest TV screen I had ever seen added to my sense of being overwhelmed with all that American family life had to offer.

I learned about different cultures from my medical chief resident, who came from India. He introduced me to curry dishes and pizza. I was fascinated watching his dexterity while he ate his rice with his fingers. "You would have made a good surgeon," I told him, but he would give a contemptuous sneer, as he wanted no part of it. His short stature and quick agility were offset by his constant rubbing of his gray beard. He seemed a wise old sage who had fun hanging around the nurses' stations and teasing them. He taught me how to research the vast literature on any given subject or some specific and weird syndrome like Wegener's granulomatosis.

Besides plenty of practice in acute patient care under the supervision of senior residents, I received my first paycheck ever. I was paid a hundred and twenty-five dollars per week for about seventy hours of work. Suddenly I felt rich. With my first money I bought a London Fog trench coat for my mother at the most elaborate department store in town. I could hardly wait to go home for Christmas and show it to her. I also bought a Swiss wristwatch for her birthday the following May. It was my way of paying my parents back for their doing without for six years to support my studies. My father was most content if I brought him a bottle of Scotch and a carton of cigarettes from the airport duty free.

Back in Ireland, my mother didn't have to wait long for the next day of rain to proudly wear her new coat into town. The watch she treasured for the rest of her life. It kept us connected around the clock whenever she glanced at it, minus six hours to allow for the different time zone. To this day I am still in the possession of her old, square watch, which has a timeless design. For a few years I simply kept it in a drawer and forgot about it, until one day when I wanted to wear it again. It had stood still for a long time. I brought it to the jeweler for a new battery. He pointed out that I just needed to wind it manually to make it tick. I felt instantly old-fashioned and walked out with a smile—and on time.

My year at St. Vincent's was called a rotating internship, with six months of internal medicine and six months of surgery. The first six months of medicine crawled. Medical rounds started leisurely after everyone on the team had coffee. I found that we stood in place a long time, tossing around different diagnoses like mental exercise balls. The updated lab reports would fill the gaps later in the day. The senior resident was so relaxed he would have done equally well as a yoga teacher. Any sense of accomplishment was intangible. I felt suspended in a nebulous vacuum that kept me afloat between fuzzy chest X-rays and the patient bedside. There was no real beginning and no end to extended medical care. I longed for definitive action and visible evidence for making a difference in the patient's recovery from illness.

A surgical scar was an obvious hallmark of having changed the course of disease. Surgical rounds started at 6:30 AM sharp. It was more like a military operation. We rapidly raced from room to room and hardly gave the patients time to wake up. Still half-asleep, the patients had not lined up their own questions yet. Senior residents were already in scrubs. More likely, they never changed them from the night before. Surgeons were dressed in expensive suits with shirts and ties. They looked successful and in charge as they snapped their fingers. A quick look at the surgical wound and the charted vital signs were all the surgeons needed to know about their progress. Best of all was the verdict, "You will be discharged this morning after breakfast."

I could hardly wait to get my foot in the operating room and put on scrubs. I was always more interested in the typical urgency of surgery. The scalpel had a sharp lip as it slid determinedly through the skin. Only once did I feel close to fainting. I had been holding a heavy steel retractor to expose the gallbladder underneath the liver's edge too long. I was hungry and tired from having been up all night on call. Beads of sweat crawled up the back of my neck and marched boldly across my forehead. Inside my mask my breath got hotter by the minute and melted into more moisture on my brow. Suddenly my legs felt like Jell-O, unable to keep me upright. My pride gave way to a muffled request to sit down. The chief of surgery was trying to clip the bile duct. He dismissed the retractor to another pair of hands without looking up and told me to sit down with my head between my knees. This time-tested maneuver saved me the embarrassment of falling off the edge of the operating table. After a few minutes of air and a glass of orange juice, I dutifully returned to finish the case.

Occasionally I had spare time to visit with the anesthesiologist. He was less outgoing than the surgeons as he dialed in invisible magical potions with the flow meters of his machine. He became much friendlier once he learned that I was interested in his specialty.

He had his own relationship with the patients, who were now at his mercy. Few patients spoke. Either they were too scared or so deeply sedated that words were beyond their grasp. "You'll be going to sleep now, and we'll wake you up when it's over," sounded like a predictable, impersonal routine. Judging by his comfort around the surgeons, he had been there a long time. Placing the mask on the patient's face looked easy, until he let me try it one day. The patient's chin collapsed instantly, and no air was going in or out of the chest. He took over, lifted the chin with one swoop, and squeezed the bag. The chest rose like a hot air balloon. I could tell he preferred to work by himself. If there had been a door, he would have kept it closed. But there was just an ether screen between him and the surgical field. Now I understand. I feel territorial if visitors step into the small footprint around my anesthesia machine and into a space wired with electrodes and pulse oximetry. There exists an almost sacred triangle between the patient, the monitor, and the anesthesiologist. Outsiders cut unintentionally through the subtle energy that any anesthesiologist holds on to for the patient's dear life.

Lost Letters

From the day I arrived in the United States as an intern to the day my father passed away fourteen years later, I made regular phone calls to our living room at Glenbeg House. Initially I could hardly afford these weekly phone calls to Ireland. Once I was established in private practice, the phone bill was not an issue. However, sometimes I dialed almost the entire number, and hung up before the last digit. I needed more time to compose myself before I tried it again. When the connection was finally established, my voice felt weak as I uttered the first word. I worried the entire day how I would be received at the other end of the wire that connected my father and me momentarily. As our voices played out well-rehearsed roles, we both longed to link our hearts.

Letters were safer. They had the distinct advantage of allowing any personal disclosure at my own pace. I could think without being interrupted by his premature judgment, which sometimes hit me with blunt force before I could finish what I wanted to say. Letters gave me space to craft my words carefully and take a lesser risk of upsetting my father.

As I wrote about my more substantial paycheck and completed rotations during my residency training, I became an expert at writing what would please him, rather than the strenuous uphill climb it seemed to me. I knew that any mention of my chronic fatigue or the nausea at the sight of bloody guts would not elicit much empathy. My father's response of keeping a stiff upper lip was predictable. My discomfort around cool and case-hardened surgeons would be disregarded as childish and thin-skinned. I learned to protect myself from the blows to my fragile self from the person whose approval I ached for the most.

Instead I edited the details of who took me on dates and how I spent my weekends. My weekly reports resembled a picture-perfect life and job in America, sometimes far removed from my real life. I was capable of distorting the facts in my favor, anything to make

24.5.1958

Lieber Papi!

Wie geht es Dir? Aus dem schönen Tessin will ich Dir ein Briefchen schreiben. Hier ist es wunder= schön. Ich hatte eine sehr gute Fahrt (von der ich die längste Zeit geschlafen habe.) In Luzern bin ich aufgewacht. Als ich in den Speisewagen ging war ich sehr glücklich daß ich in (einem) einem Schlaf= wagen fahren durfte. Es schlief mit mir noch eine alte Oma die aber nur bis Basel fuhr. Zur Ge= sellschaft noch eine Dänin. Ich dachte es mir gleich denn sie hatte einen ganz schmutzigen Rock an. Doch wieder auf den Speisewagen zu kommen. Ich war froh (nachdem ich sechs Wagons durchquert hatte vollgestopft mit jungen rauchenden singenden und lachenden Italienern) als ich wieder in meinem Abteil war. Erschöpft schmiss ich mich auf mein ungemachtes Bett und bereitete die Dänin darauf vor daß sie nicht durchkommt (sie wollte auch frühstücken). Am Lugarner Bahnhof holten Kamm und Omi mich ab. Als ich sie sah ließ ich alles liegen und stehen und steuert auf sie los. Der Garten ist kaum wieder zu erkennen. Der Azaleen= strauch ist eine wahre Pracht. Es ist wirklich wie

Early letter to my father, age 12

him proud of me and keep his "bravo" coming my way. Sometimes I dared to be honest and wrote from the heart about how lonely I felt with the distance between us. Those were the letters that seemed to trouble him the most.

I always tried to write neatly, in a straight line, not slanting up or down, to avoid his harsh criticism of my being on an emotional roller coaster. He would call me seriously disturbed. The spacing of the address on the envelope was important also. At a glance, he was able to make a diagnosis about my mental state. He forgot that I was the only physician in the family. He would diagnose me with anything from being in a hurry to being emotionally out of kilter. Worst of all, it was construed as evidence of not caring enough.

Should I address him as "Dear Dad" That seemed too casual. At least "Dearest Daddy" or "Beloved Dad." They were all lies. Often I didn't feel like writing at all. It upset my entire day, waiting to be inspired, finding the right paper, pen, and the words.

What was my life really like, then? I tried my best to keep up the traditions most valued at home. Besides my work, I made a point of attending classical concerts, reading inspirational biographies, and being socially available in professional circles. However, my attempts to create a well-balanced social life did not replace the homesickness.

My father had always been an avid reader. I remember the books he highly recommended. However, I had little interest or usefulness for the study of Celestial Navigation, which was his Bible. It had nothing to say about spirituality. I remember the stack of books next to my father's nightstand and the smell of stale cigarettes. Both got in the way when I knelt down beside his bed to kiss him good night. My father always reached for more than I was willing to give as I hovered over the sharp edge of the bed. I bent over the edge of decency. Tangled sheets and chocolate wrappers were the evidence of his insatiable cravings and restless nights that made all of us hush the next day, tiptoeing around the house. To this day, I too keep a stack of books next to my bed on different topics I want to read.

Years later my mother was planning to come for her annual visit to the States. The time had come when I longed to reread my letters written over the years and to recycle how far I had come. I wanted to retrace my thoughts with an air of maturity and acknowledge my own journey toward my personal freedom all mapped out, step by step.

I called my mother. "Mom, please pack my letters in your

suitcase." There was silence at the other end of the telephone … a pause before she explained. There was so much to move when she gave up the house after our father died. Somehow the letters were lost mysteriously. Most likely my mother's gentle nature would conceal their final destination, to spare me a reminder of my father's lectures. I imagined that perhaps she burned them in the living room fireplace.

I envisioned the letters catching the flames, going up in smoke, the ashes being carried by the same wind that carried my father's ashes out to the sea. I liked the idea that ashes of life-long misunderstandings might be dispersed by nature to a better place. Fire and rain would then recycle for me what I have been unable to do.

Gone was all tangible evidence of my efforts at being the best daughter I knew how. My letters were documents of my early victories as a young doctor that I could look back on whenever I recalled my father's battle cry to rise above mediocrity. It was a testimony of loyalty and whatever tenderness I could gather for him. It was unimaginable that it all went up in a puff of smoke.

Since my father died, now over twenty years ago, I have had to grow up all over again without him.

One might point out that it is not fair game to portray my father as harsh, autocratic, and volatile now that he is far beyond his own defense. With the perspective of maturity came my appreciation for his continual quest to encourage focus, hard work, and excellence. It was only recently that I found a reference to his character in astrology, which I now offer lovingly in his justification. Being a Sagittarius, he is brilliantly described by Patty Greenall and Cat Javaor, both professional astrologers:

> There is always an element of the guru residing in the heart of even the wildest Sagittarius. The world view of a Sagittarius is very different from that of almost anyone else ..... Sagittarians are intrepid travelers on land, sea and air; their passport makes very interesting reading, it's bound to be full of entry and exit stamps from many different countries … Because of their far-reaching enthusiasm, and their need to stretch way beyond normal human expectations they often appear larger than life and over the top …. Almost everything they do, they do in a big way. Even when they lose their temper, they do it so they almost

explode. Unfortunately for those around them .... the aftershocks reverberate for a long time after they've forgotten whatever it was that got them angry in the first place . ... It's in their nature to expect the best and they succeed at the most extraordinary feats. [4]

Having experienced the entire spectrum of this celestial constellation embodied in my father, I now believe that the chemistry between us was more fashioned by fate than personal discord and that the balance now tips in favor of his well-intentioned ambition for my success in life despite his rages.

4   From *Sagittarius*, Octopus Publishing Group, London *Copyright* by Patty Greenall and Cat Javor, p16-18, 2004

Voice of the Ocean

My father's voice ...
... an imaginary attempt to reconcile.

"I am ancient, the soul of all mankind.
Salty and gray, sometimes blue.
In perpetual motion that boils in a storm.
Recede and return around obstacles to make my mark.
Agitated or calm, people don't hear me unless
They desire to know the deep, deep mystery
That lies beneath the sandy surface of my breast.

"You are here today. I welcome your visit.
I have roared and shouted at you for years,
Seeking your friendship, your forgiveness,
For the expression of my wild imagination,
Seeking your closeness.

"You stand in front of me,
While I keep rolling at your feet.
Together we walk the beach
As I kiss your ankles with my waves.

"We both breathe the same air, soak in the same rain.
Let the sun melt the last 'berg' of ice between us
That makes me quiver and makes you shiver in the cold.

"My prayer is just a whisper beneath the surface noise.
May I always be near you,
As you drift into the quicksand of the world.
Be safe! Be great! Keep writing!
This is my gift to you."

Chapter Two

Going Under

"May your work assume a proper space in your life.
Instead of owning you or using you
May it challenge and refine you
Bringing you every day further
Into the wonder of your heart."

John O'Donohue[5]

An "Off-stage" Drama

It was early in my residency training as an anesthesiologist that I was exposed to the high charge of emergencies. I remember the feverish, frenzied alert that ran through the department like wildfire. A young woman was en route by ambulance in acute respiratory distress. She was a twenty-three-year-old student at the University School of Drama who had defeated her dormitory roommates in a macabre game. The objective was to determine who could eat the most hamburgers without even pausing for water. She had managed to consume fourteen of them without any liquids to aid digestion.

As a junior resident, I was alarmed that the specialty I had chosen would sooner or later confront me with being at the helm, single-handed if necessary, of such an unnerving situation. It demanded cool composure, great skill, and meticulous performance under the unforgiving scrutiny of crusty surgeons. I was allowed on the set for a learning experience of how to perform a so-called "awake intubation." This apparently traumatic procedure requires the anesthesiologist to secure the airway first with the patient sedated but awake to retain a full gag reflex while an endotracheal tube is inserted into the trachea. Under normal circumstances, this procedure is executed with the patient fully asleep and relaxed. However, if the patient is known to have a full stomach, one runs the risk of

---

5   From TO BLESS THE SPACE BETWEEN US: A BOOK OF BLESSINGS
     by John O'Donohue, For a New Position p23 © 2008 by John O'Donohue.
     Used by permission of Doubleday, a division of Random, House,Inc.

massive vomiting and aspiration of stomach contents into the lung, a most serious and dreaded complication. This unnerving technique has now been replaced by an awake fiberoptic intubation that, with proper sedation, is much less taxing on the patient.

I was glad to see my favorite senior mentor assigned to this case. I remember him as the most compassionate staff person of all. He had a gentle, quiet way about him and large hands to handle the most challenging cases.

For this emergency he had painstakingly set up every piece of equipment he could find in the supply room. Every conceivable drug that might be needed was neatly drawn up in a labeled syringe. A variety of endotracheal tubes were lined up in different sizes to ensure a successful pass through the vocal cords into the trachea. It was of critical importance to get this maneuver right with the first attempt.

As they wheeled the patient in, her wavy red hair licked her pale complexion like brilliant flames. She squirmed against the mattress of the stretcher. Much like a young woman in labor, she was panting little breaths, unable to take full ones, hands on her abdomen in apparent agony. Her lips and fingers were blue. There was no room for her lungs to expand and take in the normal amount of air, with the pressure of her hugely distended stomach pressing against the diaphragm. Her abdomen was like a tight, over-inflated balloon covered with mottled purple skin, stretched and compressed far beyond its elastic capacity.

I can still hear the calm voice of my senior hero as he instructed the frightened girl to open her mouth one more time so he could get a better view for what he needed to do. By now she was weakened from the struggle to breathe against the self-imposed rock to offer much resistance to the probing at the back of her throat. Between his expeditious skill and the patient's fatigue, my mentor swiftly slipped the tube into the trachea and sealed it with an attached cuff to prevent any vomit from entering the lung.

I thought I was included at the scene merely as an observing bystander. Instead, I was called to action. Once the airway was secured, it was my cue to propel enough sodium pentothal into the intravenous line to obliterate consciousness within seconds. I pushed it rapidly, with a great relief at ending her misery, at least for now. Within the same few seconds, the stomach sphincter relaxed and as expected, opened the floodgate. The stomach released a stream of sour brackish fluid with solid particles that were too large for any suction apparatus. They had to be scooped up with gloves and towels. Because of the extreme distension, the surgeons held their scalpels impatiently, ready to slash a vertical incision from ribcage to pubic bone. It was difficult for me to mechanically ventilate the lungs, which could not be expanded easily. It was just one of the reasons why the blood that oozed from the incision looked ominously dark instead of bright cherry red. The normal oxygenation of the blood was compromised by the pressure of the stomach that had compressed all small blood vessels and their blood flow.

Finally the stomach was opened, much like a pregnant uterus during a Cesarian section. The toxic contents seriously threatened the young woman's life. It was hard to catch a breath in the sudden, overwhelming stench that could not be disguised with sprinkles of peppermint oil on the floor surrounding the surgical field.

As several buckets of the foul, undigested material were removed, it became apparent that the entire stomach wall had turned gangrenous and necrotic from lack of blood supply under pressure. The delicate lining appeared nonviable and had partially sloughed off. The only chance to salvage the digestive tract was to remove the entire stomach and plan some future reconstructive surgery at a later date to restore some function. At this point we feared for her survival.

Until now I was numbed by the impact on my sense of sight and smell and the urgency of this drama that played out in front of me. As the situation stabilized, I felt a personal pang of guilt, since I had experienced sporadic episodes of overeating to the point of physical discomfort. During periods of prolonged stress and times of sleep deprivation, I'd found it easy to rationalize binging on junk food, always within reach on the wards. I had never given it much thought that it might develop into a demoralizing habit and promised myself to be more careful in the future. Although the comfort of food seemed a harmless instinctive survival skill to ward off mounting anxiety at home and to uphold my academic scaffold, this habitual eating pattern threatened to crack my own professional shell. When I embraced certain physical, emotional, and spiritual principles to discern the true nature of my hunger, I was able to get back on track.

I was puzzled whether this young woman's motive was driven by a quiet, suicidal desperation or just a frivolous moment to impress her peers. Prolonged hospital confinement, probably for months, and a long period of rehabilitation with counseling might shed some light on the question. Her physical recovery would depend on the success of some later surgery and the viability of some kind of surgical repair between her esophagus and the small intestine. It was obvious that she would never eat normally again.

All my senses were heavily taxed. The square metal frame, called an ether screen, that separates the surgical field from the anesthesia territory by a green drape around the head and neck of the patient did nothing to separate us from this grotesque scene. All of a sudden the surgeons' voices turned into a distant, chaotic commotion, and I felt sick. This time I knew that I quickly had to leave the room.

It was plain curiosity that prompted me to visit her a few days later in the intensive care unit. I was relieved to find her still too heavily sedated to realize the full impact of what she had done. Her body needed complete stillness to fight the shock of the sepsis. Her long red hair had lost its luster and lay limp and matted with perspiration against the pillow. I was moved by the thought that she had fallen victim to an innocent longing to seize center stage. Acting out her short career in drama, she had become a living tragedy with a personal lasting lesson for me.

I finished rounds in the ICU and wrote orders for new ventilator settings and more blood gases, to the satisfaction of the nurse in charge. It was a habit of mine to also make rounds in the staff lounge. I felt justified in replenishing myself with whatever was free for all. During the nights it was most often cold pizza. At midmorning it was a square, pink box filled with sugar-laden sponges.

After my visit with the young woman, I simply needed a place to sit down quietly. I needed to digest this food-related catastrophe. The most obvious place was the staff lounge. This time I never touched a morsel.

Years later a painting in a vibrant and eye-catching orange burst of color, titled "Tanya with Chocolate Cake" by Ken Kewley, provided a flashback of my own early coping skills.

Tanya with Chocolate Cake

Her sense of self is suspended,
Vaguely anchored by the fork in midair
Between a bottomless pit and the last shred of sanity.
She is trapped inside an orange balloon of anger,
Ready to burst,
Fueled by dark and sticky chocolate cake.

She is already lost,
in her intention to complete the onerous task,
Like jumping off a cliff into oblivion.
A subtle stupor drives her down a one-way street,
Deeper and deeper into the fog.
There is no return.

Her cerebral halo has been dimmed
As the light fades from her forehead into a brown shadow.
Her eyes gaze blankly backwards into the past.
Her vision is two-dimensional
And oscillates between the bitterness of childhood trauma
And the sweetness of the chocolate cake
That makes her as sick as her father's angry words
And his hot hands and kisses that burned her flesh.

Tanya with Chocolate Cake

Copyright Ken Kewley, Courtesy of Lori Bookstein Fine Art

Bend, Don't Break!

Now that I was established in my career, I had moved from my first towel- sized studio apartment to my own house in the suburbs of Boston. My second -hand spinet piano had been upgraded to a black baby grand and the car I drove to commute had heated leather seats. Most important, I now shared my life with a husband who, being a talented artist, filled my days with bursts of color. Even though I was now surrounded with certain luxuries, I could never honestly say that I had arrived. Any day in the OR could be a humbling experience.

Nights on call, now few and far apart, often reminded me of the early days when I worked every second or third night. Back then I slept in call rooms often resembling a stuffy closet, sometimes bunk beds in obstetrics, where the sheets were always ruffled from the previous resident. I still remember the fragrance of almonds of a certain lotion that was provided in the call room of my internship. I would sniff it in the drug store from time to time, just to remind me how far I had come.

Since I worked with a large anesthesia group, night calls, dispersed amongst us, were few and far apart. But if emergencies ran late into the night, I often chose to stay rather than drive home. At this hospital there was no designated call room. I borrowed blankets from the blanket warmer in the recovery room and found an empty patient room on a floor not fully occupied. There the nurses often handed me a toothbrush, toothpaste, and a bar of soap for a shower, with a promise to wake me up on time.

I remember one particular Sunday when I rolled out of my hospital bed at six AM. Physically limp from fatigue, I had felt like a patient myself the previous night as I sank mindlessly into the rubbery pillow. I longed for rest but slept poorly on the lumpy mattress. It had been a long, sixteen-hour shift in the operating room. I tried to keep pace with surgeons who scheduled imminent emergencies, nurses, and patients, each with their own demands. The back muscles that supported my spine strained all day to hold up my professional demeanor for the duration of twenty-five surgical cases. Twenty-five patients had been entrusted into my hands, until I returned them safely to their families.

An eighty-five-year-old lady with restless legs syndrome had twitched and twisted uncontrollably on the narrow stretcher. It was obvious that she would not be able to hold still for her intended eye surgery. Once under the microscope, the slightest motion of the head and the eye distorts the field of vision like an earthquake. Her heart was too frail to tolerate the stress of general anesthesia; therefore this option was contraindicated as a feasible alternative.

Her daughter wrung her hands as she begged me to find a way to proceed. The eye surgery had to be done on this day. Her mother would never return a second time. Besides, she had taken special time off from work as a librarian from our hospital library. I knew her well and envied her quiet job and her wooly cardigans. She was always soft-spoken and extremely efficient. She could retrieve and copy any article from some foreign medical journal that had collected dust in the archives. She always delivered it with a smile and a sense of a mission accomplished. Until this day I did not know about her husband, who was blind. She took care of him at home, as well as her cranky mother who seemed agitated in body and mind beyond reassurance. I had to find her surgeon to determine if he could do the operation swiftly rather than slowly. He said he would do his best. I stuck to my principle of safety and would keep her sedated instead of putting her to sleep in her frail state. I was prepared to keep her from moving by holding her arms and legs wrapped under the cotton blanket, but the sedative calmed her down sufficiently for both of us to relax.

Meanwhile, another woman arrived with her mother-in-law in the patient holding area. She wished her well with one last hug. Her voice sounded familiar. As I turned around, I recognized the face. The color of her hair had changed from brunette to ash blonde. My face remained concealed behind my mask and I promptly retreated back to my task.

It had been seven years since I sat in the office with her and her husband. It was a chilling hour for me, trying to answer questions about the complication that had occurred. An accidental needle puncture left her husband with a permanent injury. It was a known but remote risk of the procedure, which rarely led to this devastating occurrence. It was months before I received official notice of their pending lawsuit. I remember my dry throat on the telephone, sleepless nights when I imagined myself on the witness stand, exposed and unprotected by all the hard work of my flawless career. It meant nothing at that time. It all came back to me with the same nauseating blow as it did then.

At the time I received the bad news I could barely carry on with my daily work routine. Every ounce of confidence that I had gathered over the years was suddenly wiped out. I lost my usual appetite for weeks and felt exhausted. Perhaps she would not recognize me at this moment in a different setting. Somehow we all survived. Fortunately, at this moment another patient urgently needed my attention. There was no time to think about it now.

A Spanish-speaking lady was beating her clenched fist vigorously at her chest. She was in obvious pain. The closest translator was the son, who informed me that the chest pain began after the surgery under local anesthesia. After an initial evaluation of her vital signs I initiated the recommended protocol for ruling out a heart attack. This entailed batteries of tests, further consults, and poorly translated explanations to the bewildered family. The medicine I gave her seemed to take effect immediately and allowed her to relax. Meanwhile an impatient surgeon, with plans to take his youngster to baseball practice on Saturday afternoon, wanted to know why his case was delayed by my tardy service.

But that was all yesterday. Sneakers on my feet, beeper in my pocket, I felt ready to step into the sunshine out of the gray, giant, concrete building. The huge, square structure with small vertical windows was not unlike a modern version of the old historic jail right next to it. The first breath of the crisp morning air quickly revived my spirit. Over the bridge to the Esplanade by the river, the noise of the traffic subsided. I was thankful not to encounter any homeless people this morning, curled up in a sad pile. Somehow I always felt responsible for them, too. This morning I longed to be free of all blame while I was walking. How fortunate I was compared to the homeless. A gnawing sense of guilt stirred my conscience when I saw their helpless bodies, too sick and too tired to move themselves to a better place.

Out there with me this morning were others, running and walking, their minds and bodies committed to health and wellness. Only a few returned my cheery hello, offered in a spirit of camaraderie. Across the river, the sunlit dome of the Massachusetts Institute of Technology reminded me of a jumbo fried egg, sunny side up. It was considered the home of brilliant brains that explored and exploded beyond earthly boundaries into space and oceans. Compared to them, I felt brainless. Some of their brainchildren will be revisited by ordinary minds as history and tangible objects in the Museum of Science, at my back now.

Still walking away from yesterday, I met a horizontal tree. Its sturdy trunk was bent at an angle defying all laws of physics and gravity. Blown by many windy seasons into a grotesque shape, it was still firmly rooted. It was unshakable. Its twisted branches reached far and low over the water's edge. It bent but did not break. New limbs with new roots provided further support to carry the burden, grown heavier over the years. It was still growing. I noticed delicate buds, ready to unfold their leaves and follow their destiny for another season.

I was thinking about the strength of the tree as I headed back toward the hospital. I wanted to suck up its strength and take it with me for the day. I have heard of people who hug trees. Surely they were weirdoes—or maybe not. I could try it myself. No one was looking. I picked the next slender linden tree and quickly put my arms around it. The rough bark scratched my bare arms. I was disappointed that I could not feel the magic. Looking at my watch, I thought about home. It was too early to call my husband, who was still asleep. Maybe I should have breakfast before the next patient and surgeon needed my further assistance.

Morning Rush

I started my day in the locker room for female physicians. Scrub pants had recently been switched to a cheaper brand. They were loaded with static and clung to my legs. An unused shower stall with wire hangers bent out of shape served as a closet to hang my heavy winter coat.

In the narrow galley kitchen off the OR lounge, I took my turn standing in line with the nurses to stuff their recycled plastic lunch bags into the fridge. The door was worn out and wouldn't close unless I slammed it shut. This was where doctors and nurses met on common ground to exchange family news or concerns about upcoming cases or problem patients. They shared half-empty jars of peanut butter with scooped trails of plastic knives next to torn packages of stale saltines. The crumbs were usually scattered all over the counter.

In the lounge, huge windows to the outside world looked down eight stories onto an icy river without sailboats and a stream of headlights stalled in traffic, paralyzed by the morning freeze. Conservative newspapers and tabloids were spilled on the table and were embellished with morning chatter. One of the nurses had been up all night with her sick child and arrived in a depleted state. Somebody's car would not get in gear, together with its owner. Slippery roads and unusual delays on the subway caused others to arrive in a state of panic. Some brought catalogues for planting seeds in the spring or pictures of their new state-of-the-art stove. All shared over coffee—shared their new hairdo and their cat that needed medication for her thyroid gland for twenty dollars a month. Some ate cereal out of zip-lock bags and burned raisin toast. Then breakfast was over. A last slam of the metal doors could be heard from the locker room before we descended the stairs to the bowels of the OR.

In the holding area, crying children were held by anxious parents who were on the verge of crying themselves. Babies stretched their arms and legs in midair as usual. Older ones, in their clean, wrinkled hospital Johnnies, played with clowns, teddy bears, and disposable diapers brought just in case.

On adults we started IVs with a balanced salt solution in all kinds of hands. In the elderly, hands were speckled with age spots and mapped with tortuous veins. In heavy smokers, their yellow stains were a telltale sign before I looked at the chart or asked the question. Sometimes wedding rings would not come off from plump hands with swollen fingers and had to be taped securely. Some hands were cold and clammy. In young female patients I often wondered if the metallic copper-colored nail polish would allow the oxygen probe on the finger to pick up its mandatory signal. In a certain disease, namely scleroderma, the skin could be stretched so tightly across the hand that it developed a marble-like, shiny translucency. Sometimes I came across a warm, firm handshake despite the patient's compromised position on the stretcher. The patient's hand was often the first indication of what kind of challenges might be expected during the course of an anesthetic. Once the IV was placed and the entire team assembled, we were ready to roll down the hallway to the assigned OR. By now the patient was adequately sedated to slip from the sheets into our caring arms.

Two-faced Reconstructive Surgery

Part One

There were no flowers or potted plants in surgical suite number four, yet it was steamy, hot, a windowless greenhouse. The room temperature was set at seventy-five degrees to prevent excessive heat loss from the patient, while he remained anesthetized for twelve hours' estimated surgical time. During long surgical cases patients were always vulnerable to drop their body temperature significantly. This would occur by radiation of body heat into the room environment. In addition, patients under anesthesia would reduce their basic metabolic rate and lack their normal shivering mechanism. Adequate circulation throughout all major organs, and especially the muscle tissues, was critical during this kind of operation. It could easily be compromised in a cooler environment, as the blood vessels tended to constrict spontaneously to protect against further heat loss.

Having witnessed surgery over twenty years, including open-heart and neurosurgery, I still found this type of reconstructive cancer surgery difficult to witness. It was oppressive to breathe in this stifling heat with the mask that covered my mouth and nose. Hot and humid air escaped behind the mask and fogged up my protective goggles, which blurred my vision. The crisp monitor trace lost its edge. When I removed my goggles, I felt instantly cooler. Without the goggles my focus sharpened on the surgical field and the stark reality for the patient who was under my care. Only the surgeons knew from experience that they had the upper hand.

The neck gaped wide open, spread out in front of me like two pages of an anatomy book. I was inches away from the bloody but controlled battlefield with cancer. The patient's chart documented the presence of the tumor around his larynx. Without this radical intervention, he would eventually choke to death. As an onlooker, my eye was not trained to distinguish healthy tissue from microscopic tumor cells, but surgeons could feel the hardened tissue matrix and nodes between their fingers.

The tumor was first diagnosed in May, after so many years of smoking two-and-a-half packs a day. The patient was a forty-nine-year-old male. I hardly knew the person whom I had kept alive, a minute at a time, since I started this case. His body was completely covered by surgical drapes.

His wife waited upstairs in the lounge reserved for relatives, next to the cafeteria. Most likely she was restless, since surgery had started at eight AM. I wondered if she pleaded with him every time he lit up again. For a while she probably paced back and forth from the cafeteria to the elevator, riding up and down with the friendly voice that announced each floor for people without vision. She had tried to call the operating room, but the surgeon didn't want to be interrupted. He told the nurse curtly that he already left a message three hours ago that the patient was doing fine.

When I thought of myself as a stranger to the patient, I felt uninvited during this radical invasion, but as a professional I was needed to keep him asleep for the remainder of this surgical procedure. Someone needed to ensure guaranteed unconsciousness to a pain that no one could endure. Qualified with the necessary skills and experience, I had been assigned as the anesthesiologist in charge of this case.

I saw the remains of a face, once the window of this patient's personality. It was cut and disfigured beyond recognition; nothing made sense anymore. There were no visible familiar landmarks, only a bulky mass of flesh without contours of any kind. The corners of the lips hung loosely, almost disconnected from the chinbone that was split in half to gain access to the inside of the gaping cavity that was once a mouth.

While I stared at this ghoulish disfigurement, I wondered about the person inside this body, severed from his senses. While all the senses were temporarily dormant by anesthesia, some were permanently obliterated by the necessary surgery to remove the cancer. Where did his senses go? Suspended somewhere in space until it was time to wake him up? Eyes that still could see once awake now moved with his dreams behind closed lids. Eyes that had gathered images over a lifetime and committed them to memory would still capture familiar smiles on other faces, but never again his own in a mirrored reflection. His accustomed face was not his anymore. Where could one go without a face? For a while he would have to recognize himself by the mention of his name, the memory of his face, maybe some old photographs. A long road lay ahead of him to acquaint himself with his new identity. I wished I could keep him asleep until he had healed.

The senses of touch, sight, and hearing would have to compensate the patient's capacity to pursue any pleasure. Taste and smell would be blunted beyond usefulness. The sensory nerve endings of delicate flavors and fragrances had been amputated by necessity. His face that had laughed and cried with graphic lines of emotions would have to channel them some other way from within the confines of a body and a face mutilated by disease. Ears would amplify the careless laughter and trivial chatter of ordinary pleasures beyond his reach. His cries would have no voice.

To what territory would he retreat and still feel like life was worth living? Into the surgeon's hands and the mysterious skill of an anesthesiologist he never met? Hardly! More likely he had risen to the challenge with desperate faith and sheer determination to survive and return to his family. He had chosen to live.

The patient's chin and tongue, after having been partially removed, were being reconstructed with a new muscle flap dissected from the belly of his forearm. A team of four plastic surgeons competed with one of the most aggressive forms of cancer, caused by the toxic combination of cigarettes and alcohol, which now threatened to destroy the entire face with simultaneous invasion of the body.

The success of this operation depended on the viability of a flap of muscle and skin tissue that already had been tediously dissected from the forearm. The flap, without its own blood supply, was then transplanted to the primary surgical site of the face, where the blood vessels were reconnected under the microscope to the carotid artery and jugular vein in the neck. The bulk of the muscle mass was reshaped into new facial features, filling the void where the tumor had been removed.

Even though visually I could connect with the patient by looking at his head, I ascertained the patient's physical presence by scanning the uninterrupted function of his vital organs. His steady, regular heartbeat marched undeterred across the screen in a green wave. His kidneys trickled the predicted amount of urine into the plastic bag on the floor every hour. Attached to his forearm and his index finger were wires and probes that verified a sufficient level of oxygen being pumped with each heartbeat inside his physical shell. I saw a flaccid hand within my reach. Would he care if I held his hand for silent support instead of keeping to myself? I grasped it lightly while I thought about his close family who would have to provide extended care and support that would be crucial to his recovery over the next few months.

Behind the mask I was faceless, also. I actually wore two masks. The first was a thick cotton mask stretched across my face and mouth. It moved with my breath like a flag that gave me permission to be on the set. The other invisible mask I slipped on as soon as I entered the operating room. It was a solemn facial expression of intense concern for the safety of my patients. My smile for patients and colleagues behind this imperceptible mask was more often restrained and professional than spontaneous. Sometimes my own unexpected laughter caught me by surprise as a refreshing relief from the intensity of the environment. But most of the time I would consider it inappropriate. It would be equally inappropriate to complain about the sharp pain I felt in my back during such a long procedure. Instead I endured it quietly together with the patient, bonded under the surgeon's knife, while I briefly held on to the patient's hand for mutual comfort. The anesthetic I delivered, charged by the hour, wiped out consciousness, blocked out pain. But did I bring compassion? It was not billable and came freely given, but did it matter? Or should I think about getting out on time to pick up groceries for dinner? No one would ever know the difference except me.

The patient had signed the informed consent for this procedure with trust and hope. We, as a surgical team, had advanced beyond return. The only way out of this shattered self was with the help of the surgeon's skilled and confident hands. You would not recognize the level of skill enclosed by these hands from just a handshake or watching them pay a parking ticket and open the door. Their years of arduous training started by tying the first square knot over and over, day after day and endless nights, until the repetitious motion became a natural, effortless continuum.

The surgeons didn't apologize for how far they had gone. They had contemplated the risk during the initial evaluation of the patient's status and explained to the patient what he needed to know. It was up to them to salvage a certain quality of life. They were not available for questions now; there were many more hours to go. Lost in concentration, they had forgotten any sense of time. On a day like this, there was no other schedule, no personal agenda beyond this patient's face.

The surgeon looked up from the field while his gloved fingers felt for a newly created pulse in the tissue mass that was once an arm. A delicate junction of blood vessels, sutured under the microscope for two hours, bounced rhythmically as blood again flowed into the transplanted artery. It revitalized the forearm that was now to become a face. Blood spattered from a fine arterial spray when he, with a blank gaze from behind his mask, released the clamp. He measured tissue viability with his fingers. I imagined the surgeon's mouth felt like a cotton ball. But he didn't ask for orange juice—didn't even think about it. His intellect had moved into his hands.

He used his words sparingly to communicate progress with the other surgeons who stood around the patient's head. Other fingers came to his aid where his own were not adequate. They seemed natural extensions of his hands that knew the next move without being told, like two pianists who performed a four-handed concert.

The small, slender hand of the scrub nurse quietly slipped in between, agile like a dancer, always ready, never in the way. She held the forceps, carefully cleaned it, removed the used one, and wiped it clean again with a damp cotton sponge. She found its place on a tray with dozens of others, all lined up neatly, waiting their turn. She too was waiting her turn for a chance to date one of the surgical residents who would find her attractive face behind her mask. As she kept wiping the instrument, she wondered if she could afford a new car this year, along with the monthly cost of the shared apartment.

The technical blended with the artistic in this un-choreographed surgical dance. Function and form guided the surgeons as they tried to mold and shape the forearm into a face. By the surgeon's admission, it was a poor substitute for the original tissue. Still, ten years ago this reconstructive option was completely unavailable. My mind fast forwarded into the future and wondered what miracles would be forthcoming for such a patient twenty years from now.

Suddenly I was startled by a series of repeated clicks and flashes. A professional photographer had quietly found her way into the restricted field, off limits to laypeople. She must have been invited, since the surgeons didn't object to her presence. She seemed to know operating room etiquette as she whispered for permission to climb on a stool in order to reach sharper angles. I ignored my vague interest in learning about her special assignment, as this was no time to engage in conversation. Her photo frames would be filled with additional drama that was already firmly imprinted on my mind. The loose encounter with her untitled project was soon forgotten.

Part Two

A few weeks later, I barely noticed an invitation taped to the door of the surgical staff lounge. It announced a photography exhibit assembled by Sage on Wednesday, from ten to four. It was an odd name that reminded me of a grayish-green pungent medicinal herb or a virtuous woman full of wisdom.

As I took the stairs to the lounge, the black-and-white exhibit displayed on four walls demanded my full attention. Large-format portraits penetrated patients who had survived one of the most drastic surgical procedures, reconstructive plastic surgery for head and neck cancer. It was a compelling collage of an irreversible diagnosis that had merged into victory. The pictures showed personal transformations from panic to composure.

Each photographic essay documented a patient's heroic story of survival and his or her own personality in a series of four progressive photographs. The pre-operative photo portrayed a disclosure of an attitude of inner strength, real or posed. This was not a candid camera shot. I wondered about the patients' harsh reality after the click of the camera had stopped. An opposite image of days of despair was not apparent from the silent pictures.

The side profile of the lady with a silk scarf tied around her head to hide her lost hair reflected dignity. Her shoulders were straight as she held her chin up high. I applauded her determination and her will to prevail. I marveled at her courage to turn full front with a facial defect that had sacrificed half her nose and an entire eye for a chance of survival. In her hand she held a custom-tailored facial prosthesis, a mask behind which she could take refuge. The last photo showed a perfect fit of the prosthesis in place. This was not a masquerade. This was her new face for the rest of her life, a face that could not frown upon the occasional tactless remark overheard in public. Behind the face lay concentrated courage to outlast the stares directed toward her.

The next series of four photos was taken at various stages, before, during, and after surgery. The first photo revealed focused fear in the patient's eyes, haunted by the aggressive tumor. The second and third photos moved to a radical disfigurement, haunting to the onlooker. A phantom-like face lit up by white surgical light emerged out of the bleak blackness of its background. The upper eyelids were held open by two gloved fingers. Vacant eyes stared as from a coma, immobile and expressionless. What would those eyes see upon wakeup? Postoperative swelling would keep them mercifully shut until the shock subsided.

These pictures displayed a scene that was often all I could witness while I took care of such patients: a convoluted mass of tissue beyond recognition that appeared disconnected from the person deeply anesthetized. I observed zigzag suture lines and isolated muscles weighted down by heavy clamps. In the final photo the patient had resurfaced and appeared healed and socially acceptable with a proud smile. Positioned behind her, a relative's pair of hands were placed on her shoulders like living shoulder pads, epaulettes for bravery.

I moved in slow motion. I wanted to grasp the preciousness of life that lit up these faces, and I acknowledged each of them as a hero.

Next was a man in his early sixties. He had a friendly, ordinary face with an innocent trust in his eyes. He wore a plaid work shirt buttoned loosely around his neck. He appeared emaciated from the advanced cancer, the loss of appetite, or maybe a drinking habit. He was a plain-looking man who typically might come down to the operating room clean-shaven, smelling of inexpensive aftershave. I imagined he was the type of patient who would quietly submit to the necessary preoperative procedures. He probably would not complain when the intravenous was started or a more painful arterial line was placed. It would be merciful if he did not fully comprehend the magnitude of his disease.

The two intraoperative shots were wide-angle scenes of the surgical field, like photos that you might find on a double page of a current news and action-oriented magazine. Overhead lights, heads with square paper caps huddled together over lots of hardware. The anesthesiologist remained out of focus. Only I knew that she was there in the background with her silent mission. I remained unnoticed for the most part, vaguely recognized for a split second, the duration of a click of a camera, during a twelve-hour case that left me physically fatigued and depleted emotionally. It was unlikely that I would see the outcome that took months of intense postoperative follow-up to allow for the healing process to occur. And yet it was a hard-earned privilege to be an anesthesia member of this surgical team.

The final shot detailed the ultimate outcome. It was the same patient, with a spirited smile underneath a cowboy hat that brimmed with confidence. He had positively re-entered the world of the living. Applause for the surgeons. Applause for the photographer for having captured this patient's lost and found spirit so vividly. I wished I could meet this patient and tell him how much his survival meant to me. It broadened the perspective of my role beyond the walls of the operating room, even though I knew that I might never see him again.

Part Three

It was a busy day at the preoperative clinic on the ninth floor. I counted thirty-five patients to be cleared for safe anesthesia before they underwent their elective surgical procedures that day. Patients of all ages and sizes brought their pain, their fears, and their relatives.

Some of them didn't speak English, and others didn't want to speak. Sometimes patients didn't wish to participate in their own care and assumed a more passive role that might relieve them of any ordeal. Empathy on my part did not always come naturally for patients who demonstrated little interest in basic self-care. Some appeared unshapely and bloated from too much food and alcohol. Their lungs exhaled a stale smell of nicotine. Shriveled skin like dry tobacco leaves and yellow-stained fingertips were telltale signs. After years of self-abuse, surgical intervention was not intended to reverse the process but alleviate the consequences that might otherwise escalate into a life-threatening emergency.

My role was to assess the relative anesthesia risk, depending on the patient's physical status, and propose a safe and pain-free anesthetic. As I went through a litany of routine questions, I overheard the nurse's intake interview across the hall with a male patient. His speech sounded garbled. Curiosity drew me to his cubicle, as I already sensed that this would take additional time. Next to the patient lay a chart that burst out of its cover with records from previous surgical procedures and an obviously complicated history. It would be easier to extract the needed information from the chart than making demands on his speech impediment. I extended a hand and a smile as I introduced myself as the anesthesiologist. Somewhere I had seen this face before. Then I recognized the toothless smile from under the cowboy hat. Health insurance did not cover the cost for a replacement set of teeth.

I was genuinely pleased to meet him, to hear more about his

experience since his major facial reconstruction. He answered my questions incomprehensibly. His new tongue could not make many of the sounds necessary for speech. I was unable to comprehend his new language that had been fabricated by necessity. His frustration was obvious. Maybe fitting him with new teeth would make it better. I wanted to know how he was getting along in the world, but we could hardly communicate.

There was a deep sadness in the recognition of the stark reality. Again I wanted to hold his hand and offer comfort, which seemed inappropriately inadequate. As I examined him further, I found twisted tissue inside his mouth that severely restricted his speech. His breath smelled clean. There was no grossly apparent evidence of recurrent cancer. I took refuge in the safety of explaining the details of the impending procedure intended to improve his speech. He had heard it all before and knew what to expect. He did not question my proposed plan when I asked him to entrust his life into our hands again with his signature. While he read the list of potential complications, I searched the chart for clues of his well-being. He did not represent what I had interpreted from his photograph. There was a distressing discrepancy between his physical appearance and his function. It startled me and slowed me down. Eventually we both moved on with a shared sense of hope that the procedure to release tissue would restore a better speech pattern. On the back of my schedule, I jotted down his telephone number with the earnest intention of checking on his progress.

I remember another patient from the photographs. Betty liked to make regular visits to the hospital cafeteria. Her cosmetic outcome was fair at best; however, her spirit of resilience captivated the entire audience when she told her story at the annual medical staff meeting. She was brilliant when she served as a witness of an incredible and arduous journey to support and encourage other fellow victims.

A few days later I was waiting in the operating room with the chief surgeon of the reconstructive team for his next patient to arrive. There was so much I wanted to tell him—how much I admired his surgical skill and incredible stamina to sustain the patient's morale during the months of their regenerative transformation. I wanted to tell him about the fresh enthusiasm amongst the staff, sparked by the respectable results in the photographs. Only with a vague embarrassment did I mention my personal conflict, the recent encounter with a patient with such limited speech function underneath the bravado of the cowboy hat. He understood my unspoken allegation. However, he was well-equipped with reassuring facts of long-term research that particularly addressed the of quality of life in these patients. According to his experience, a convincing number of patients were able to resume an almost normal lifestyle within a year of major reconstructive surgery. Remembering that none of these options existed twenty years ago, I felt comforted with a new vision of what the next decade of accelerated surgical technology might achieve.

The doors of the elevator opened. Our next patient, scheduled for facial reconstruction, had arrived.

Eyedrops and Tears

Wearing black glasses on black skin, he was dressed more appropriately for a funeral than for his surgical appointment. He wore a black suit over a shirt that was once white but now was gray. It had lost most of its buttons from too many laundry cycles and was held together at the collar with a black tie, none of which he could see. He resembled a sinister black tower with nothing but darkness around him. He had lost his vision despite multiple surgical attempts over the years to save his sight. Darkness came out of his mouth as he flung hostile language at me, which had nothing to do with my present assignment to prepare him for yet another surgical procedure on his eyes. He was still stunned by a collective disappointment about his previous five corneal transplants that had failed. He had no vision in his right eye and was here to face another three hours of surgery on that eye with nothing but a vague, guarded promise of improvement. There was a slight possibility that his sight might recover from light perception to hand motion.

He could not see me as I moved from behind my desk and sat close to him on the corner of the table, hoping that he could somehow sense my attempt to help him through yet another ordeal. No, he had not taken his blood pressure medicines this morning and did not want to answer any more questions that had been asked too many times in different doctors' offices. The answers I needed had been lost in a paper shuffle somewhere between underpaid secretaries and broken fax machines that delivered smudged sheets of paper. They were even more illegible than a doctor's worst penmanship. I could sense that my patient was not willing to volunteer any answers.

There was resignation in his voice, which was his last trail to the outside world from the massive prison he carried around himself. No matter how hard he punched his fists against the wall, he could not penetrate the wall behind which there was no outside world to be found. He could not fight the frustration one more day or one more hour before he sank into the black oblivion of general anesthesia. This

man needed deep sleep. He needed a break from the fierce bitterness that rampaged in every cell of his body and consumed his spirit while he resigned himself into the capable hands of the little surgeon who rarely spoke but always smiled.

Nobody had escorted the patient this morning. Instead, he came alone by subway, having alienated all friends, neighbors, and family. Over the years he had turned into a black menace, with all his pent-up anger waiting to rip.

I saw him again sometime later, in the next cubicle with the nurse who cautiously asked him more questions about his medical history. The automated blood pressure cuff squeezed his arm for a mechanical answer. He recognized my voice. "I'm really sorry, Ma'am," he mumbled, a sorry stream of apologies tumbling across his thick and dry lips.

I told him, "Not to worry, you must be getting just a bit anxious about your operation."

I was happy for him that he found an untapped softness, buried somewhere deep inside of him, overgrown by the black stubble on his unshaven face. Behind his dark, shielded glasses, his eyes were wet from eyedrops mixed with tears. I reassured him with a squeeze of my hand that he had nothing to apologize for.

I was not pleased with myself and felt that I had not succeeded in diminishing his anxiety or made any impact on his long history of darkness. The tight time constraint of the preoperative anesthesia interview pushed me along like a piece of luggage on a conveyor belt. The next patient was ready and needed to be seen. I resolved to inquire about the outcome of this dark and sad man's surgery the next time I saw the surgeon involved with his case. However, as the days slipped by, my initial sense of genuine concern faded. It was some time before I came across the surgeon, and by then I could not remember the patient's name.

Anesthesia for AIDS

There was no applause for my performance. My only audience was a patient who opened his eyes and blinked as he attempted to match the surrounding cues of lights, unfamiliar voices, and a strange bed. He looked disoriented as I helped him find the missing piece of the jigsaw puzzle. Calmly, I reassured him that his surgery was finished and he was doing fine. We were off to a bad start before I put him to sleep.

His battle with AIDS for the past eleven years had rendered him intolerant of the slightest pain. He recoiled with uninhibited screams, heaving his body off the stretcher, like a woman in labor who can't be reached with words. This is how he reacted to the minuscule needle puncture of Novocain used to numb the skin before I inserted the IV. What normally takes no time at all became a drawn-out ordeal for him. To tap into a vein beneath his black, leathery skin, marred with criss-cross scars from intravenous drug abuse and chemotherapy for many years, now became my struggle. As I tried to beat the clock against the expense of every idle minute of operating room time, my patient obviously became more upset with each failed attempt. He lashed out with angry obscenities directed at me that made me feel like a helpless beginner. The required meticulous technique to dispose properly of any sharp exposed needles and any blood- contaminated gauze made me unusually clumsy.

It would only take one drop of the patient's blood to come into contact with the slightest open wound, as minuscule as a paper cut, to put me at risk of living with the uncertainty of having been infected with AIDS.

A colleague of mine, who with a glance recognized my dilemma, quietly offered assistance. With our combined experience of over forty years, we succeeded in establishing intravenous access. Sometimes good bedside manner can be useless until the intravenous sedation gets the chemical advantage. The drug most commonly used for this purpose, however, could be hazardous in this situation, because it interacts with the anti-viral medicines for patients with AIDS. I injected it into the IV and let it drip cautiously until I reached the desired effect. But even a small amount, which a healthy patient would hardly notice, was enough to put my patient to sleep almost instantly. I could hardly rouse him and noticed his shallow breathing. Quickly, we moved into the operating room to attach an oxygen monitor and supplement his oxygen level with a facemask. With all monitors established, I could proceed to anesthetize him fully for surgery. A shielded mask, goggles, and double gloves protected me from any coughing into my face while I inserted a tube into his trachea in order to breathe for him while he was under anesthesia.

The surgeon walked in with his junior residents, discussing current sports events. He knew the patient was asleep and ready for him, and he could take all the time he needed. There was no hurry. He appeared relaxed as he approached the patient with another injection to control potential bleeding from the delicate membranes that lined his nose. This time, I was confident that he would not move, since I had carried him safely to a deeper level with a steady inflow of anesthetic gases and intravenous narcotics.

Like a pilot having reached altitude as he switches to cruise control, I settled into the regular beat of the monitor, as familiar to me as my own heartbeat. The slightest variation of rhythm or pitch alerted my attention, as automatically as a conditioned reflex. Instantly, it could interrupt my current thought process like a built-in alarm. When the patient's heartbeat was steady, it would allow me to reflect on my surroundings beyond the monitor. For a moment I questioned myself why I was still there, after so many years of self-sacrifice. Depending on the intensity of the day, the answer was too multifaceted to dwell on it. It was more comfortable to watch the monitor.

I recognized the patient's nasal deformity, shaped flat and concave, instead of a normal bridge. I would hardly have noticed it, if it had not been pointed out to me. While the surgeon had moved on to discuss the drawbacks of healthcare management, I searched the chart again for the actual reason for the surgical procedure beyond a cosmetic improvement. In my mind, I wanted to justify the risk of putting this patient to sleep with all his medical complexities, on a journey beyond his understanding.

I wanted to defend my role in creating a potential risk situation for other healthcare workers who would take care of him post-operatively. Suddenly I wished I was joining my sister for a vacation in southern France, where her two healthy boys discovered crabs under rocks on the beach. They all seemed as far away as another planet.

Mostly, I wondered if this procedure would improve his quality of life, when he returned to that jobless life within the confines of an apartment in an undesirable neighborhood. I wondered how many friends remained to help him with his groceries. I imagined a shrinking circle of support that offered him rides to the doctors while his illness invaded more organs and functions of his body. Very few would still be willing to shake his hand or give him a hug. I wished I could keep him anesthetized for the duration of his progressive illness and not disturb his dreams, to spare him any suffering to come or the return to his lonely existence.

Back to reality, I tried to find a more comfortable position on my three-legged black stool, which provided little support for my back muscles that screamed quietly. I had finished recording the sequence of events that put this patient to sleep and flawlessly logged all his vital signs from the computer. My thoughts turned to planning his precise wake-up, approximately one hour from now. It would have to coincide with the last few surgical sutures and the application of a wing-shaped cast over the newly elevated nasal bone.

It was like a precision landing, a gentle touchdown without a bounce. There could be no coughing when I removed the artificial airway—that could disseminate the AIDS virus into eyes of innocent bystanders. One bout of coughing could also reactivate bleeding from the fresh operative site in his nose, as the patient strained to catch his breath. Worse than that, it could cause a dangerous spasm of his vocal cords that could prevent the inflow of vital oxygen into his lungs. His arms would have to be secured, to prevent out-of-control thrashing about. I had to suction out his stomach and remove any blood that might have trickled down from the back of his nose.

Twenty minutes before wake-up time, I started slowly to reduce the anesthetic gases and wean the patient off the mechanical ventilator, until he gradually resumed his own breathing pattern. At the same time, I gave him one last dose of intravenous narcotic, to let him wake up without the dreaded pain. Also, a special medication was given to prevent nausea and vomiting in the post-operative period. As the surgeons left the field for a quick break of stale coffee in the lounge, I moved to the head of the patient to fully control his wake-up.

A slowly controlled wake-up would prevent explosive coughing as I got ready to remove the artificial airway from his throat. He shivered under the thin cotton blanket. On the way to the recovery room, I replaced it with layers of warm blankets and wrapped him like a child. Two nurses wearing gloves and shielded masks were ready to take over his care after I gave a detailed report of the anesthesia given. There were no special thanks for a patient with AIDS who was well sedated and not coughing or being sick all over the nurses, but I knew that the nurses were appreciative. A relieved look on their faces said it all. As I walked away, I gathered the paperwork to file it and scanned the large schedule board for the name of my next patient.

Anesthesia for Children

Although I was well trained in putting children to sleep, there was always the responsibility lurking at the back of my mind to get them through the perils of anesthesia unharmed. This sense of responsibility never faded. The games I played with the children in the holding area were partly motivated by gaining their trust for the few moments while they went to sleep. At some point the innocent game turned into serious business.

This was not so one night when I babysat my one-year-old nephew. We searched for golden stars on the blue pages of his book of bedtime stories. We found them, more than we had hoped for. We didn't even care about the stories, just the stars. There were shooting stars, little stars, and big stars that you could sit on and take a ride into fairyland. We lost count, there were so many, and when we reached the end of the book, we started again at the beginning. They just kept falling out of the pages and onto us.

Eventually the stars made him yawn; his eyelids became heavy and droopy, just like the first stage of anesthesia. When his head fell against my shoulder, I caught it softly with my hand. I was well accustomed to this first light sleep, where any movement can stir a child rudely out of his dreams. I held him gently and observed his staccato breathing pattern until it smoothened into a more regular rhythm. Now he was firmly planted on a star in his world of dreams. I felt safe in stretching out slowly on the bed. He sensed the motion and snuggled his head with damp, curly hair against my neck. His short little arm and hand settled on my shoulder while I held his back with my other hand. I was used to seeing children asleep under my care, but this was different. It was a natural sleep without drugs, mild coercion, or the pain of surgery after wake-up. It was a free gift to me without having to walk the tight rope of putting children to sleep to administer anesthesia.

Pediatric anesthesia did not exist as a subspecialty when I completed my anesthesia residency twenty-five years ago. At that time, every anesthesiologist was expected to be equally adept at the entire patient spectrum, from infancy to geriatrics. We applied similar physiologic principles to children as to adults but different dosages of drugs and a lot of common sense.

Nowadays, whenever available, children who come for surgery are anesthetized by pediatric anesthesiologists who have elected to take one additional year of fellowship training in pediatric anesthesia after the general three-year residency in anesthesiology. There is a high demand for an edge of expertise in this relatively new subspecialty.

Today parents frequently request a pediatric anesthesiologist and settle reluctantly for someone who just offers twenty years of experience instead of a subspecialty diploma. In such a case it is ultimately the responsibility of the anesthesiologist to refer the patient to a more qualified colleague if the required technical skill or the medical management is outside of his or her comfort zone or usual practice. Sometimes parents call ahead of time at the anesthesia office to find out the name of the anesthesiologist assigned to their child's care. It gives them the opportunity to check the background and/or any past or present litigation process through a national databank for physicians. It can be a humbling experience for a physician. Whenever the office staff notifies a physician prior to such an encounter with the family, it can raise a defensiveness that may affect the patient's care, especially since any subsequent litigation may be totally unrelated to the care the individual was capable of giving. I know some unfortunate cases beyond anyone's control that amounted to nothing but bad luck.

In particular, I remember the frightened parent of a two-year old scheduled for insertion of ear tubes to treat chronic ear infections. The parent asked me if I was a pediatric anesthesiologist. The question did make me bristle, particularly since the twenty-minute procedure involved a straightforward technique of introducing the anesthetic gas via a facemask and did not require any complex skills. In my encounters with such parents, I have to pocket my professional pride and just be sensitive to their concern. Instead of defending my skill, I must become an instant caretaker of the parent and make every effort to offer reassurance backed by facts rather than emotion. Most of all, I never let it interfere with my care of their child and just focus on the child's needs and safety.

During my residency training, it was natural to keep the babies warm by turning up the room temperature until surgeons and nurses started to complain about it, or placing a more direct heat lamp, jokingly called the "French Fry Warmer," a measured distance above their little bodies. It provided sustained warmth while we placed the monitor electrodes on their chests and started the intravenous, which sometimes took more than one try. Baby veins that need to be cannulated with an IV catheter are about one millimeter in diameter and tend to hide in pudgy fists of baby fat. We wrapped a wooden tongue blade with gauze and taped it to the baby's arm, to create little arm-boards to stabilize the delicate intravenous.

At that time, cotton hats to keep the head warm were quickly fashioned out of a piece of soft "stockinet" with a knot at one end. For basic equipment, the baby mask used to be a molded black rubber mask. We now have advanced to a clear transparent vinyl mask, which is less frightening for children. This also has the advantage of allowing us to better observe the child's color or any untoward events, such as potential retching while the child goes to sleep. Unlike the old days, we do now have an entire menu of bottled flavors, such as banana cream, watermelon, or bubble gum to flavor a child's mask.

Only one parent is allowed to escort the child to the operating room while we begin the anesthesia induction. It has taken years of academic discussion to determine if having a parent present is actually beneficial to the child. The main objective is to minimize child-parent separation, which I still remember as a devastating experience when I had my tonsils out at age four. My mother simply vanished behind a milky glass door that shut, merciless despite my cries and outstretched arms.

It can be difficult for parents to see their child lose consciousness in a stranger's arms, but consistent with all studies, it is better to place the emotional burden on the parents rather than on the children and do everything possible to prevent a sense of abandonment. When the child enters the operating room with a parent, all of us stop what we are doing to avoid frightening them. For a few minutes, the clock stops to allow a brief playtime instead.

We have all sorts of magical tricks to divert their attention from the sterile environment and the bright lights. The goal is to send them to sleep with giggles rather than tears. One of the children's favorite games is to change all the colored graphics on the computer until they find a favorite. Another popular distraction is the finger clip with a red light that measures oxygen saturation. The children are allowed to shake it in the air until its regular waveform resembles an abstract drawing on the screen. We do silly things, such as making them count and multiply and ask them if they are married yet. The most popular act is "Rocky," a slinky, furry, squirrel-like animal that seems to come to life in the arms of one nurse anesthetist, who can be as silly with the children as he is serious once the patient goes to sleep. Rocky jumps and squeaks, the fur over his wire skeleton already threadbare from years of making children laugh. Another nurse anesthetist makes me laugh every time he places the mask on the child's face just for a split second. He quickly takes it off and asks, "Are you asleep yet?" He then acts totally surprised as they shake their heads, laughing.

Once we have established a reasonable amount of trust, we proceed to introduce the anesthetic gas through the mask, which enters the lungs, where it is then absorbed into the bloodstream, and finally delivered to the cerebral circulation until the child falls asleep. At this point we send the parent off with a last kiss on their child's cheek. We then turn to our respective concentrated tasks of securing intravenous access and a safe airway before we turn the child over to the surgeon.

Unlike providing anesthesia for adults, when giving anesthesia for children, one must expect unbridled personalities. Children are more unpredictable with their defenses. Without playtime they may put up a fight to ward off the unknown with any strength of their imagination. Adults have learned to accept the unavoidable. On the other hand, children are usually much healthier and lack the diffuse, degenerative disease that is a natural process with progressive age. Taking care of children can be most rewarding, and the children often elicit my utmost empathy as they march like brave little heroes, hand in hand with me through their surgical experience.

For the sophisticated anesthesiologist, there are many subtle but distinct differences between anesthetizing children and adults. As a general rule, children are more at risk and require greater skill and vigilance, because the physiological make-up of children, especially their autonomic nervous system, is more reactive to physical and pharmacological intervention.

One day, at the end of a long, hard week, I was not enchanted with my Friday assignment at our surgical center. Sixteen children were scheduled for tonsils, adenoids, ear tubes, and strabismus surgery in three operating rooms. My challenge was to satisfy three different surgeons with great efficiency. They were anxious to finish on time to see more patients back at their offices in a few hours. Sometimes a prolonged discussion about a child with a simple cold can gobble up fifteen minutes of precious time. I also had to supervise three different nurse anesthetists with varying skill levels.

I had to meet and interview sixteen parents, admit sixteen children, and sneak in a playful rapport while I examined them. I would also somehow have to complete the paperwork accurately and obtain an informed consent from the parents. Even during this highly personal interaction with the parents and children, I had to remain physically available at a moment's notice to supervise the anesthesia induction of another child as he or she went to sleep. I also had to keep my ears attuned to any excessive crying coming from the recovery room and stand by for rescue medication to treat unexpected levels of pain or nausea.

With much trepidation about the day but a firm resolve to stay focused, I stepped out of the elevator and climbed over several children and toys on the floor of the small pre-op waiting lounge. The children, too young for pre-op anxiety, seemed to be having a good time, while the parents sat anxiously or leaned against the wall, wrapped in their own concerns. Grandmothers held diaper bags and storybooks and added some comfort by their mere presence.

My first sign of hope that I would have a good day was when five-year-old Nicholas adorned me with a sticky blue paper ring around my little finger. I wore it proudly until later in the morning, when it drained down the sink while I washed my hands.

The first challenge of the day was a twelve-year-old girl with Down's syndrome; she had a short, obese stature and elderly parents of equally short stature. The girl's excessive weight, which was part of the syndrome's typical endocrine dysfunction, worried me. It would take a long time to get her to sleep by inhaling the anesthesia gas through a mask, before we could even attempt to place the intravenous line sometimes urgently needed during the induction phase of anesthesia.

The parents were extremely protective of her, and together we decided it would be wise to pre-medicate her with a liquid syrupy sedative. Without it, we would risk a struggle with her effort to defend herself from any perceived bodily harm. Her father was not shy about telling me what was best for his daughter, but I was glad that she seemed most relaxed staying close to him. Sometimes it was best to listen to suggestions from well-meaning parents rather than assuming a wrongful authority. With his reassuring endearments, the patient went to sleep smoothly.

After her successful operation and an uneventful recovery, the father shook my hand and thanked me profusely for being attentive to his suggestions for her care. With obvious relief and a big smile, he whisked his daughter in a massive wheelchair back to the elevator. He didn't know that I too was greatly relieved to have this case behind me without any mishaps. I knew they would be back for another procedure before too long and made a mental note to look out for them.

With a lighter heart, I turned to the next patient. When asked into the room for the pre-op interview, children often skip and bounce through the door fearlessly, although the shy ones hold Mom's hand. Mothers, often composed for the sake of their child, proceed in a calm but questioning manner. Dads usually follow, frequently with a baseball hat pulled far down the forehead to disguise any fear.

Since most children were admitted the morning of surgery, I always looked forward to the colorful array of their outfits. I love the pudgy baby necks that bulge out from their white cotton T-shirts while they lean their heads against their mother's shoulder and wonder why they are up so early in the morning. They just know that something is up.

I remember the twelve-year-old black girl in tight, stylish jeans and a neatly checkered red blouse, a perfect back-to-school outfit. She mentioned that it took her mother four hours to braid her hair the African way. I wondered if the daughter returned the favor to her mother. That would explain the extraordinary closeness between them. At twelve years old, she seemed agreeable to go to sleep with the intravenous just like the adults. She was willing to take a chance and did not surprise me with her brave attitude. Often I can tell how far I can challenge a youngster just by watching the interaction with the parent. The more relaxed the parents are, the better the children do when they go to sleep. It is an intense and accurate snapshot of the child's environment at home.

The best days in anesthesia are routine days when all procedures go smoothly. We simply mark these days as uneventful, which is not an indicator of a busy or a light schedule. I was surprised how quickly the pediatric day at the Surgicenter flew by. Since the surgeons left as usual, without a word of thanks, I felt like giving myself a pat on the shoulder for a day well done. I left for home tired but deeply rewarded by a good day. Sometimes the sudden appearance of a flock of children in one day is all I need to remind me how precious they are and that all of us were little miracles at some forgotten time.

A few days later, still feeling good about my pediatric day at the Surgicenter, I called a longtime friend and colleague to confirm our plans for a social visit that afternoon. She sounded shaky on the phone, like a frightened child who had awakened from a bad dream. But it was not a dream. It was the stark reality of a disastrous, potentially fatal experience in a two-year-old boy during a routine tonsil operation. My friend had been in charge of supervising a case executed by one of our most competent senior nurse anesthetists, with over twenty years of experience. Many considered him the best of them all. I could not imagine what went wrong. As I listened to my friend's account of the child, who at the end of a routine tonsil procedure developed a sudden onset of heart irregularities that almost came to a fatal standstill, I sank to my knees and sat on the floor next to the phone. When something happens to a colleague whose skill I deeply respect, it is the same shock as if it had happened to me. A team of physicians had rushed to the scene in response to the emergency call. Resuscitative drugs and chest compressions restored a regular heartbeat, and the patient was stabilized before being transferred to the intensive care unit.

After some further investigation, it was speculated that the event might have been surgically related, but the burden of proof was on my colleague's shoulders. Fortunately, the patient was discharged home the next day, and there were no further consequences.

Within the "family" of a department, such an event triggers a shock wave to all members. Individuals react differently. As I spoke the next day to another senior staff member who assisted with the resuscitation, he appeared cool and rather than discussing it, simply told me he "took care of business." It is unspoken knowledge among us that if we are in it for the long haul, we are all victims of the statistical evidence that promises the encounter of a serious complication and litigation at some point of our career. Such an occurrence is not spoken of as a catastrophe, but its brutal effect on all concerned is camouflaged in cushy terms such as an "adverse event" or "critical incident." Of course, there is a strict protocol of conduct to adhere to that delays an emotional outburst until the patient is taken care of, the family is informed, and the written documentation is completed. There are guidelines on how to approach the family and how to talk to colleagues without getting into a bigger mess. Emotional support from colleagues is usually tentative and restricted to all-knowing, empathic eye contact. Additional emotional counseling is preferably dealt with on one's own time and credit card.

My friend and I kept our engagement that afternoon to baby-sit for a two-year-old boy, who was in town for a visit with a distant cousin of mine. At my friend's apartment, we both crouched on our hands and knees to steer him away from glass tabletops and other sharp objects. We gladly let him explore all the kitchen drawers and helped him pull out zip-lock bags and red coasters with white polka dots.

We encircled him with protective boundaries that were playful, much less critical than in the OR. We felt far removed from the fulcrum of the teeter-totter between life and death, and dared to swing happily on the seat of life. The safety margin seemed harmless compared to our mighty responsibility for any child under anesthesia.

We didn't mind the half-chewed crumbs of animal crackers on the white carpet. While we watched him closely, we celebrated the curiosity of a healthy child. As we chased him from the living room back to the kitchen, my friend stopped, looked at me, and remarked that she had not seen such a joyful smile on my face for a long time. This playful interaction with a healthy child was a form of unspoken therapy for both of us. It gave us permission to be children for a short while and good reason to laugh.

Two Children I Won't Forget (Part One)

I was already caught up in the micro-management of my departure for another night on call, packing shampoo and a midnight snack. I had ten minutes left to iron my scrubs when the phone rang. I did not want to take a phone call, since in my head I was already in the hospital. Nevertheless, I picked it up, expecting to cut off a telemarketer and firmly let him know that I was not available

Time stopped when my colleague told me on the phone what had happened the previous night, after I had left at midnight.

She talked about a little four-year-old boy I had seen in the pre-op holding area. He and his mother had squeezed into a wheelchair together while they waited for a stretcher. He squirmed in her arms to the point that he got rid of his hospital Johnny. All I could see were his skinny ribs.

I knew that my colleague and long-time friend, who had no children of her own but cared about them more than anything else in her solitary lifestyle, would give the best anesthesia possible. We had trained together at one of the best residency training programs in the country more than thirty years ago. Even then we dreamed of having our own children when we huddled together in the call room, sharing an orange to pick up energy for the remainder of the night. Over the years we compensated for our childless careers by caring for our pediatric patients with the utmost gentleness, as if they were our own, at least for the day. We found the biggest trucks for toddlers and blew up balloons of surgical gloves. We renamed the dolls and rolled bandages around the paws of teddy bears.

Already, at the age of four, this little boy had required a cochlear implant for congenital deafness. This had been accomplished in another state but had left him with facial paralysis from surgical nerve damage. It was our surgeon's challenge to redo the cochlear implant and possibly reverse the facial paralysis by decompressing the facial nerve.

The child had been under anesthesia for a few hours. It was after midnight when she returned the child to the recovery room and sent me on my way home after I finished my own case. When I passed through on my way to the locker room, he was still asleep in his crib. All I could see was a white, round plastic shell that covered his left ear. His mom was on her way down to be present when he woke up.

This morning my friend told me that she witnessed his wake-up. His eyelids opened partially with a slight flutter of his long lashes. His little hand was awake enough to communicate with his mom in sign language. We expected him to convey pain or discomfort. He took us by surprise when he simply signed "I love you." He never cried.

As I hung up the phone, I marveled at my friend's skill to keep this little boy so fearless and comfortable. I wondered what magic potion she had given him besides the standard pediatric dose of anesthesia. I concluded that under her genuine loving care he never felt a moment of distress. It is also reasonably sound to assume that he never heard a harsh word in his life.

Two Children I Won't Forget (Part Two)

The nurse in charge had warned me as I was about to see a one-year-old patient in room 1021.

I thought I understood and armed myself with a stethoscope. As soon as I entered the room, my internal alarm shot up a notch. Piles of adult and baby clothes were scattered all over the floor in the room, with more tossed aside in the bathroom. An offensive smell prevented me from taking a deep breath. The narrow bedside table was covered with litter, torn open gooey candy bars, and other junk food left over from Halloween a few days ago. Standing upright amidst all was a half a bottle of blue juice and some in other rainbow colors, at 9:30 AM.

Mother, tall and thin in a surgical scrub suit, held on to the crib. With her free hand she grasped a white towel around her wet hair. The nurses had put the infant back in the crib after they found it crawling on the floor amongst the strewn clothes while the mother took a shower. Even after the shower, she appeared very restless and agitated, as if on the run. She seemed in a hurry to get the operation over with. If we could not start it within the next two hours, she needed to go home to a suburb north of town and come back later. She was determined to get out of the confinement of this room. Her face had a drawn, ashen look from exhaustion. Multiple scabs on her face were proof of her chronic itchiness. Scars on her arms confirmed the nurses' collective suspicion of self-administered drugs.

Meanwhile the baby bopped up and down in the crib as if it was having fun. It had a chubby red face, partly from an untreated infection in the neck with recent episodes of fever. Since no one had been able to start an intravenous on his equally chubby hands and feet, he was also becoming dehydrated, which only worsened his flush and his fever. The baby seemed delighted to see me and greeted me with a beaming smile of innocence. I wanted to pick him up and hold him close. When I called him by name, his mother corrected me: his name was Max and not Alex as printed on his chart. The background noise of domestic confusion became more urgent in my head. I struck a soothing, mellow chord to which Max responded in his own way. He stretched out his little sausage arms as if to say, "Take me away from here."

The baby needed general anesthesia, first to start a reliable intravenous that would last several days for antibiotic medication which the mother neglected to give by mouth, as directed. Max also needed to be asleep for a fifteen-minute CT scan to determine the exact source of his infection. Since this procedure was urgent but not an emergency, it was scheduled for 1:00 PM, as soon as we had staff available.

This period of time allowed mother a four-hour window to go home and come back. It was also a safe margin of time to feed the baby some clear apple juice to restore his hydration. The mother hurriedly signed the informed consent for anesthesia and almost bolted out the door "to fetch some clean underwear."

At one o'clock we sent for Max to be brought down to the X-ray department. Max arrived in his crib, escorted by two caring nurses. I was glad that his mother had not made it back in time. My assistant and I removed his faded blue jumpsuit and wrapped him in a clean blanket.

As we held the clear plastic mask on his face, it turned even redder with the effort to squirm away from it. His eyes opened wide with sudden terror. He shook his arms with livid fists and kicked his legs in midair with all the strength he could muster until he finally went to sleep. Despite his short-lived but intense distress, we were stunned. Max never cried. We almost did as we shook our heads with an unspoken sadness.

Our common-sense psychology led us to believe that his stress response was so blunted by abuse that any crying triggered some unthinkable punishment. When the baby returned safely to the recovery room, we were relieved to overhear the nurses whisper Chapter BD53. This meant immediate involvement of social service for the purpose of domestic intervention.

It occurred to me that while both children were handicapped in different ways, I witnessed two extremes of maternal love and abuse. Both resulted in the absence of the spontaneous crying I would expect under each circumstance. I welcomed the next child who cried while going to sleep.

The Caretaker

The expression on the face of the nurse who called me to OR seventeen resembled a pushed panic button. It told me there was no time to waste. Had I not been footsteps away, I would have run. Crises like these happened too infrequently to ever get used to them. After so many years of the daily gamble with life and death, they still made me want to run the other way. However, it was my job to be there in a flash, sometimes an instant too late. Intraoperative catastrophes, like cardiac arrests, have their own momentum. They couldn't wait. In minutes I had to turn it around, do the impossible, salvage the wreckage, and act the Almighty.

Over a time span of thirty-five years, I had seen every conceivable crisis and still feared the unexpected. The fear of freezing at a crucial moment or forgetting the basics, like a seasoned actor missing his lines, never died. A fear of being held accountable for not knowing or doing enough was still a continuum from my childhood, when no tunes I ever played sounded good enough. At work, I was always a heartbeat away from disaster; there were no guarantees. I had carried this burden as a painstaking caretaker since childhood.

It took seconds in room seventeen to assess the mess. Patient and surgeon seemed out of control. An irate surgeon yelled at the patient and me, "Stop the vomiting. Stop the retching." The patient couldn't stop it, and neither could I. The nurse's eyes, alarmed and with widened pupils, were upon me and demanded action. Now with resigned desperation, the surgeon bemoaned the open eye, ready to receive a corneal transplant. He had high hopes of saving the woman's last chance for vision, fading fast from her destructive diabetic disease.

The nurse had already given the most potent intravenous drug to stop the nausea, a double dose. I was on my knees, covered underneath sterile drapes, to suction the flood of ominous, bilious material that pooled in the clear plastic oxygen mask. I didn't care about the universal precautions of gloves. I just wanted to prevent it from spilling into the operative site of the eye and silently plead for help. No spill had occurred, but the violent retching has dislodged the contents of the eye and caused a hemorrhage. Too late; the damage was done. The retching had stopped, and so had the hope of ever restoring the patient's vision.

They started without me, while I attended the weekly mandatory departmental case presentation and discussion for educational purposes. I learned about an extremely rare transfusion reaction, so rare that I had never encountered it in thirty years of practice. It could cause damage to lung tissue but was usually completely reversible. The damage that had occurred to this patient's eye was not.

Just at this moment, I would have paid anything to restore this woman's vision, to give her the pleasure of seeing smiles, flowers, and grandchildren for the last few years of her life. At the age of seventy-four, she liked to watch television while she endured the tedious process of kidney dialysis three times a week. So brave, so unfortunate.

The remainder of the procedure was carried to the end in painful silence. Dozens of stitches were placed in a circular fashion with a suture invisible to the naked eye, tracked by the power of the microscope. It resembled stitching together a burst bubble. There was nothing for me to do but to attend to others who needed me. Outside, a nurse questioned my silence. "You don't seem yourself today." No explanation could convey my distress; therefore, I dropped any dutiful answer. My mind was already piqued by relentless questions. Would the outcome have been different had I been there from the beginning with a different strategy? Not knowing the circumstances, I righteously left this patient to the care of a colleague on duty that time.

I arrived at the hospital early enough to leisurely check my clinical assignment for the day before walking over for the medical conference. The weekly grand rounds took place in the adjacent building of the most famous teaching hospital, in an old amphitheater from the last century. Its tall, polished wooden benches, like church pews, held up legions of sleep-deprived residents over the years.

It was ten minutes of seven, just enough time to make a mental note of my assignments for the day while I balanced a cup of black coffee that burned my tongue. On the gray magnetic board that covered half a wall, clinical assignments for twenty operating rooms were listed. Names of staff and patients were lined up, ready to move forward, like pieces of chess. It was mostly a random match, except an occasional request from a relative or a friend who knew so and so. The arbitrary shuffle could be called anything from luck or, depending on the outcome, an act of providence for patients and staff alike.

My assignment included room seventeen at nine-thirty, after the conference. A colleague of mine, scheduled to supervise room seventeen until that time, had called in sick. Another attending in charge of the entire schedule this morning had an equally proficient colleague available to share the limited workload until then. For a brief moment I considered staying and offering a helping hand to get started. But we agreed, as we often do, that one of them would get my case started and I should go to the conference. After all, he was in charge. If help was needed, he could page me. My beeper remained quiet for the duration of the conference.

It was past noon when the patient was admitted to the recovery room. I felt physical hunger but no desire to eat. This was my first face-to-face encounter with the patient I didn't even know but just met under the disguise of the surgical drapes and undignified circumstances. Her face looked solemn. She sat up straight like the bolt that already hit her with the bad news. The operation had failed, and she knew it. Her lips were pinched tight, holding it all in, determined not to spill her anger and frustration. I could not tell whether she was more distraught with herself for getting sick to her stomach at the worst of times or at the doctors for not preventing it somehow.

Silently I was tormented by the same question. After I had stabilized her retching in the OR, I searched for my colleague in charge at the start of this case. He looked perplexed and detached when I told him the bad turn of events.

Having been through the grueling ordeal of a lawsuit myself ten years ago has made me conscientious, often beyond the call of duty, leaving no page unturned in patient care. On examination of the woman's record, it became clear that she had a previous history of nausea in the operating room, so severe that the planned procedure had to be cancelled in the recent past. Today she had come for another chance. We could offer her full general anesthesia, which would eliminate the immediate risk of nausea while the surgery was in progress and deal with it after the transplant was in place. However, she was considered a poor candidate for a general anesthesia, with increased risk factors because of her extensive illness. There was not an easy way out. Keeping her awake with local anesthesia to the eye was the most feasible alternative.

Now I felt the blame for it all. Most of my life I was the first to grab unsolicited blame when something went wrong.

I softly put my hand on her shoulder. I was afraid for her and for me as I offered a humble sorry and a glass of water to rinse her mouth. She could not see the green stain of bile still on the white cotton blanket. The metal patch with the pattern of peek-through holes that covered up the disaster looked innocent to by-standers but grotesque to me. I reluctantly signed my name on her record and herewith assumed full medico-legal responsibility. What was I thinking of? Had I totally lost my mind? Someone had to take responsibility, and I was there. I arrived after the fact and did what could be done. There was just a vague sense of uneasiness after I had signed, with the innocence of signing a check at the grocery store, that this was not smart on my part. I also wrote her postoperative insulin orders and called her medical doctor for future follow-up. My mind worked flawlessly helping her but not myself.

A discussion with the surgeon, who had regained his composure, confirmed that the damage was irreparable and nothing would change that stark reality.

I was off duty unusually early—plenty of time to take in my favorite yoga class on the way home. I had looked forward to it all week, to gather the final strength to complete my duties the last day before the weekend. But today I felt the need to do something for someone else. On my way home, I gladly drove the extra mile for a visit at the nursing home to take my mother-in-law out for coffee. She seemed overjoyed with the unexpected visit. I told her everything. At eighty-three, she was not concerned about the details. She just listened without judgment and told me she loved me. With genuine love and a deep gratitude, I scooped up her laundry and drove home. Oh yes, I heard her occasional grumble about her roommate who took her hangers or the soggy tuna fish sandwich for dinner. It occurred to me that she had been the lucky one today.

The Holding Area

All week I had been longing to turn over at 4:30 AM. On Saturday I woke up at 4:45 AM, unable to get back to sleep. I felt quite depleted. A sore throat and a congested head made me wonder what happened. As I replayed the events of the week, I realized that it was just business as usual, with routine cases. Just five days ago, I felt invincible after a weekend trip to South Carolina to celebrate New Year's with friends.

The first day back I was given a full caseload of twenty-five patients for mostly cataract surgery. Also, an anesthesia colleague called in from a peripheral community hospital. He was interested in an opportunity to observe our anesthesia procedure for ambulatory eye surgery. He had found time this morning and announced his visit unexpectedly. It would be easy on any given day to find excuses why it might be inconvenient, but I surprised him by simply saying, "Yes, by all means, come over this morning."

I was challenged to juggle priorities all day. It took single-minded focus to keep up with the patient load and the rapid case turnover yet still give each patient my undivided attention, as if she or he were the only ones I had to take care for. Between cases, I pointed out various anatomical landmarks to my student in the bony orbit of a skull that I kept for teaching purposes under my desk in a fancy paper bag.

It was an attitude and a habit of mine to help out wherever I can. If time allowed I might start an intravenous in the holding area for a colleague who was still engaged with another patient and felt rushed to start the next one. It was a trivial gesture of courtesy. At the same time, it allowed me to strike up a casual conversation. I was always curious to visualize the lifestyle that belongs to each patient. Lifestyles varied greatly, from a battle for survival in our sickest patients to a momentary glimpse of the rich and famous, who have traveled from another continent to receive the best medical care money can buy. None of them is immune to preoperative anxiety.

Some patients bestowed upon me a unique gift of revealing the personality beneath their skimpy hospital gown that barely covered their bodies. One time I was privileged to meet a patient who was a well-known psychologist for crisis intervention and bereavement counseling at national disaster sites. We talked about my mother, who was afflicted with Alzheimer's disease. He shared his expertise as author of a book on the same subject and about his joy of writing. He had observed my interaction with other patients and colleagues and told me that judging by my smile, it was apparent how much I loved my work. He noticed that I seemed to do much more than just my job. It was something I was not aware of, but I was pleasantly surprised that I still projected certain vitality. He seemed interested in my own writing progress. He offered his advice any time over coffee, as he visited the hospital regularly for his own study of characters.

This encounter was a rare but precious connection of a spiritual nature, in which we both realized each other's capacity as caretakers and psychologists taught by life. He rose above his own anxiety about his upcoming surgery with faith and trust, while I interrupted my routine. I willingly chose to linger beside his stretcher instead of sipping a cup of coffee in isolation during my scheduled break time.

More often, the preoperative interview consisted of a series of routine questions in the least amount of time possible. Sometimes the only meaningful connection was deliberate eye contact on my part—a blend of warmth, confidence, compassion, or reassurance, whatever seemed most appropriate the instant I met the patient. It was not always acknowledged by patients, who might be too shy or scared to enter such intimacy while they lay on a stretcher with no place to go but into an unknown tunnel. Patients were cornered at this moment and faced it each in their own way.

Sometimes I had to detach emotionally from the task ahead, like the middle-aged man this week who faced a twelve-hour radical cancer procedure of the head and neck with unimaginable facial disfigurement. It would be his only chance of survival. He only spoke Russian, and the only way to communicate with him was by means of an interpreter. By necessity I kept my comments to a minimum while I obtained the pertinent data from his chart. I briefly introduced myself and explained that I would take the best possible care of him. He returned my greeting with a trustful twinkle in his eyes and a natural smile that reassured me that everything would turn out all right, more so than I was able to do for him. From then on I simply merged into my role dictated by the protocol of the procedure.

I always felt disappointed when on occasion the preoperative interview did not reach a satisfactory level of mutual trust and understanding. I sensed it most often with parents of small children, when no words of mine seemed adequate to reassure the parents of their child's safety. I then made a conscious decision not to let the parents' fear undermine my professional judgment. I felt more confident in street clothes with a starched white coat and the stethoscope around my neck than in scrub clothes, when most of them assumed I was a nurse. An understated nametag was helpful. In all cases, my task represented a significant threat to their child, sometimes more so than the surgeon they had selected with trust that he could help.

There were, unfortunately, rare parents who did not seem to care who I was or what I did, like the burly father of a fourteen-year-old black boy who had his back turned to his son at the far corner of the holding area. It was shortly after the Christmas holidays, and his black, shiny leather jacket still smelled new, still stiff from the rack in the store. As I identified him as the father, he barely answered with a nod. His eyes were fixed on the floor, both hands in both pockets of the leather jacket, while he pulled the tooth-like edges of his zipper across his massive stomach.

I did not expect much cooperation to begin with and just asked him some simple questions about his son. Did he have any previous surgery, any allergies, any medications he might be on, or any recent coughs or a cold? He could not answer some of the questions and turned to his son to find the answers that might bridge the glaring gap of interest in his son's well-being that did not escape me.

When he asked me if he could leave and come back later, I wanted to send him on a long journey, but not without mention that parents usually wait in the hospital. I gave him a specific time to return, and he was gone. He was gone before I had time to start the intravenous, which could be scary for young patients despite many promises to first numb the skin. Not having children of my own, I was not always sure how to strike the right chord with teenagers, but care and gentleness usually succeeded. While I proceeded with the intravenous in the least threatening manner, I asked him about the holidays. I asked him about the Christmas presents he had received and can still feel the shock and the rage when he simply answered, "None."

He was a quiet patient. After he answered a few trivial questions with a nod and a shake of his head, I did not persist. Instead I brought him an extra warm blanket and stood by his bedside with a fierce urge to protect him. We proceeded with a mutual understanding.

"Just Knock Them Out"

An unidentified resident stretched out in the supine position, already occupied the full-length leather sofa. He had just joined the training program in July and was too sleepy to introduce himself. Only the love seat in the opposite corner was left for me to curl up on while I waited for my cup of ginger tea to cool off. It was a flavor I found soothing in times of extraordinary stress or fatigue. Much against my usual disposition, I wanted to bark at the cleaning lady who carried on the loudest conversation in Haitian with her male buddy across the hall, as she proceeded to wheel a huge vacuum cleaner into the surgical lounge at ten-thirty at night. She had to finish before eleven PM, and without mercy turned up all lights I had dimmed just minutes ago. I had come up from the OR suite to rest, while a colleague relieved me for fifteen minutes.

It was a tedious case of an eyelid reconstruction, which moved along ever so slowly with the tiniest stitches under local anesthesia. It did not hold my interest. I pulled the crumpled paper mask over my eyes to block out the bright light while I endured the shrieking noise from the vacuum cleaner that had often sent me hiding under the kitchen sink when I was a small child.

My perceived stress was not triggered by the patients or the cases I needed to do but the unyielding authority of the hospital. Staffing was determined by a budget rather than the real need to help the doctors do their work. It was not a unique attitude of this particular institution but rather a sign of the times, where managed care and the bottom figure controlled activities at most hospitals. Even administrators were cornered by the system. Once in a while they appeared sheepishly at the OR desk to assess our business with an unspoken attitude of, "Just knock them out."

I grew up in the medical world where a supporting staff assisted physicians with respect and pride in doing so. The nuns of a religious order lived on the premises and would gladly be of service around the clock, while they served tea and sandwiches. Now cases had to be staggered into the night with a skeleton crew. We were simply told by the administration to deal with it, "it" meaning a predictable twelve-hour shift with added emergency cases to follow.

My bad humor over the vacuum cleaner did not change my assignment. After fifteen minutes I had no choice but to head back downstairs, finish the case, and set up for another. My frail, elderly patient with the droopy eyelids had nothing to eat or drink since her dish of ice cream the previous night. Her bravery made me feel childish. I wondered if she liked the portable music the surgeon had brought to make the long night more entertaining. She did not complain, while I was not in the mood to listen to the triumphant march of Verdi's "Aida" that bounced off the tiled walls of OR 15. There was nothing to do but sit on my three-legged stool and reminisce how much I was all fired up when I went to see the opera at age sixteen. I was brimming with ideals, youth, and ambition. Now I just wanted to pull the blanket over my head and not have to come back in the morning to deal with "it."

I was surprised when the little old lady thanked me profusely at the end of the case and told me that I was terrific. Back in her room, she could look past the fact that it desperately needed a new coat of paint. Green mold of financial cutbacks invaded other patient rooms that remained empty, waiting for an occasional overnight admission.

Hospitals are not entirely healthy places anymore. The profits barely cover nurses' salaries, despite being chronically understaffed and overworked. Patients fear not only lack of attention but also medical errors in their care that might occur with the constant turnover of temporary help hired from agencies. Changes in a hospital environment are more often discernible to old timers who many years ago took pride when they stepped into the lobby of their respective hospitals.

Some doctors appear spiritually depleted. Ever-increasing workloads and time constraints force them to function far from their idealistic goals that made them proudly take the Hippocratic Oath. Some are seized with deep resentment that medicine has become a free-for-all commodity, advertising side effects of cardiac drugs on television along with veggie-burgers and termite control. This was once considered privileged information for physicians only.

As far as managers of healthcare conglomerates are concerned, doctors have little to offer beyond the most time-efficient execution of their specialties. Anyone with proper training can do it. If I were to hang my stethoscope on a doornail for good, someone else would gladly step into my place with youthful vigor, pumped with current knowledge about the latest anesthesia technology. A young physician would take over my patients and replace my hands without much effort, in a seamless transition. However, hard-earned clinical judgment and experience are qualities not so transparent at the next credential committee. The human element is hardly needed anymore. It consumes precious time when the next procedure could be accelerated. Spiritual emergencies are dealt with elsewhere, at a therapist's office from nine to five, with a buzzer that rudely interrupts the patient's stream of consciousness at the forty-five-minute mark.

And yet my own spiritual quest has been an important ingredient I call on each day in my practice as anesthesiologist. It comes as additional support that I extend quietly to patients without being asked. My good intention to see them through their procedure safely hovers over them invisibly during their temporary disconnected reality. It might come as late as a last eye contact or the touch of my hand on their forehead just before they go to sleep, but it is always present. I make myself available as someone to hang on to, someone they can trust. I appear as a human being who instills faith in something other than the patient's own vulnerability, at a time when he or she needs to let go.

Of course there is also the patient who on the chart just missed the 300-pound mark. He checks in at 297 pounds, when in reality the scale can't differentiate the last three pounds. One more meal will banish the illusion. He already has lost faith in anyone or anything including himself. He also tells me, "Just knock me out!"

I got the impression if it was forever, it would be all right by him. As I explained the great number of complications that might occur with general anesthesia, starting with his risky airway and how much safer it would be to operate on his eye condition under local anesthesia with intravenous sedation, he showed not the slightest interest in cooperating for his own safety. He preferred to be numb and unconscious, the more and the longer the better. He already chose to anesthetize himself with food, which has made him more miserable instead. He has picked a poor substitute for spirituality, perhaps the only salvation for his physical and mental agony.

And yet he has survived not only his chronic state of morbid obesity but also the general anesthesia, which turned out to be extremely difficult. He could have died from it. But I had asked for help before we started. I recruited a colleague to assist me with some added physical strength required to handle his massive neck. I also needed another pair of hands to reach across his mountainous chest to inject the intravenous sedative. I prayed for God to guide us safely through this procedure. I have been in the OR long enough to know that anything can go wrong at any moment. In a patient like this there is no margin of error. His physiology was so deranged, his reserves already depleted before any additional stress. Any mishap or transient loss of oxygenation could be fatal and irreversible. I was grateful for the second pair of hands of my colleague. He worked swiftly to manipulate the crucial airway in its proper place when my own physical strength was failing from the fatigue of pulling up his jaw until he was fully relaxed. After a difficult start, the case went smoothly.

The patient woke up, however, extremely agitated, grabbing the oxygen mask with both arms, ripping the electrodes off his chest, disoriented, and out of control. He was still too incoherent to comprehend our calls to lie still and keep his arms down. His body heaved with the sheer strength of his weight and slammed back against the side of the stretcher. Heavy sedation was not an option, as it might obstruct his air passage now that I had removed the endotracheal tube. He needed to be sedated very gradually with incremental doses of a drug that would relax him without compromising his respiratory drive. Over the next fifteen minutes he calmed down and gave up the fight possibly against his own nightmares, his aching eye, and his physical discomfort.

I walked away with a bruised hand and a sharp pain in my back. The nurses urged me to file an incident report in case of an injury that might become more apparent the following day. I declined, knowing that I would recover merely with the gratitude that nothing serious happened to this patient. Instead, I made a note on the anesthesia record to alert any future colleagues to avoid general anesthesia if at all possible for any further eye procedures. This time he narrowly escaped a bad turn, but he was too high a risk to "knock him out" again just because he was not willing to cooperate. It was also a much tighter margin of safety for me than I am conditioned to and a narrow escape from the boomerang of litigation that would be propelled into action the instant something went wrong.

Without much discussion, I made a conscious effort to add this case to my mental file of similar gray areas of judgment and clinical experience that I had gathered with sweaty palms over years of practice. Clinical experience and spiritual strength don't earn high marks anymore on the tally of usefulness of "docs" hired by administrators. But at times, I dare say, they may still save lives.

Bedside Manner

We all assembled from different places. While the inmates started to stir in their cells, we doctors clicked the garage door buttons of our suburban homes to beat the traffic on the way to the hospital. Even before six AM the expressway was already a long stretch of slowing down. Perhaps the old term –freeway- better describes the privilege to travel anywhere, anytime, which I often take for granted.

I turned off the radio. The scandalous news of the abuse of prisoners in Iraq disturbed and offended my sense of moral values. I wondered what twisted fate or trauma it takes to strip the last stitch of human dignity, even in prisoners of war. I didn't feel like pursuing such a loaded subject any further by talking to myself in the car. Instead, I quietly prepared myself mentally for any challenges that might test my skills as an anesthesiologist in the OR today. I didn't know it would be on a different level than a medical complexity.

While the doctors and nurses arrived in the hospital lobby in professional-looking attire with an air of pride and confidence, the handcuffed prisoner in his orange jumpsuit shuffled in, escorted by a guard in uniform. Together they were directed to the back elevator for general deliveries. There was no need to raise any unnecessary concern in other patients already anxious about their own operation.

Once the surgical team changed into OR scrubs and the prisoner into his hospital gown, the social gap narrowed instantly as we gathered for the same purpose. Our goal was to repair the prisoner's detached retina. It was not so much that he had noticed a deterioration of his vision at arm's length in his narrow cell, but the recurrent flocks of black floaters when he closed his eyes. As they buzzed incessantly across his field of vision like black flies, they made him more restless than usual. No amount of willpower could chase them away. When the doctor explained the cause, he felt relieved to find that he was not going mad in the confinement of his cell after all.

As I was assigned to take care of him, a colleague in charge of pre-op interviews called to alert me to his arrival. She summarized his unremarkable medical history in a time capsule of a minute. She mentioned that he seemed sensitive to questioning, which turned him irritable and agitated. The harmless question of whether he had anything to eat or drink after midnight would in any other patient make the stomach growl, at worst. But maybe in him the mere intention to be truthful might remind him of the probing interrogations it took to unravel his crime. Was it an armed burglary or the unspeakable act of rape or murder?

My natural curiosity to picture the crime scene had to be curbed by my obligation to render equal medical care to all. At the same time, I didn't quite trust my own ability to dismiss any prejudice in my approach to this patient, with his dark history. There were no courses in anesthesia residency that addressed bedside manner for convicts. With my assignment for the day came an uncalled opportunity to respond to the moral question I had left unanswered earlier in my head in my car. Instinctively, I knew that I must separate his medical from his personal history and provide the same flawless anesthesia and warm blankets as to any other patient.

I approached the stretcher slowly, so as not to cause alarm. Physically he appeared old and tired. I realized that the blanket I had brought probably served more to cover my own unease. At best it would cover his vulnerability and helped to lend some dignity. His cheeks were sunken in from the lack of a proper dental prosthesis. He looked pale and emaciated from the lack of sunshine, a shadow of the threat I had imagined. Maybe he had lost interest in the boring menu of starches and undefined soups that all tasted the same, no matter what color.

The guard with a ruddy complexion stood by with arms crossed, assuming a posture of significant importance. Did he escort him to prevent him from bolting? He could not if he wanted to. Underneath the cotton blanket he was shackled with a heavy chain around his once white socks. The shackles were limp and worn out, but today they served to anchor him into relaxation on the stretcher.

I shook hands with Saul. His biblical name seemed to soften the first gesture to treat him like any other patient. His handcuffs were removed for the procedure to allow us to apply our monitoring equipment. While I gathered my tools to start the IV I wondered if these were the same hands had strangled, stabbed, or shot the life out of a victim. I chose to use the kind approach to my IV start, with an extra dose of Novocain. Pain does not bring out the best in us. I cringed at the thought of bringing out the worst in him.

As I proceeded, Saul turned out to be a friendly patient who enjoyed the routine kindness of the staff. His veins were hard to find amongst the convoluted tattoos that covered both arms. He didn't flinch with the start of the intravenous. He seemed to trust me. He tolerated the next injection to numb his eye much better than the medical questions that seemed to needle a more sensitive area of his psyche. We fussed over him with pillows, blankets, and kind words. We wanted him to really enjoy his one-day outing into the world. We joked that he might even like our care enough to return for another procedure. The open-ended invitation seemed to please him.

His eye surgery was scheduled under local anesthesia, supplemented with intravenous sedation. The surgeon was a delicate woman with extraordinarily gifted hands. Even though she had operated tirelessly for over twenty years, her child-like enthusiasm had been preserved by the purity of her intention. The love for her patients and the commitment to restore compromised vision in as many patients as her waking hours allow had made her ageless. Once she looked through the pupil to the back of the eye under the microscope, she found a world only known to a few. It was her hard-earned privilege to access this fragile territory called retina, which makes no distinction between a lifetime of felonies or good deeds.

Saul lay motionless for the next two hours, assisted somewhat by minimum sedation. He knew it was in his best interest to let the surgeon do her work undisturbed. His shackles never rattled once, while the guard fell asleep on the metal stool in the corner of the darkened room.

While I monitor a patient under conscious sedation, my threshold of allowing any pain or discomfort to occur is zero. I had to discard the curious impulse to even question if I would raise the threshold in a man who was convicted to years in prison. Would I prolong his discomfort by holding back the appropriate dose of narcotic? I was relieved to conclude that I was not capable of such subtle mistreatment. There cannot be any variable margin for personal judgment in the practice of anesthesia. While under my care, he was as innocent as the child I had treated earlier in the day.

Saul reminds me not to pass silent judgment on any patient—even those who have become prisoners of morbid obesity, the addiction of alcohol, or a cancer related to excessive smoking. He reminds me that I know nothing about the mental torture of AIDS. All are entitled to the best care I have to offer. They all deserve a few hours' break from a life that has dealt them a hand that is too overwhelming. Perhaps they've thrown away better choices and exposed their emotional despair with destructive behavior hurled toward self and others.

While under my care, they will not only receive good anesthesia, but I also wish to heal the gaping wound that is not documented in the medical record. I can do it by adjusting their pillow and untying the knots in the back of the hospital gown that hurt to lie on. I can do it by lingering at their bedside until the last set of surgical instruments has been autoclaved. I can remain there in supportive silence instead of turning away and catching another piece of useless gossip on the way to the lounge. I can do it with a willingness to drop my own shackles of prejudice.

When the prisoner arrived in the morning, the obvious intent was to improve his vision. It is hard to know whether an unusual dose of care and expertise might also change his insight about his past. Sometimes kindness has a second chance. I was hopeful that the benefit of our procedure would outweigh his natural tendency to slip back into darkness. Maybe we opened the door and let in enough light for him to see the world outside again.

A New Job Description

Recently I was invited to an informational meeting of the deacon's ministry team of our church. The invitation was prompted by a recent conversation with our minister about my spiritual journey being in need of a new spark. My spiritual practice consisted mostly of attending Sunday worship and daily prayer, dictated by my mood or my schedule. Lately the stress at the hospital seemed unbearable, and I looked forward to my spiritual medicine on Sundays.

We met in the church library as a circle of seasoned deacons and other church members who were also considering participating in this ministry. It would consist of assisting our minister with the sacraments of communion and baptism, as well as some pastoral care for church members who are either homebound or hospitalized. Other duties might include overseeing a smooth Sunday worship, working behind the scenes as greeters and coffee makers, and making other last-minute adjustments.

The evening's theme revolved around doors that had closed in our lives, while others had opened. There were stories about job losses, illnesses, and retirement. We shared our common solution of finding new fulfillment in service for God. There was also an unspoken concern about not taking on more than we could handle with our present responsibilities to families or careers.

As for myself, I had shouldered a strenuous medical career for the past thirty years as an anesthesiologist. I had been struggling with the ever-increasing demands on the doctor-patient relationship. My colleagues and I sometimes have felt pushed to the edge of compromise of patient safety. It requires constant vigilance and an attitude of defense to maintain the standard of medicine we were taught. The field of medicine I had chosen for humanitarian purposes was changing into a profit-based business, where I often felt that I functioned as a depersonalized nonentity, juggling endless schedules. There was a huge void in my primary interest to act as a caring human being who loves to comfort people in need.

I longed for a place where I could serve and heal with a heart on God's terms. If the practice of modern medicine would preclude me from functioning as a humane healer, maybe I could find a niche in a more spiritual environment.

These were my thoughts at the meeting, and I bounced home with a new sense of purpose. We were encouraged to pray about it and return in two weeks with our decision. I was so excited that I missed a good night's sleep. I drove to the hospital extra early the next morning to see all the children preoperatively who were scheduled for day-surgery. It is a difficult assignment; we are pressured to get the children to the operating room on time. Any child who has a complicated medical history compounded by anxious parents can take a huge chunk of precisely allocated time.

Such was the case with Benjamin, a two-year-old with such a rare form of bone marrow cancer that I had to look up the implications for anesthesia in a textbook of uncommon diseases. In his short little life he already had endured several bone marrow biopsies, aggressive chemotherapy, steroid therapy, and several operations of other organs involved. This sounded complicated. When I walked into the room, a young-looking couple huddled in the corner by the window watching the first morning sun on the river. They were holding a small blue bundle in their arms. The mother's face was a long stretch of worry with a faint smile that tried to stay open despite the next obstacle in her baby's fight for life.

As I introduced myself, I immediately sensed that she had many concerns but she knew how to quietly endure my routine inquiry to provide the information I needed. They diligently answered my questions about the baby's last food intake, allergies, recent colds, and previous anesthetic history. Having studied the case history before I met the parents, I was quite aware of the challenges and kept my questions curtailed. While we were talking, the baby took me in quietly with the same big brown eyes as the parents and didn't cry. Dad also had some questions but waited politely for his turn. There were several issues; the baby already had an indwelling intravenous catheter used for chemotherapy. Mom wanted us to use it to start the anesthesia with some intravenous medication. This was not our usual way to anesthetize a two-year-old; they normally inhale an anesthetic gas given with a mask. But I could find no reason not to consider her option. More difficult to honor was her request that the baby would be put to sleep while in her arms. This might present a problem for my assistant staff. I knew they would insist on placing the baby on the operating room table with all the monitoring devices attached. There were other issues about the recovery room and medications that might be used.

After we had reached a satisfactory mutual understanding of how we might proceed safely and keep everyone happy at the same time, it was time for closure. I lingered to express my empathy on how difficult it must be to take care of such a sick infant with so many special needs and my admiration for what they had already shouldered to get this far. Prompted by a sincere curiosity, I innocently asked if they had any other children. The parents proudly announced that they had six other children. I fell into an incredulous silence. I was struck with awe and respect and immediately thought that I would never be able to endure such a burden. I just didn't want to move but instead to somehow communicate comfort, courage, and even hope with my silence.

I will never know what exactly prompted their next action. Both parents looked me straight in the eye and asked me if we could pray together. We huddled our three heads together around the baby, six arms on six shoulders, and all took a turn asking God to help us through this day and to take care of this precious sick child. There was a soft, warm darkness between our heads, and with the child on Mom's shoulder and God's presence palpable amongst us, we all felt safe and protected and ready to take the next step.

Benjamin was peacefully anesthetized in Mom's arms and woke up in her arms after successful surgery.

I thought about my invitation to the ministry of pastoral care and realized that I had just stepped up to the plate. God, in his graceful way, had expanded my job description with a powerful reminder that he is my ultimate employer.

Close Call

I sat down next to the prickly chestnut on a bench in the grassy quadrangle of the hospital courtyard. The normal hustle and bustle of white coats or blue scrubs that stroll for a brief break of sunshine at lunchtime was reduced to an unusual stillness this Saturday. During the week I often wondered about the groundbreaking significance of the brainy conversations of doctors and researchers that spilled all over the lawn and echoed off the historic stone walls of the old hospital building erected in 1836.

This morning only the uniformed crew of New England Satellite Systems sat around their van parked in the shade. Close by, little boys were running at a dizzying speed around the trunks of chestnuts, playing hide and seek tricks on their mothers, who could not keep up with their high heels. Others fed pigeons with leftover pieces of bagels. A cool breeze encouraged me to take a deep breath and made me realize the preciousness of the moment as I tried to balance a tipsy Styrofoam tray with a bowl of chicken soup and salad on my knees.

My knees were still quite shaky. I felt weak from a fight with a heavyweight prisoner that lasted all night. Just when we finished the last scheduled case of the day, around ten PM on Friday, my pager beeped. It didn't jolt me anymore the way it used to, when I started my residency training in anesthesia. Last night it announced the arrival of a young, healthy patient with an acute ruptured eye injury, an almost routine emergency at our hospital. The nursing supervisor informed me that he was a prisoner, not an unusual patient population subject to eye trauma. Since I was familiar with the precautionary entourage of security personnel that would accompany such a patient, this call did not disturb me greatly. In fact, I sometimes enjoyed making these patients feel special during their necessary field trip to the hospital and lavished them with a high degree of kindness and warm blankets.

When the patient arrived, all I could see was a huge black arm from under a heap of blankets and bare feet with shackles that hung loosely over the edge of the stretcher.

As I approached the patient, whose name was Jonah, I wanted to appear very skilled and professional in front of the prison guards, who all stood around with folded arms watching me provide an interesting evening away from their station. As I interviewed the patient with routine questions related to anesthesia, he held his right eye and was obviously in acute pain. He mumbled to answer my questions and admitted to intravenous drug abuse up to six months ago. This made it difficult to find an intravenous access under his toughened, leathery skin. Just as I congratulated myself for having succeeded on the first try, he showered me with juicy vulgarities well within earshot of everyone around me. I immediately reached for the pain relieving sedative I had brought along, which promptly saved me from further profanities.

I recently read scientific proof that personal prejudice is mobilized at an unconscious level and registers in our brain chemistry, even if we consider ourselves immune to holding any bias against race or color. I wondered about my subtle reluctance to take care of this man who had gotten into a stupid brawl at the prison, but then attributed my vague disinterest in starting this case to merely being fatigued after a long day.

When I took him to the OR and attached the cardiac monitor, I never bothered trying to decipher the multicolored tattoos on his chest wall. Instead I focused on how impressive I would be to have this big burly man sound asleep in seconds. An array of all the right drugs for this purpose was lined up neatly on the anesthesia machine. I felt well prepared. I wanted to proceed quickly, as I was also concerned about the prison guard who sweated in the corner of the room after pulling a tight scrub gown over his bulky uniform. His glasses had already turned steamy behind the mask. The quicker the better, I thought, to get on with this case. Better for everyone concerned. Better to get the patient out of his painful misery, the prison guard out of the room before he fainted, the surgeons to operate, and me to bed eventually.

As predicted, I rendered the patient unconscious in less than a minute. I needed both hands to lift up his massive jaw and neck to keep his airway patent while my assistant nurse anesthetist squeezed the bag with oxygen. It was time to intubate and secure his airway with the endotracheal tube. After I had given the proper muscle relaxant, I looked down his throat. His fleshy tongue was so large that I had difficulty identifying the normal anatomical landmarks of his larynx. When I finally recognized my target, it was so far down his throat that it was out of reach for me. No matter how hard I tried, the tissues kept slipping away from me. The first try I ended up with the tube in his esophagus. A second try with different equipment was equally unsuccessful. Some blood and/or stomach contents in the back of his throat started to obscure my vision even further. The necessary suction to clear the airway and prevent any aspiration stole precious time. At this instant I knew intuitively that I was quickly heading for the most dangerous emergency of losing this man's airway. There was no one other than myself to perform a slash tracheostomy if things got worse. I was solely responsible for getting to this point and had to do something fast and effective not to lose more ground.

I was able to maintain marginal oxygen levels by placing the mask back on his face and holding on to his jaw with both hands while the nurse continued to squeeze the bag. This maneuver bartered me a few minutes to make a decision. Should I reverse the process, wake him up, and postpone the procedure to avoid a disaster? Should I try to get help I was unlikely to find at the twelfth hour on a Friday night? It would take too long to expedite someone from the teaching hospital across the street with the technical skill that I needed within minutes. I ordered the nurse to call our in-house emergency room on the chance that an ear, nose, and throat surgeon might still be on duty. Fortunately, a senior resident was still on call and appeared with strong hands and new confidence, both of which were failing me quickly. As he recognized my dilemma, he also struggled but managed to get the tube in the airway.

From then on the surgery proceeded uneventfully except for the tragic finding that the eye could not be salvaged. All the surgeons could do for this young man was to stabilize the wound and make plans to bring him back within forty-eight hours for the removal of his eye.

I felt full of remorse for this patient, now deeply anesthetized. First for the stupendous injury inflicted on him by some violent vengeful prisoners who hurled a bar of soap buried in a sock at his head and his eye. Asleep or not, I had gravely aggravated his situation by arriving at such a dead-end where he not only lost his eye but almost lost his life while under my care.

We almost killed each other. I almost killed him with my professional cockiness of years of experience, my cavalier "can do anything" attitude. All of a sudden I was all alone, all incompetent, all powerless while a life threatened to slip away under my hands. Quietly! He would never know that he never woke up. Would I be behind bars to explain, to serve time? The severity of the jury's sentence would hardly make a difference, for at that fatal instant I would have created my own life sentence.

In our struggle for air, he came within inches of my face and almost wiped out my cushy life, my fine reputation as a capable, caring physician, my confidence, my self-worth, and my sanity. The future dangled much promise. The cards I held in my hands pictured a new home in six months, a new car on Saturday, and a sunny retirement within less than five years. I could see it all vanish in an instant and instead see myself buried by the haunting mass of black flesh that came out of prison for one night to wreck my career.

His pulse raced fast throughout the procedure. His lungs felt as stiff as a balloon filled with lead. They hardly moved. His oxygen level held steady at a marginal level, while his breath sounded coarse. I heard ominous crackles at the bases of his lungs. There was substantial suspicion that he probably aspirated some stomach contents while I struggled to stabilize his airway. This proposed a new set of daunting problems.

How would he fare when it was time to wake him up? Would his oxygen level hold up or had I further compromised his respiratory reserve with an acute aspiration pneumonia in his lungs? The only effective way to assist in such a situation is by providing mechanical ventilation with a respirator until the acute inflammation has subsided.

If I opted to leave the tube in place for that purpose, it meant a full admission to the ICU. It was a lot to organize at 1:30 AM. The nurses proceeded to clean up the equipment and supplies, anxious to get home, while I made some phone calls to put my plan into action. At this point I had no confidence in my skill to resuscitate this man in another emergency situation. My decision was irrevocable. I had to go the long way. Lack of sleep and a mildly disgruntled staff was a small price to pay to save a man's life. I never doubted that he deserved the best care.

We transported him to the ICU and sedated him enough for the night, as he slept innocently. The ventilator hissed confidently as it delivered each full breath on time, without any effort on the patient's part. There was no tension on the shackles resting limp at his ankles. The findings on the chest X-ray and a new team of experts would determine in the morning when it was safe and appropriate to let him wake up and pull out the breathing tube.

As soon as he returned, wide-awake and stable back in his hospital room, I paid him a post-op visit. I wanted to learn more about him and find out if he remembered anything about his emergency surgery. Pharmacological amnesia is a drug-induced, merciful phenomenon. Most patients don't recall any peri-operative events. When I entered the bright, sunny room the patient sat up over the edge of the bed, dangling his feet, as if he was testing the waters. As I reintroduced myself, he vaguely remembered me but not much of anything that had happened to him. He did not recall being on the ventilator until the next morning. He wanted to know about his eye, hoping maybe that I would have better news than confirming the loss of his eye. Instead I told him, "You still have one good one, and if you take good care of it, it will last you a lifetime."

There was a great, dark sadness that hung over him like a black cloud. The sunshine that fell on his back from the window could not penetrate the darkness that surrounded him. Instead of words coming out of his mouth, tears were rolling down his cheeks. I wanted to comfort him. I wanted to hug him but held on to my stethoscope. While I was ever so grateful that he was even alive on this day, I had no business telling him what a narrow escape he had had from a far bigger disaster. I lingered in the room. Eventually I mustered enough courage to ask him how it happened. This is what he told me:

"I was the runner for food distribution for the prisoners and sent one tray to a cell. It was not enough food, and he came after me. I was just minding my own business, playing chess with another guy." I thought to myself, *I like the game of chess. It is stimulating and thought provoking, non-violent, and requires a certain strategy.* My patient burst into loud sobs as he told me that he was planning on being discharged this week. At first I thought he meant from the hospital but then he explained to me that he was going to be discharged from the prison after one more hearing with the probate.

Six months had passed since my visit with this patient. Life was good. I had since moved into a new home, I had no apparent enemies, the stock market seemed on the rebound, and my work schedule was manageable. And yet I thought about Jonah. Why should I care about a prisoner who got hit with a bar of soap? For whatever reason, he was still on my mind and disturbed me to the point that I picked up the phone and called the penitentiary. I wanted to know if he told the truth about being discharged. I wanted to know if his tears were genuine. I wanted to know if this unfortunate twist of fate had reformed him and made his life better, not worse. I wanted to know that even though he lost his eye, his life was better now. I wanted to know that he was better off alive than dead. I needed to know that I could finally lay down the blame.

The officer from the infirmary at the penitentiary told me that he was discharged in September and she had not heard from him since. She sounded cagey, as if she expected in the near future to hand him his orange suit once again. She described him as a regular and gave me a phone number of a relative. I did not call—not right now, I told myself.

Sometimes I wondered if anesthesia was the ideal specialty for me. At the outset of my career I imagined it had many favorable features. It would provide enough patient contact to satisfy the humanitarian gifts I had to offer but not tie me down to the bedside of the chronically ill and their families. I could tailor my own level of involvement with patients but always have the option to walk away. I dreamed of a flexible schedule, having my own family to raise, and still sparkling in my white coat. I didn't know the cost of fear and terror of losing a life, the sheer weight of responsibility that seemed crushing at times.

There was a long stretch of time in the middle of my career when I sent for application forms, wrote resumes, and penned letters with the intention to switch my specialty to psychiatry. It was a phase when I was not committed with heart and soul to what I was doing. One might call it a career menopause; I never liked the term "burnout." There was a time when I was willing to do anything to get off the fragile teeter-totter that squeaked too loudly between consciousness and coma. How much risk and liability could be lurking in a softly lit office with a box of tissues and a vase with fresh flowers on my desk, while I would listen to stories of dysfunctional families? It seemed it would have been a better choice to ease emotional pain than taking patients to the brink of their physical resilience. I longed not to live in fear. Was it less menacing to carry the patient's mental burden or keep the heartbeat going in the OR, no matter what illness or surgical challenge the patient was subjected to? These questions could sometimes keep me occupied for the duration of some long cases or else could keep me awake at night.

Today I know that sometimes I care beyond reason, carry more than my share. I started young with my father, when I carried his slippers around the house with the hope of softening the next blow.

But it was only a matter of time before his fist opened to flash across my cheek.

Here it was, six months later, and I still cared about the life of a one-eyed prisoner whose medical record had already traveled to the basement of another building for filed storage. My emotional capacity would have soaked up the psychiatric sagas like a sponge and dripped and dripped like a leaky faucet into my dreams. There too I could have lost lives. Someone always jumps off a cliff or a building or takes rat poison in the prison of a stale smoky hotel room.

For the most part, however, the good outcome of patients allowed me to walk away at the end of the day with a sense of completion. Until now my specialty had not exceeded my "carry-on" capacity.

It had been a whole year since my encounter with Jonah. He still hung on to me, and I to him. Like a lost, homeless person, he seemed to have nowhere to go but loitered in the back of my mind. I often thought of him when I got off the subway and walked by the old historic prison wall, now the partial façade of a new hotel. In my mind I imagined him waiting for a job, waiting for a cup of coffee, waiting for me to speak to him. Why did I still think about the prisoner who landed with shackled feet on my operating room table? I considered him "unfinished business" and needed to do something about it.

I still had his home phone number tucked away between some pages. One morning I retrieved it and dialed the number of the relative. It only rang twice before a woman picked up the phone. She sounded heavy and tired. I didn't really want to talk to her or explain too much as to my relationship with Jonah. Better not get involved. I just wanted a happy ending for him and a clear conscience for me. I wanted to move on to a new story a fresh start. Instead, his sister sounded sad.

She didn't mind telling me that Jonah was back in jail. She said he got out for a little while, out on the street, back into trouble. She said he had no place to go. With two children of her own, she could not take him in.

"What kind of trouble?" I asked.

"Yeah, a bit of drugs; he just don't take care of himself, but he's a good person. He's got a good heart."

I said, "I know he is."

Latching on to my faith in him like a lifesaver, she thought maybe I could talk to him and encourage him.

Just two days before I had written to a friend and went on about making a difference in someone's life. Here was a brazen opportunity.

I thought about jumping in with both feet and wanted to rescue him. Rather than acting impulsively, maybe it was a better to wait for some divine inspiration to give me direction. In any case, I could not think about it now, as I headed out the door for a physical therapy appointment. As I lay down on the table with my icepack, the piped music caught my attention. It played Paul McCartney's, "Let It Be."

I learned many lessons from Jonah. I learned that despite years of experience and my best efforts, I could still find myself in a situation beyond my strength and capability. In medicine there is no such thing as a routine procedure. The ultimate outcome of this serious occurrence that was getting out of my hands was resolved by the timely appearance of another pair of hands as quickly as it arose.

After thinking about the lasting impact of this incident on my psyche, I was more convinced than ever that the specialty I chose was well suited for my emotional capacity to care about patients.

A year later, I was still grateful that I had been allowed to continue my comfortable life uninterrupted. It made me appreciate the privilege to take care of each patient as a new opportunity to just say, "Thank you."

I also learned to reach out beyond the professional etiquette and got to know someone who made a difference in my life. And as far as making a difference in his life, I already had. I didn't kill him.

A Recent Nightmare

The skin of my hands is scaly and dry, cracked at the fingertips.
Nails variously broken and split, hands aging.
The diamond looks out of place.
Rough hands from hand-washing ritual between patients,
Brown paper towels, never taking time to dry.

This is not lady-like.
I must make an appointment, maybe on Saturday,
for some pampering.
Between a piano lesson
and a visit to the nursing home,

I reach in my pocket for soothing lotion,
recommended for fishermen and nurses.
I am neither, just doing my job.
Doing a good job for twenty-five years.

My patient is safe. He sleeps deeply
under the care of my seasoned, experienced hands,
while skilled surgeons are reshaping his nose.
A healthy young man,
not old and diseased with a tired heart and a clouded mind.
I have steered sick patients with utmost vigilance,
through the maze of their necessary and unnecessary surgery.
It was a hard week. A crowded morning.
I look forward to lunch.

The new sculptured chin and nose meet approval by all in the room.
The final touch is a beak-shaped cast over the bridge of the nose.
A big circular bandage around chin and head
with a bulk of fluffy gauze piled underneath.

Narcotics were properly spaced throughout the procedure.
All gases off, just pure oxygen.
Time to wake up.

Soon he resumes his own respiration.
Upon calling his name he opens his eyes.
Looking into my eyes.
Silently begging to remove the airway from his irritated throat.

Like a pilot waiting for the right second to rotate for touchdown,
I decide it is safe to remove it.
He returns to somnolence.
His own airway begins to obstruct. No air going through.
Big tongue in the way. Vocal cords shut in a spasm.
Color deteriorates with each failed breath.
Rapidly changing from crimson to dusky to blue.
Even the oxygen given by mask is useless.
I can't lift his jaw out of dilemma,
cushioned with the bulky dressing.
No matter how hard I pull on his jaw with all the strength I can muster,
press down the mask and have the nurse squeeze the bag flushed
with oxygen,
nothing goes through.
Sheer terror, but I must act.
Do I call for help? It takes too long.
How many seconds do I have?
Do something before the pulse weakens, slows down.

I beg the patient, don't do this to me.
He is in trouble, drowning in my hands.
A million fears race through my head,
already preparing my defense.
Verdict: Misjudged the landing.
Should have left the tube in longer.
Let him remove it himself.
I call for the drug to relieve the deadly spasm;
I shout at the nurse to push it in fast.

A few more seconds seem like eternity
before his color returns.
He opens his eyes and asks: Is it over?

They already sent for my next patient.
I am scheduled twenty minutes for lunch.
But I can't eat while my whole body trembles.

A Difficult Airway Course

Close Call
At best, a second attempt, a second pair of hands.
Sometimes just a missed lunch.
Sometimes a bloody nuisance.
A change of topic from politics and recipes.
A bottle of wine for a colleague who bails me out.
"No one is perfect" does not apply in this deal.
My reputation is salvaged after the patient is discharged.
Whatever happened is still rational, forgivable, and forgettable.

Potential Fatality
A last heartbeat of hope,
Hurled into desperate action.
Cold metal in my hand
Silver blade stained with dark blood.
Green oxygen misses the window.

There is nothing to say as failure hovers in silence.
Hides behind eye contact avoided by all.
A medical mission suddenly severed.
Disrupted schedule, disrupted life, no more allies.

MD discharged home, unemployable.
Forsaken into a lifetime of therapy.
A nauseous nightmare with a mangled outcome.
Irretrievable, professional ruin.
This must not happen!

A Different Slant on OR Walls

"You always start with a clean green towel!"

I can still hear the voice of my mentor, who on my first day of residency correctly assumed that I knew nothing about anesthesia. I remember the cold cavernous OR with white-tiled walls and glass cabinets filled with sterile supplies. The fluorescent light stung my eyes. None of it deterred me from my burning desire to learn. I was eager to start my first case. The towel idea seemed trivial at the time. It was not what I expected when I applied at Yale for my anesthesia training. It was a humble beginning of a career that would often bring me to my knees with fatigue, dicey decisions, or sheer terror. It was a neat way to start each day.

Now, three decades later, I still begin my day with the same ritual and the same eagerness. The crisscross, woven texture of the typical green OR towel has not changed. Even now it still feels the same to me, as I spread it out on the square stainless top of the anesthesia machine and iron out the folds with my hands.

The towel ritual sometimes reminds me of the nuns at boarding school in Ireland. They hustled and bustled about silently as they prepared the altar for early morning mass in the blue-and-white chapel. I always admired the white crispness of the starched hand-embroidered cloth as they laid it across the granite altar. Next a flowing black robe with almost no face would deliver a bursting bouquet of yellow chrysanthemums. Two pale, soft hands appeared from the long black sleeves to light honey-colored candles. Together with the flowers they released a sweet fragrance that forgave everything before we started mass.

Like the nun, I too dash nearly faceless behind my mask in the spirit of service. I take much pride in setting up the anesthesia equipment as neatly as I was taught in my early days of training.

Setup time is a window where my focus sharpens on the task ahead. I draw up an array of drugs and selective airway equipment with deliberate care, much like preparing for the arrival of a guest who deserves and appreciates nothing but the best. I know where to find cushioned arm-boards for oversized people and little cotton hats to keep a baby's head warm.

The towel has become my daily ritual to soften the environment for my patients and for myself. I try to make my workspace personal. I keep it clean. I create a fresh experience each day. It is a modest gesture, not unlike a silent prayer. The cacophony of morning chatter that bounces of the walls in the adjacent ORs fades with my intention to conduct the best anesthesia of my lifetime. The urgent sound of my beeper abruptly announces the arrival of my first patient, and I am ready.

Sometimes a nagging apprehension grabs hold of me the morning of a long day. It vanishes once I engage in my task. By the early afternoon, with still some hours to go, a wave of weariness can surge in like a tide. My straight-laced posture while I sit on the edge of my stool melts into an amorphous lump, like a wedge of Brie that has sat in the sun too long. At this time my mind can slip into a secret whirlpool. The gray tile walls around me begin to close in. I am reminded of a poem I read:

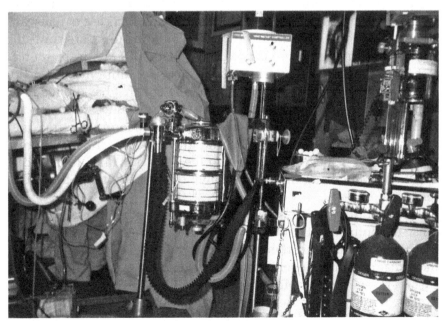

Typical space around an anesthesia machine

Walls

by C. P. Cavafy[6]
With no consideration, no pity, no shame,
they've built walls all around me, thick and high.
And now I sit here hopeless, I can't think of anything else.
This fate gnaws my mind, because I had so much to do outside.
When they were building the walls, how could I not have noticed?
But I never heard the builders, not a sound.
Imperceptibly they've closed me off from the outside world.

I might as well sit down. Since I have left the world of color, there is a discernible loneliness that hangs around like a bad case of nausea. I have wandered around the same hospital building for years now, still looking for flowers. There is not even a blade of grass to be found, just hard, unforgiving pavement to be pounded until my feet ache. Sharp pain shoots up into my right hip, the one that has dragged the leaden ball of responsibility around for years, chained to the ankle. There are twenty operating rooms, all in monochromatic gray tile, with tightly packed grouting, neutral gray. Seventeen percent gray, easy on the eyes, never offensive, but the walls don't talk to me. I can shout all I want, bang my fists and my head against it, but the bricks remain silent.

The eight-by-ten-inch window in the heavy gray door adds to my sense of confinement. At these times I feel chained to the anesthesia machine, knowing that there is no relief in sight. I entertain plans for the remainder of the evening, next weekend, or my next vacation to sustain myself in my solitary sentence behind the screen of surgical drapes. My ears, ever alert to the slightest change in monitor pitch,

---

6   KEELEY, EDMUND; *C.P. CAVAFY.* © 1975 by Edmund Keeley and Phillip Sherrard. Reprinted by permission of Princeton University Press.

jolt me out of my absent-minded daydream. I resume my posture of vigilance that I vow to each patient.

Since the initial green towel era I have mastered the necessary knowledge and technical skills to conduct a safe and reliable anesthesia practice. I have enjoyed my encounters with remarkable patients and regretted the all-too-brief time spent with them, dictated by a driving OR schedule. I have a bank account that pays the bills. The two letters MD behind my name raise the threshold of respect and politeness when I check into a hotel. The same letters raise both eyebrows of the police officer who issues me a speeding ticket as I race back and forth from the hospital, trying to make time for something else in my life. I can be obsessed with the search for the part of me that is missing in action. I want to break down the wall around me and lift each tile to discover what lies beyond saving the lives of others. I want to save myself.

I have searched for creative ways to rejuvenate my spirit. It seems cracked and glued by years of being an eyewitness to the ruthless invasion of disease in once-healthy bodies, the bloody mess of it all, and the heartbreak of families who face the inevitable end of a loved one.

It is not so much that I have sought pleasure or luxury outside the OR. Over the years I have found that simple pleasures, like my insatiable appetite to smell the cool morning air, quickly restore my spirit. I found peace of mind in nature's backyard rather than in crowded places. I often craved solitude and stillness to settle into the single-mindedness required to shoulder the sometimes-fragile lives of my patients.

I have taken in the long view of the flat marshland that spreads like carpet and changes color with each season to the south of our living room. Sheets of blue ice melt into muddy browns before the marsh turns into a tender green, usually not before May. The brassy copper wetlands in the fall reflect the richness of the soil and the miracles that lie quietly hidden beneath its surface. The tidal river that swells and ebbs with undeterred predictability comforts me, no matter how many bodies and families fall apart. Nature's broad landscape gives me relief from the microscopic focus needed for the minuscule detail in the care of a premature infant, the five-minute set-up for a bleeding tonsil, and the urgent "trach" to rescue the patient who rapidly loses his airway.

There are days off when I like to stroll through the museum and study how painters and their subjects have testified on canvas that they lived through shipwrecks, bloody battles, and cold winter nights. I see a family settled down on a wooden bench in front of a simple table with a jug of water, a bowl of purple grapes, and a crusty loaf of bread that looks fresh with cracked paint. Or I can find them on their knees in prayer in a cathedral where a diagonal shaft of light lifts their shoulders and their spirit, which in turn lifts mine. One of my favorite paintings is Vermeer's "Girl with the Pearl Earring." As I linger and look at her face, I wish I could comfort her:

When I call you by name, your face turns halfway
Toward a gentle voice it doesn't know.
A voice of forgiveness out of the blue nowhere.
A voice that knows the silent suffering inside.

There is still a child beneath the cracked fissures of paint on your
      face.
But your search of the truth has outlasted your perpetrator.
Your face is halfway there in the light.
The quiet accusation in your eyes drowns in the shimmer of your
      tears,
About to spill into the creviced canvas landscape all around you.

I know you did not steal the earring.
It was given to you, in exchange for your services.
Your youth, your freedom, your girlhood.
And now it burns a hole in your ear and your soul,
A festering wound that takes a lifetime to heal.

You may feel cornered, framed on your canvas bed.
But the mirrored light of a martyr is firmly fixed on your face.
You stepped beyond backbreaking, skin scraping,
Joint swelling pain of your daily chores,
Scrubbing and serving for thankless others.
Quietly you endured while you climbed up and down the ladder.

Today you resemble no less than a noble queen
With your head wrapped in silk,
Your shoulders cloaked with dignity in blue and gold.

Fine art and other staged cultural highlights provided an uplifting and distracting hiatus from my usual colorless observation deck. For a long time I needed such outings to sustain me.

But my perspective about my work environment has fundamentally shifted since world-wide terrorism blew apart the neatly assembled jigsaw puzzle of our lives with a volcano of violence. It has now been years since 9/11 and yet it continues to spew its corrosive lava at our doorsteps. I now look at all the flags that decorate our homes as band-aids for our wounded spirit. Together we move about without the security we used to take for granted in almost any geographic place. While all of us strive to make our daily contribution to whatever mission we believe in, a malicious mastermind has spent equal time between dawn and dusk to engineer more mass destruction.

During the past thirty years I have established deep roots in a country that has written and spoken volumes of liberty between the striped lines of its flag, cornered only by the stars. And now I seem afloat again above the billowing smoke and ashes that keep smoldering, in search for a safe place to anchor my spirit.

Death is an easy choice, the choice of an instant. It is a choice that asks no questions and demands no more answers. I think about the time it takes me and my fellow physicians to carry three thousand patients to a safer place within their own bodies. I reflect on the care, the passion, and the daily commitment to steer them in a healthier direction, so they may continue their lives as functioning members of society, each with their own contributions to make to their families and to the world. And then one madman blows three thousand bodies and souls apart in an explosion of such hatred that it stops the world in its tracks. Only the sun seems to keep moving, and even the sun feels cold. I can't dwell on it. I must go on and find other human beings at the far perimeter of the rubble, warm them up, and lift their sunken spirits.

As we march through each day, held up by the scaffold of our routines, there is no obvious disruption of the OR schedule. But if I look closely, it moves at a kinder pace. Doctors and patients need more time to make a more meaningful human connection. Staff members restore long-forgotten eye contact amongst each other to acknowledge their common mission. They add an invisible minute to their coffee break to extend the courtesy to listen to a colleague.

Instead of feeling imprisoned within the confines of the gray tile walls of the OR, now I often feel safe and protected. I consider it my newfound sanctuary. I appreciate the stillness of the surgeon's concentrated effort to direct the laser beam to the microscopic hemorrhage at the back of the patient's retina. I am content to offer silent emotional support to my anesthetized patient, as well as to the surgeon as he finds his way through the pathological landscape.

Catastrophic news penetrates the dense walls of the inner sanctum of the hospital at a slower speed than lightning. Suicide bombers have not disrupted any surgical procedure in our OR. No TV scenes of starving children who kneel in a heap of rubble are apparent on my monitor. It just displays a regular sinus rhythm at a comfortable pace. The hissing ventilator takes care of the patient's respiration without my help. The intravenous drugs deliver the proper sedation, as promised on the package insert. For a handful of days I can feel secure in my orderly, non-violent environment— as if nothing shatters the outside world. I feel as safe as I did back in the chapel at boarding school. As I unfold my green towel in the morning and smooth out its wrinkles, I can believe for a moment that my world has not changed.

Chapter Three

In Search of Balance: Coming To

For Equilibrium

Like the joy of the sea coming home to shore,
May the relief of laughter rinse through your soul.
As the wind loves to call things to dance,
May your gravity be lightened by grace.

John O'Donohue[7]

On the Far Side of the Water

It was a sunny boat ride to Monhegan. *Elizabeth Anne's* pristine white paint caused such a glare that it gave me good reason to put on my fancy new sunglasses and my denim hat. Instantly cool, I accepted the fact that I had to share my bench seat on the bow with a cocker spaniel who panted all the way, either from lack of water or more likely from a nervous disposition. The moderate speed, the gentle swell, and the warm breeze put all of us at ease.

I, too, had been apprehensive about spending three days on one square mile of trees and rocks with my husband, who thrived on action. Besides, lately I had the urge to run away from everybody, including myself, unable to resolve the complexity of the demands at my job and neglecting my role at home. Recently, I often felt remorseful coming home to a bare refrigerator that offered limp zucchini and outdated cottage cheese. Droopy geraniums crumbled in my hand when I picked their parched leaves. I felt that I was not measuring up to my own expectations at any place and was losing sleep and strength.

It was easy to recognize the outline of the island's whale-shaped topography with Manana, its neighboring island situated to the west. The lengthy façade of the proud Island Inn dominated the bluff above

7   From TO BLESS THE SPACE BETWEEN US: A BOOK OF BLESSINGS by John O'Donohue, p 127 © 2008 by John O'Donohue. Used by permission of Doubleday, a division of Random House,,Inc.

the harbor. With its three stories of weathered gray shingles and white windows, it resembled a stretched ocean liner in dry dock.

At low tide the Spartan landing pier protruded from the rocky shore above eye level. All I could see was sturdy piling covered with a wet and slimy coat of algae and seaweed. There was a flurry of activity that was taking place on the wharf: pick-up trucks backing up close to the edge with confidence; men with muscles in T-shirts shouting orders as our boat approached the pier. Finally they caught the lines and pulled us in.

I arrived at the wharf tired, stressed, and overdressed, with a suitcase on wheels on an unpaved hill of gravel. Clusters of friends sipped lemonade and slush on the deck of the nearby Barnacle Cafe, too caught up in their own contagious laughter to notice my embarrassment. I was eager to change my clothes and my attitude into something less formal, something unpretentious. I mumbled some vague apology about my heavy suitcase, with an assortment of books for every mood I might encounter, as the young man hauled it onto the back of a truck.

The worn, wide tires of the two rusted luggage pick-up trucks, dispatched from the only two inns on the island, were grinding their way uphill on sand and crushed stone in slow motion. The trucks behaved like loaded camels, dusty, thirsty, and in need of a shower, just like me. There was no automated carwash on the island for the entire fleet of twenty pick-up trucks registered in Monhegan. The only vehicles necessary on this island were for the purpose of utility. Everyone else walked.

Extreme people search for extreme places. And so I arrived, with no expectations other than some unpublished dreams about my desire to write, to stand still in one place where I could trust that my husband, who came to paint, would also find a respite. It was a place where fluid but powerful natural boundaries contained water and sky. And yet on the far side of the water, the distance had no limits. It was a place where local customs were still ruled by common sense and an instinctive decency.

My walk toward the inn started out stiff-jointed, but I was willing to become part of this landscape. It was just a few hundred feet away, but not being conditioned for hiking, I felt anxious about the climb to the lighthouse, which seemed to rise straight up from the inn at a steep incline. The round natural stone monument with its red cap glowed in the late afternoon sun and smiled.

The squeaky screen door of the inn opened and slammed shut

as I went to retrieve the only suitcase on wheels from a heap of bags in the low-ceilinged lobby. The historic inn already commanded the harbor view in the black-and-white vintage postcards on the shelf next to the registration desk, which we checked out during check-in. My husband remarked on the scarce vegetation at that time, whereas I noticed the ladies in veiled hats and long skirts sweeping the dusty road on their way to meet the boats and their men. There were old photos of fishermen, bent over and taking stock of the catch in the wooden dredge. A circle of lobstermen mended their nets as they made plans for trap day. It was an obvious and customary way to provide for family, something to do during the day, something to eat at night. Of course, it is all different now down by the wharf, where the Barnacle Cafe serves cappuccino to curious day-trippers.

While I stepped back outside from the lobby to find our own cottage, apart from the main house, shouts of good-byes of new and old friends down at the wharf receded across the water toward our boat that pulled away and turned northwest back to Port Clyde.

By now, my feet were firmly planted on the island and didn't want to leave. On the far side of the water, back on the mainland, I lately suffered from too many choices, too many cars, too many stores, too many phone calls from people who were out of touch with themselves. I wanted to find a sanctuary far away from the screaming world of business, where driven people hold out their greedy hands for fat paychecks and more jobs and the less-fortunate panhandlers push for homes for the homeless. All the way to San Francisco, they line the streets and pile more guilt on the shoulders of passersby, who frantically race from one cup of coffee to the next without glancing sideways. They have put on their blinders, so as not to get startled by social misfits all around them. They try to forget that some of them might be their children. I yearned for a weekend of simplicity in an old-fashioned village.

Our cottage, painted blue with white lace in white windows all drenched in sun, was full of promise. It overlooked a sunken green meadow that would turn into a large, steamy soup bowl the next morning, holding sun-filtered mist. As we ventured out, much to my delight, I found Main Street lined with lobster pots and apple trees instead of meters.

At the end of the winding, unpaved Main Street I found an unlocked church that welcomed a prayer anytime and offered one silently on a velvet cushion. The old stove pipe that traveled along the ceiling, across the pews on the right, promised warmth in the winter. There was a musty smell that leaked from the pages of the old hymnbooks and missals, published at the turn of the century, printed principles that had stood the test of time for a hundred years. It was a humble church, where I knew that our contribution would be put to use for a new roof and a new double bed for the parsonage. We found a grocery store that sold bean soup and herb tea and another general store where locals played cribbage, interrupted by storytelling and laughter. They sat next to each other in wooden booths, painted pink, and drank coffee from their own mugs. The mugs were stacked on a shelf next to the counter, more or less clean, with a handwritten sign that read, "Mugs for locals only."

On our way back to the cottage I was enchanted to find a library with an open screen door, where time-proof wisdom lined the shelves, free for the taking—a place for me where I could abandon all sense of time and responsibility. The screensaver on my computer at home is a daily reminder that "Literature is the memory of humanity." The quote inspires me to pass on my legacy by writing down my memoirs about events that shaped my life and moved me, since I don't have children of my own. Over the years I never tired of reading different versions of the same human story that continues to unravel the mysteries of love and pain. The library was located conveniently next to an art gallery with art supplies for every medium my husband might want to dabble in. I trusted that he, too, merged with the landscape on canvas.

On our way back to the cottage, I wanted to thumb-tack my name on the community bulletin board on the sun-faded shingled tool shed on Main Street. Not my business card, just my name and my willingness to be part of this community. I could clean vegetables, be a librarian, or just listen to where other visitors came from, where they were going, or why they were here.

The end of a long day turned into a black velvet dark night. There were no streetlights or garish fluorescent enticements that distracted from the brilliant splendor and magic of the starlit sky that I had not seen for years.

I brought sneakers and socks to walk the trails. The excitement of meeting the sunrise on time at Whitehead made it easy for us to get up early the next morning. The clean nip in the air quickly woke up the rest of the senses. We climbed the hill past the lighthouse and across the old athletic field. On this island any destination is reachable: rocks on cliffs that I can touch, new heights, different light, new perspectives.

We were on time to salute the sun as it billowed over the horizon in its full splendor. On the far side of the water, it cast a glittery path toward me, and I felt my feet could walk on water that morning. Next to the steep cliff that had stood as its witness for centuries, we paused for a human second to worship it. Standing at the edge, 160 feet below me, a whirlpool of liquid thunder showered new power all over me, frothy and wild. And yet I felt secure with all the turmoil at my feet. As I stood on top of the cliff, it could reach me even though it went on forever. I could watch it with detachment and not become part of it. I was grateful not to be swept away by it, out of control, struggling before I drowned in it. I could breathe easy up here; I was safe. No adversary could reach me here. The rocks were like newfound friends. I knew they would be here next year to renew my strength and answer my questions with their stoic posture, as they'd been there for generations.

As I looked up to the top of another twenty feet of vertical cliff, I spotted a woman who sat erect with folded legs in motionless meditation. She had become a breathing extension of the rock. Just for an instant I envied her sublime peak, but I knew that I could return anytime and that the same rock would be there for me also. Within a few steps I found another rock that protruded at an angle from a vertical cliff and settled into its perfect chair. My back realigned itself against the warm stone behind me. While I closed my eyes my husband captured me at peace on my perch in a photograph. We left quietly, like leaving church before the final blessing, and headed back to the inn for a hearty breakfast. At the first turn of the trail the sound of the roaring surf faded quickly and we reclaimed our own voices to share our experience. Different eyes, different angles multiplied our joy.

Back at the inn, I pondered the experience in a white Adirondack chair, with its wide armrest that comfortably held both my arm and a luxurious second cup of tea after breakfast. By now I had closed and opened my eyes a hundred times to imprint the view of the quiet harbor firmly in my mind and record the chimes of the halyards to memory. Sailboats moved gently with the tide in stationary circles. Red buoys bopped up and down like balloons filled with dreams of the boats and their respective owners, like me looking on the far side of the water, still waiting to reach the horizon. It remained as elusive as my efforts to find the perfect balance between my career as an anesthesiologist and my personal life.

Seagulls gracefully led the way toward the open ocean, uttering stuttering, mournful cries while they were coming and going. I have listened to monitors of heartbeats in the operating room too long and could not distinguish the calls from looms or gulls. But I trusted that together they would do all the crying for me that I had not done for years.

It occurred to me to find a dory stacked by the cove and take a spin around the harbor, perhaps to explore Manana Island. I wanted to venture a bit out of my comfort zone that had been getting tighter and tighter, like an unforgiving belt after a recent overindulgence. It needed to be loosened so I could breathe in the sweet salt air.

I took off my watch and put it in my pocket. I had forgotten how to trust my senses, to eat when hungry, rest when tired, write down my thoughts as they occurred, pray any time of the day. It takes more than three days to not feel the constraint of having to account for every minute, more than a weekend to unlearn being propelled into an unconscious circle of compulsive competition with faceless others and with a dishonored self. This island offered me an opportunity to regain a strong, lean body and leave with a revised list of values. It would sustain me when I returned to a world of ATMs that spoke English and Spanish but not the language of the living.

I always liked directions as to which way to go. On Monhegan I found handwritten messages everywhere. "If our dog Mandy lies in front of the screen door, exit through the one next to it."

The gallery I visited in the early afternoon was officially closed for a wedding that took place that day. On my way over I had seen the wedding guests carrying gifts up the hill in colored bags. There were buckets with sunflowers and daisies in a wheelbarrow that the young guests pulled, the older guests pushed. There were trays of homemade sandwiches and pastries. The women were wearing long skirts and sensible shoes with hats for the festivity or in case the sun burned through the fog.

The door to the gallery was left open, either in a hurry or for me to walk in. The artist had left a note tacked to the screen door that answered all my questions. The note said: "Yes, the winters are long but provide quiet times to work the arts. They are windy rather than cold, not too much snow. And yes, we get to the mainland to deliver art, buy groceries, watch a movie, and eat Chinese food."

The sculptor's wooden heads of seagulls with their yellow painted beaks entertained me. They made me laugh and wonder when I had become so serious.

Back outside, I sneaked up to watch an elderly lady in her folding chair reading a book in the afternoon sun. She reminded me that peace sometimes sits in folding chairs. We can fold it up and take it anywhere.

On our way back we trotted up the gravel path slowly past the now-familiar cottage.

My husband took a photograph of an old painter walking uphill, hunched over by the weight of his portfolio.

We continued to walk uphill to the lighthouse, from where we could look down into the village, where misty clouds washed and hovered over the meadow as they rolled toward the west to softly embrace Manana.

The fog started to surround us, and we lost the view of the white picket fence around the town cemetery. It was a good time to visit the lighthouse. It had been automated for a few years now but still stored many stories in the crevices of its unpainted cobblestones. It was still attached to the original house of the lighthouse keeper and his family, a simple white house with a red roof and an enclosed porch, which now served as a museum. It was only open from twelve to two-thirty, and I had to come back another time to fill the gaps of my curiosity about the storms, the shipwrecks, and the fishermen, their women, and their tools. There were spearheads of red Indians who inhabited the island as early as 1600.

I was touched by so many voices of the past, printed and photographed—labor pains of the birth of a community. The museum documented dark, dark nights with howling winds that drove families in and out of cottages with cold courage, curiosity, and compassion. Their handheld searchlights barely flickered, as the sea claimed lives of their loved ones. There were shipwrecks and tragedies the year I was born, and I wish I could have comforted the survivors. In a display case with old, tarnished medical instruments, I located the wire frame of an ether mask and its box with a printed warning in red: "To be used only by qualified anesthetists."

"That's me," I said and excitedly poked my husband. Thirty years ago, I learned how to give ether by mask at the very beginning of my career as an anesthesiologist. Surely I could have helped out on the island in an emergency, resuscitated a drowning victim. But I was not there then, I had just arrived. Instead, the pictures of extreme conditions and enduring faces reminded me to bear my mission, with its occasional hardships and sacrifices that are inevitable for a physician, more lightly. The stories stirred up an old intent, which over the years had become blunted by the daily routine, to find new ways to relieve suffering.

I was glad I wore my old red wool jacket with its black cuffs that were starting to fray. None of the colors matched this morning, but I was warm. At last, I fit in with the rest of the crowd who gathered at the wharf to embark on *Laura B.* to take us back to the mainland. As the newlyweds boarded the boat, the woman, with her arms full of flowers from the wedding, gave them away to departing friends and strangers—strangers who were sudden friends just for the moment. The sunflowers still held up their perky heads, while the goldenrod and purple cosmos drooped wet and heavy from two days of fog. Waving arms and shouts flew up in the air as the boat pushed off the dock. I was about to slip into a quiet sadness, when a young lad climbed on top of the piling and with a joyful yell, took the jump into the water. The flower lady was right behind him, flowers, skirt, and all. I wondered if this was a tradition. Now I understood the color of her hair, bleached by sun and saltwater. I had just seen her early this morning from my bedroom window, long before sunrise, still in her nightgown and bare feet, stealing flowers with a flashlight from her own garden. There was another island wedding today, the bride veiled in fog.

You may call it providential, the way this island was first presented on my coffee table in a magazine called *Southern Accent*. It is one of many complimentary issues that my husband receives at the ad agency. He brings it home occasionally, as it reminds him of his favorite barrier island in South Carolina, where we vacation in the winter or the spring. I also like the flat beach walk with views of the lighthouse on Hilton Head on the far side of the water. I like the shrouds of Spanish moss suspended in ancient oak trees and the fairways dotted with bunkers throughout the marsh. I particularly like the formidable mansion from the turn of the century that was barged all the way up Savannah River from St. Simon's Island, where it was purchased for a dollar. Now it proudly presides over surrounding new low-country construction. At some time or another during every visit to this island I reminded my husband how much I missed a quaint old village with a church and a library, until he showed me the illustrated write-up on Monhegan in this magazine and made plans to bring me there, a place where life was still the same as it was depicted in the old vintage postcards that I found in the lobby when we arrived. This weekend had fulfilled all its promises of a newfound peace, new strength, and clarity of mind. Back at home, we pored over the photographs taken on our island weekend. Our favorite by far was the black-and-white study of the old painter who shuffled uphill.

I was moved by his spirit to still create something memorable and was inspired to dedicate a poem to him without his knowing.

Life Is Short and Art Is Long,
on Monhegan Island

Almost at a standstill, he slowly shuffles uphill alone.
He catches his breath under the broad canopy of the chestnut tree.
From its dark shade, he steps into the spotlight of a remote
     audience.
His wide-brimmed hat protects him from the glare,
while his eyes search for more images to fill the last frame.

His bent spine carries the load of his life's work
strapped across his frail shoulder.
A portfolio wider than his back and his oversized coat.
A portfolio zippered shut like a cloistered oyster.
Unfinished sketches, with neutral patches of possibilities in the time
     that remains.
Still strong enough to lift the brush that strokes the canvas with jittery
     pastels.

A young, tall man strolls downhill; cool, in undefined whites,
empty-handed, with no apparent purpose.

Beyond the corner of the wooden fence under the chestnut tree,
a sturdy sculpture of stacked round stone, unlike the painter's brittle
     vertebrae,
promises strength for one more day.

Life Is Short-Art Is Long

Sea Smoke

The boat at the end of the town wharf promised to launch us to Friendship Island. It was ugly beyond description. It was so unsightly that I used the last shots on my throw-away camera to record it. Pictures spoke louder than words. The partially sober, round-bellied captain wore a blue T-shirt stretched beyond comfort—even he called it a tub. It didn't deserve a name. The heavy, greasy diesel fumes turned my stomach. It was the same smell that always made me nauseous on my father's sailboat when we motored out for the entire day.

I could hardly decipher the rusty letters against the blisters of dull red paint that after all did spell the name *Sea Smoke* on the hull. It was smoky, all right. Aft to the pilot house of rotted wood with salt-crusted window panes there was open seating. Chipped iron flakes stuck to puddles of engine oil and grease on the corroded floor. There was no evidence of any recent repairs or maintenance.

I hesitated to place my new cooler and my white canvas bag with my writing utensils anywhere. The captain ordered us to move it all to the center of the floor, including me and six strangers who had come from elsewhere for the same writer's workshop.

Was this smoky tub seaworthy? Our local host, a robust female first mate, emerged from the shore office. She seemed to know Stevie, the captain, well. Both seemed anxious to get us aboard and to the island, to allow Stevie to return to the pub. I sat on the edge of my cooler, closed my eyes, and turned my face to the sun.

Stevie made a skillful approach at the private pier, something he could do easily while more asleep than awake. I jumped off into the warm welcome of my teacher. Good riddance to *Sea Smoke*; you are a character!

Only then did I learn that two other writers had gotten lost in the White Mountains and were still in New Hampshire. With better directions, they would join us later. We delayed our first impulse to write while we nibbled on water crackers with green bean and almond pâté.

The pitchers of water looked cool with their floats of lemon slices and mint leaves. Two hours later, with a trained eye, the innkeeper spotted *Sea Smoke* on course toward the house. The tide was low now, almost too low to navigate to the pier. *Sea Smoke* appeared less ugly from the distance off the deck. Its brick-colored paint had a warm glow in the evening sun. It almost looked quaint. I watched its second approach in shallow waters, inches away from hidden rocks.

They made it, with not much luggage to carry ashore—two backpacks, a pillow, a bundled sleeping bag, and an overstuffed paper bag with paints and brushes. *Sea Smoke* cast off quickly and bounced back to the main shore as the captain fully opened the throttle. We closed the circle of writers.

My journey with *Sea Smoke* had been richly rewarded. There was ocean all around me. It spoke to me with its language of waves. A steady breeze blew away heavy thoughts more quickly than I could dwell on them. It was a place to return to childhood pleasures.

Closer to the shore, warm rocks provided a place to rest. I tossed a few branches of driftwood for a stray dog in and out of shallow puddles. One of the limbs caught my eye. It was a sculpture in gray, smooth to the touch but sturdy enough to make for a good walking stick. I surprised myself. As I sat on one of the rounded rocks and I laid my found treasure down at my feet, I picked up my notebook and gave this lifeless stick a voice.

Driftwood

My new surroundings are kind to my knotted limbs.
The sun warms my bones, which is all that is left of me.
Years of being tossed to and fro aimlessly by tides stronger than me,
And yet I stay afloat.

My appearance is slender, almost graceful, like a flexible spine.
Sheer endurance has turned brittleness into strength.
I am not ashamed of my nakedness, stripped to the root.
Circular silvery swirls etched by the elements give me character.

Some of my limbs are broken.
Some are torn off, dislocated from their joints
by the brutal force of collision with others.
And yet I can do without them.
The damage is done, but I rise to the surface.
Willing to move on, find a destination.
Find someone who will cherish my soul, pick me up and take me
    home.

Now I may rest in the sun.
Observe from a distance the ocean that has tossed me around all my
    life.
Today I am not thwarted by the ocean for years of abuse of my body.
It has stranded me with an ultimate knowing what is best for me.

There is company.
Other pieces of driftwood, distorted sticks, stir up gnome-like
    fantasies.
How lucky I am to still look graceful.
There are stones and rocks and shells that all say, "welcome,"
Eager to tell their own stories.
I like the large flat rock that slants at a shallow angle into the water,
Its surface dry and warm, still grainy like ossified sand.
Tiny pinheads sparkle like diamonds in the afternoon sun.
Two elongated crevices carry puddles of water
That reflect a micro-cosmos of sky and clouds.

A patch of dirt has gathered in a wide triangular fold, edged with
    moss.
A bed of grass and clover bends with the breeze that brushes it
    lightly.
From my perspective, lying low, it looks like a forest.
A patch of green for my pleasure, my private garden.

This morning, a young woman strolls from the beach house,
just a few rocks away.
She stands in front of me,
picks me up, strokes her hands up and down the entire length of my
    body.
Holds me upright.
Looks me straight in the face and walks away with me.
I hold still; her intentions seem childlike.
I trust that she will not break me in two.
Instead, I may steady her stride,
and give her the comfort and strength she is searching for.

The Swing

Behind the house there was a broken treehouse. A swing waited for a lost child as it dangled from a sturdy branch of a fir. The heavy bough spread its transparent canopy of pine needles like a market umbrella, to provide shade. Its faded blue cushion only carried shed pine needles.

There was room for me. It had been too long since I had sat in one. I heard chimes from the distant house. A heavy rope stretched from the wooden pier like a wet snake across a large rock—or was it a worn-out umbilical cord that connected me to my childhood? Today I could have it back again.

This swing in which I sat was actually more like a hammock chair. The mesh of rope was gray and weather-beaten like my hair. It still felt strong enough to carry me and my burden. It supported me and kept me in a peaceful, playful, circular motion while I thought of my father. The sound of the wind and the water drowned the pale menace. The snap of the screen door opened and closed more urgently at the house and called for dinner prepared by my friends.

I remembered the swing at home that hung suspended from the branch of a massive chestnut tree. It was one of my favorite friends when I was a child. Its memory still offered a ride. It gave me a lift toward heaven and freedom each time I stretched my feet on the rebound and caught the air underneath. Its pendulum carried me safely from my childhood to becoming a young girl. Sometimes an invisible helping hand had pushed me boldly beyond my own imagination. The momentum allowed me to rise above my own limits without much effort on my part.

There was another swing in Holland, on a beach at the North Sea, with warm, soft sand underfoot. I sat between the pillars of my brother's legs, as they were firmly planted beside my hips on the wooden plank. He took us higher and higher. I screamed to stop, but the wind and the surf from the ocean drowned my voice. I could see it coming—with the next upswing we would flip over the top.

He slowed down just in time to recover gravity. Little did I know that I would brush many such terror-stricken moments during my career, with only seconds between me and disaster. At times I felt completely out of control and powerless over the next heartbeat. And still, I reached for more: more speed, more freedom as the rush from the air rippled by my ears. There was an exhilarating fear of getting too high.

Today I just like to sit on a swing and gently brush my feet over the grass. I like the contact with the earth and feeling safe as I rock back and forth. It gives me pleasure to twist and then let it revolve and resolve its own knots. It gives me a chance to dream about the luxury of time and motion, unexplored possibilities, heights and frights, and in the end always returning to center, if I just let go.

Sunday Safari

My fellow writers and I met at the moss-covered wall. We were setting out on a silent Sunday safari through the woods to a hidden cove. Pillows of moss in the woods beckoned us to search for mushrooms. Their tarnished tops with red edges looked like helmets as they protruded from the ground. Their poisonous nature was flashy enough to leave them alone.

There were obstacles. Fallen trees across our path made me slow down and breathe. As I looked up, the treetops converged like matchsticks against the sky. I spotted spider webs, wet and suspended with the perfect symmetry of lace. On the ground beds of bright fern looked like lush peacock feathers lit in the sun. Another fallen tree obstructed my path, too high to climb over, too low to walk under. I ducked and found a pair of lost sunglasses with a blank stare, looking for their owner.

Besides birds, I heard sneakers shuffling over dead leaves. A mosquito buzzed around my ear. I moved faster to get away. Suddenly I could see a large patch of blue behind the tree trunks. We transitioned onto grass-covered trails to an orchard of apple trees and fields of fern in open spaces. Pillars of birches had their bark painted on with a loose brush of a painter's wide brush. So it seemed from the distance. Getting closer, I could see that one of them wore a necklace of red berries around dried scabs of gray.

I stepped over a wet rhubarb leaf drying in the sun. My eyes could not focus anymore in the heat of this clearing. I pulled out my shirt. The sight of the open cove ahead promised relief. The dog that had followed us from the house already splashed in the water. I wished I was he. Even sneakers and shorts were a hindrance. Everything was too hot: the sky, the dog, my new friends, and my mouth. My gaze was on the water. I didn't see it coming. The sharp corner of a rock made me lose my footing. I smashed with my whole body hard into a bigger one. I couldn't move. Something was broken for sure; something had cracked.

I Leave, I Take

A sudden departure, unpacked, unprepared.
It was less than an hour ago,
when we took pictures of each other at a hidden cove.
I rushed through the moment,
caught in the footling of impatience.
Fell on a rock, a hard, hard rock with an edge.
Stronger than me.

My breath was broken, it could not find its way.
But my friends were breathing for me, whispering, "Breathe!"
Arms from all directions holding me,
lifting me to a cool patch of grass that made me shiver.
Branches part on our quiet walk back to the house.
I take water.

I leave unexpectedly early. A hurried good-bye
to my newfound friends.
Twenty-two arms attached to eleven souls,
fly up in the air and wave words.
I am filled with words as *Sea Smoke* pulls me away.
I take them all, my friends and their words.

I take my childhood,
Discovered again on the gray, knotted swing under the pine.
On a blue cushion.
A green cushion of moss shaped like a mushroom cap.

I leave the gaps of perspective
that have kept us apart for too many years,
my father and me.
I take him home with me.
I take my bruises.

I leave the ocean in stillness;
the maddening roar of my father's restless voice has ceased.
He will not have to shout at me again
or crash at my feet,
for me to acknowledge him.
I take what is left of us and bundle it carefully under my arm,
close to my heart.

I leave a piece of driftwood, found on the beach yesterday.
It was a gift of yesterday.
Today I have no use for it.
All I see are spiky branches that poke through my canvas bag.
I leave the wooden cane behind.
I take my car keys, my notebook, some aspirin
to blunt the throbbing pain.
This time, it is strictly physical.

Last night, I had reason to dance
as I sang a lullaby to the ocean,
until it receded into stillness.
The one my father often played for me.
A melody by Brahms.
I take the memories.

Sea Smoke had steered me to this magical island. I didn't know then that *Sea Smoke* would promptly return just for me, to rescue me after my accident.

This time I felt grateful as I leaned into the vibrations against its warm engine hull.

"Soon Comes the Warm Breeze of Summer"

The sharp blade of the icy wind cuts my face
As I turn the corner by the old prison
That stands shoulder to shoulder with the infirmary.
I pick up the pace and step into the front door,
to get out of the cold.

It is warm inside, but my heart is still frozen.
Frozen by a relentless routine that demands
Urgent action, decisions, life and death decisions.
Emergencies that can't wait until I thaw out,
Warm my feet, or drink hot tea.

I push along as an ice cube,
There is no time to melt, to go with the flow.
I must remain rigid, vigilant
And move through the day with a frosty smile
While I put all my pain in the freezer until I go home.

On the way home I tell myself,
Soon comes the warm breeze of summer,
Balmy breezes that carry me to a gentler place
Where I can shed the layers one by one
And unclench tight muscles, loosen the knots.

I dream about treetops of willows
that dance like umbrellas under the golden rain of the sun.
Warm sand under my feet that molds my step,
And keeps me from running too fast,
And falling too hard.

Mission for Vision

Even though I am an early riser, being at the airport at 4:00 AM for a one-week medical mission in El Salvador meant leaving the house at 3:00 AM. Everything was packed and ready the night before. While my husband loaded the car, I ran back in the house to fetch our new digital camera. I didn't realize until much later on our journey that I never inserted the chip. All the images that appeared so memorable on the viewfinder had not been recorded. I had carefully chosen the images of faces and situations, so foreign to my usual world that I wanted to hold on to them, bring them home, and replay them with a push of a button.

What I saw could not be contained, bought, or computerized, because these chosen frames constituted the lives of people in El Salvador, faces that shifted from the patience of stones to easy smiles. Men and women walked with postures of dignity. Patients and their families sat for hours in the hot sun, crouching on the grass to lean against the narrow shade of the clinic building. They endured long hours of waiting while sustained by their hope for better vision. Some, unfortunately, had to be turned away, due to longstanding eye disease beyond the surgical possibility to reverse the damage. They carried their disappointment stoically as they quietly walked away. Their poverty taught me many lessons in simplicity and about gratitude and service. They appeared to live their lives by values that we preach on Sundays, as we go about our business aggressively and defensively for the remainder of the week.

Upon our return from our mission in El Salvador, I found eighty e-mails stacked up in my computer. The following caught my immediate attention:

> On behalf of all of us and of ASAPROSAR (rural
> health of El Salvador) I want to thank you once again
> for a terrific job and an enormous contribution to the

lives of more than a thousand people. Feel good about yourself; you deserve it.

Despite our accomplishments, there was a disturbing whisper about decreasing funds to sustain this program, instituted single-handedly by a female doctor, Vicky Guzman, who had dedicated her life to providing better healthcare to the poor. She had recognized in the 1970s that medical and surgical eye care was a high priority.

Now Vicky, after three decades of self-sacrifice and political pressure by local adversaries, looked exhausted. Her burden to sustain the care for the poor despite shrinking funds was obvious. There was an unforgettable sadness that stared at me from the eyes that had brought light and hope to so many patients.

Perhaps another painstaking mission, also grossly underfunded, called "Barefoot Angels" contributed to her sadness. The purpose of this project was to shelter those children whose parents scavenged through the rubble of the nearby dump in order to survive. They had no choice but to take their children along for a day of work from dawn to dusk, gathering as many empty cans and plastic containers as possible that they could sell at the end of the day for anywhere from three to twelve dollars. The heat of combustion of waste turned the dump into a furnace of hell during the day. Empty juice boxes were inspected for residual contents to ward off dehydration. There was always the danger of needle punctures and infection from discarded medical waste that was dumped at the same site along with soggy mattresses, old stoves, containers with chemicals, or any household garbage. This was not a playground for children just because they had no alternative. This remarkable doctor came to their rescue and found ways to fund at least a sheltered refuge, staffed with young teachers, where the children could play, learn, and laugh in safety.

With the new eye clinic and three fully functioning ORs, the intention was that the local doctors would utilize this facility and provide care to the poor during the remainder of the year. It now appeared that the local physicians demanded to be paid for tending to the needs of the poor instead of donating free care. Vicky struggled to compensate the local physicians who exerted political pressure on the existing program.

This time, my second year doing this work, our efficiency was markedly decreased by poorly maintained equipment, lack of interpreters, and a general lack of readiness for what we needed to do. To me these shortcomings did not indicate lack of commitment but battle fatigue and a cry for more help. It became clear to me that instead of withdrawing my efforts I needed to double them.

Some of the patients' examination rooms were equipped with two slit-lamps and chairs, while others had none. Opticians had to lug around faulty equipment and perform on-the-spot repairs while one hundred twenty-five dehydrated patients waited in the smoldering heat of the clinic.

Our bank of ten thousand pairs of glasses, donated over time by mostly the Lions Club and various other organizations, were sadly covered with a heavy layer of caked dust. Each pair needed a wipe of the plastic sleeve to find the catalogued prescription, now barely readable. The previous year the inventory of eyeglasses was neatly spread out in many boxes on tables on a tiled patio, adjacent to a courtyard with rosebushes and beds of marigolds. There was always a gentle breeze for rows and rows of patient patients who would wait their turn for hours. There were plenty of toys for the children scattered across the lawn.

This year the space for dispensing the eyeglasses had been moved for the entire week to an enclosed concrete pad. It was walled in by a black wall and a corrugated metal roof, not unlike an oven. The only fan that came from the kitchen acted as an exhaust for the smoke of fried plantains and other exotic home cooking. I marveled at the stamina of my husband and his colleagues, who tirelessly dispensed glasses from seven AM until dark, usually eight PM. It was a long day for the volunteers who started the day cheerfully to find and fit the correct prescription for each patient. They told me that the smile on the faces of the patients who could not see or read made it all worthwhile once the right pair of glasses was fitted and anchored behind both ears.

I slept surprisingly well on the Spartan sleeping cot in the dorm, which I shared with four of the nurses. While I heard a few muffled profanities about the lack of a proper mattress and iron struts poking them in the ribs, my back was doing well with the firm support that realigned my vertebrae into a straight column. We used coarse gray military blankets for extra padding the second night. The rigid pillow kinked my neck at such an odd angle that it had to go. A folded towel became a good enough substitute.

I woke up with the first morning light, around 6 AM, and felt rested enough to look forward to the day in the OR. The reward for getting up early was a shower that was still hot, not guaranteed to the later risers. With red rubber flip-flops on my feet, the hot water made me feel grateful and clean.

After a day or two I was the first in line in the outdoor courtyard, still in the shade, for a hearty breakfast of scrambled eggs with peppers, onions, and black bean paste with fresh papaya on the side. Conversation buzzed around mosquito bites encountered during the night, as well as complaints from the men's dormitory about the decibel levels of snoring. We had neither mosquitoes nor snoring in our dorms, just swollen ankles, which we stacked up vertically against the wall at the end of each day.

I felt proud to walk up the steep incline of the newly poured concrete ramp to the OR, which had dried just in time before our arrival. Patients of all ages, who had traveled by foot for many hours, expectantly waited their turn in and around the open-air cafeteria at the bottom of the ramp, while their relatives found some pastries. I could sense their eyes in back of me as they identified me in my scrubs as a member of the surgical team.

Although we had the advantage of the operating room being the only air-conditioned space, other problems interrupted our best plans. There we found broken microscopes that restricted cataract surgery to two rooms instead of three. Supplies we had sent were lost or misplaced. We ran out of eye pads and gauze pads. Toward the end of the week we ran out of local anesthetic solution and had to substitute a different kind rarely used in the United States.We consulted with the regional pharmacy and concluded that it was safe to proceed.

It took no time at all to check out our three anesthesia machines with my two colleagues, who were familiar with this mission from the previous years. They were well experienced in putting together a suction apparatus with an old car battery. The machines were outdated models without the modern bells and whistles, but certainly functional. The dinged rusty drawers were neatly lined with white paper towels. Our capable anesthesia technician had already stocked all shelves with a proud supply of emergency drugs. I was amazed by the extensive array of equipment assembled from a variety of generous suppliers.

The nurse in the pre-op area would find the first few patients of the day by calling out their long and melodious names. Every patient had at least three names, all duly recorded on the top of the chart. Our translators would make sure we identified the patients correctly. As they changed into their faded, recycled hospital gowns I noticed their clean undergarments bleached by the sun. It was obvious that they wore their best Sunday clothes for this occasion. Their bodies were lean, toughened by much physical labor, a scanty diet, and a stringent lifestyle.

It was tedious and time consuming to rely on a few translators to interview so many surgical patients. At one time I saw a patient with a complicated and potentially serious medical history that needed clarification. Once the translator was found, the patient did not know any details of his heart condition or why he was on blood thinners. We then had to find a relative who strolled somewhere between the garden and the kitchen to fill the gaps as best she could. Whereas a normal pre-operative interview might take five minutes, here it could easily take twenty minutes to obtain the simplest but necessary information to proceed safely.

It didn't take me long to decipher the medical record of each patient. I found the category of allergies and list of cardio pulmonary problems and "diabetica" usually checked off as healthy. I found the weight in pesos and a neatly pasted EKG strip in the back of the chart. The entire chart consisted of three pages.

I was careful that I did not take any shortcuts to my usual way of approaching any patient, irrespective of the environment or language barrier. I learned as much as I could about the patients, when they had their last meal, who had come with them for support, and how far they had traveled. I was interested in their families and how they felt about the surgery. The majority of patients answered my questions with an enthusiastic smile and squeezed my hand for approval to go ahead with whatever I needed to do.

There was no need for a lot of language. We could do what we came to do with our hands and our skills. Additional kindness could be expressed in so many other ways. A touch, a smile, even a skimpy pillow stolen from the airplane wrapped in blue OR paper under their heads was appreciated. We rigged up a compression device to soften the eye after the anesthesia was given from an old tennis ball with a rubber band that fit neatly around the patient's head. I drew up water into a syringe from a clean water bottle and dripped it into the parched mouth of a patient, knowing that he or she had traveled many hours during the night or early morning to get to this destination. I willingly scratched an itchy leg with my fingers and placed a rolled blanket under the knees.

As they lay down on an old, squeaky, wheeled stretcher, they did not complain about the missing pillow or top sheet. The parched skin of their hands and forearms was tough and sometimes required more than one attempt to start the intravenous, which he or she didn't seem to mind. After a few days, all bare feet, with their tough, leathery skin, looked the same to me. But then there were always one or two patients I remember distinctly.

This year it was Claudia, ten years old, who had sat in the OR waiting room for her strabismus repair since early morning without a bite to eat. By mid-afternoon the leftover watermelon from lunch had melted into a pink slush, with only the black pits still standing up. Because of her surgery, I could not offer her anything to eat.

With her hands she gestured a question I did not understand. Her large dark eyes, badly crossed, piqued my curiosity. So off I went to find a translator. Claudia was not looking for watermelon but a book that might be left over in one of the many boxes of donated toys. I went down to the clinic and roamed amongst the toys. Most of the books were gone, but I pulled out one with a glossy turquoise cover. It pictured a white bird that wore a red scarf. Good enough, I thought, to distract her for the moment while she waited her turn. She seemed delighted, as was I, when we discovered that the book was in Spanish with English subtitles.

Since I had a little time, we both squeezed into the green padded plastic chair. I gestured to her to read while I followed the text with my finger until I recognized the words she pronounced. I repeated them first slowly, then faster as I was able to comprehend their meaning. I was pleased with my first Spanish lesson while Claudia seemed to like the story of the bird that lost its mother and looked for it in all the wrong places. The bird even mistook an airplane as its mother. The story had a happy ending, and I still remember the words for a chicken, a dog, and a cow—a humble beginning. I helped Claudia pack the book into her pink nylon knapsack with a broken zipper.

About two hours later it was Claudia's turn. I set up the anesthesia machine as if I was about to put to sleep a famous dignitary. I wanted everything to be perfect for her—the anesthesia, the results, the surgery, and her future. Without words, I knew that she trusted me, and I was determined to deliver my best. She never flinched at the start of the intravenous and smiled all the way as she walked to the OR, covered with an oversized hospital gown that reached her ankles.

She waited for me patiently as I placed the monitors on her skinny ribs, and I was touched by the level of trust that this little girl had to offer me. I chose my dosages carefully and sensed my way into her unconsciousness until it befell her as gently as natural sleep. It pleased me enormously to observe the surgeons' meticulous attention to each fiber of her eye muscles that would keep her eyes straight as soon as she woke up. It was obvious that they operated with the utmost respect for the task ahead. They were given one chance to change this girl's life experience, and they seemed totally immersed in their commitment to a good outcome. I learned that in third-world countries such as El Salvador, a young girl with crossed eyes could easily become a social outcast, disregarded and rejected. I was glad that this was not the future fate for this young girl under our care.

I found it remarkable that generally the children scheduled for surgery behaved like mature adults, already marked by their life experience of hardship, poverty, and sharing too much responsibility and too little food with their many siblings. They did not know about the cherry-flavored anesthesia masks we use for children in the States to mask the smell of the gas. They accepted either the placement of an intravenous or the facemask on their sunny faces without any sign of distress.

After two hours all of us were pleased with the surgical correction, and I proceeded to wake Claudia up as gently as she went to sleep. As soon as she opened her eyes, we knew that we had succeeded. Her eyes looked straight at me. She seemed comfortable. When her mother appeared at her bedside, I let go of her hand and turned to my next task. There was nothing else for me to do.

A few hours later while I sat and monitored the vital signs of an elderly man for cataract surgery, I recalled the day's events in my mind. One of the nurses came in to relieve me and told me that someone wanted to see me. On the other side of the plywood door was Claudia with her pink backpack, ready to go home. Her straight eyes looked determined and intelligent. She smiled as she put her arms around me for an affectionate hug. It seemed a long moment in which we felt connected and yet so brief before we knew that we had to go our separate ways. I shall never forget her.

Another man who inspired me was a blind man who appeared almost daily in the waiting room outside the OR. Slowly he paced back and forth just a few steps while he tapped the tile floor with his white walking stick. "Uno, dos, uno, dos" was his mantra. He delivered it with great dignity and perfect timing to allow one breath in and one breath out.

It became very quiet in the waiting room; the usual chatter and laughter had ceased and the only sound was the hum of the ceiling fan. Most patients, whether they could see or not, had their eyes closed while they sank deeper and deeper into the worn-out plastic cushions and slipped into the peace of a deep relaxation. There were a few empty chairs, and I sat down to listen. I marveled at the gift this visually handicapped man brought to this circle of patients. I too had simple gifts to offer that expressed kindness or did something useful for other team members. I could get up from my anesthesia stool, walk across the sterile OR, and fan the scrub nurse with a piece of cardboard for a few minutes of cool air. She looked hot and tired in her blue scrub gown. Sometimes our opportunities are closer than we realize.

I had my moments during this campaign when I would tell myself I would never do this again. I thought making the trip a second year would be easier since I knew the assignment of my duties, the layout of the clinic, and a few words of Spanish. Instead it involved much more effort, stomach pains, and lack of sleep. Why did I bother?

Over the years I had observed much eye surgery here in the States. Somehow watching it in El Salvador carried more weight. There was more at stake. In some cases it made a difference in maintaining enough of a livelihood to provide an education for one of the children. While there are six million people who live in poverty in El Salvador, another two million have found their way to the United States and found jobs that pay enough to support their families back home.

I saw the evidence on our return trip to the airport. I noticed a new settlement of the most basic housing that consisted of four walls with a flat tile roof closely stacked together. This was a considerable improvement, where just a few years ago people still lived in cardboard boxes or wooden shacks with four poles that held up a bent piece of metal for a roof. The new housing was not a project subsidized by the local government, but by family members abroad.

After a brief vacation in Florida where I shook off the fatigue from the week's effort, it would be easy to justify wiping my hands, enjoying the gallery of digital photos from various team members, and putting the entire experience neatly on file. But I came home knowing in my heart that this was just the beginning of more work that needed to be done.

The choice was mine. I could walk away with an attitude of pride after a week of fair effort while I warmed up my bones from an extreme cold spell. I could also use this experience as a platform to initiate further work that needed to be done. I prayed that the images of people in need would not be crowded out by resuming business as usual. I felt committed to stay involved and not crawl back under cover of my proper suburban life.

A senior team member said it best: "It's like the Peace Corps advertisement; going to El Salvador is the toughest, most frustrating job you'll ever love."

I never tired all day long and couldn't wait to see and take care of as many patients as possible. An occasional "no show" was a real disappointment that I considered a lost opportunity. This was viewed differently at home, as a welcome break in a heavy schedule, which could be rebooked another day. Not so here. Every case was an irrevocable opportunity to soften a stringent life.

Somehow in these basic ORs, equipped with antique anesthesia machines, our team seemed immune to the stress that is usually on the heels of such a demanding schedule. Working late into the evenings, I was physically too tired to open any of the books I had packed as my usual travel companions. Books were my usual way to find breathing space and disconnect from any day's complexities.

Books

Various stages of my life were partly defined by the different homes, schools, and universities I lived in. I felt instantly at home in any of the above, if it contained a designated library.

My husband, usually a man of few words, can often read my unspoken wishes. At our present home in Plymouth, he proposed to appoint our rarely needed living room space as my personal library, with custom built-in bookcases from floor to ceiling.

Ever since childhood, books offered me an endless source of inspiration and quietly moved me forward while I became entranced in a motionless state.

I read once that "books were the missing slats in the fence" (Günter Grass, *Peeling the Onion*). For me books were the missing bricks in the wall that surrounded my family. All of us had fabricated a wall tight and secure against any outside opinion or intrusion. From inside we could safely observe and judge other lifestyles and behaviors. Pointing fingers at others allowed us to believe that we were superior to them all.

Only in books did I find other characters who were as fearful as I was. They became silent witnesses who never banged their heads against our wall. Invisible to others, they brought me comfort. I became engaged in their tender embraces. They lured me to places outside our family perimeter and taught me compassion. Though fictitious, I dreamed to someday experience personal freedom outside our world of critique.

My appreciation for my silent but persuasive friends is best summarized in my tribute to Arundhati Roy, author of *God of Small Things:*

She plays those words with the passion of a gambler.
Tosses them randomly up in the air and lets them tumble onto the page.
She wins every time.
There is no thought involved, just reckless abandon.
On their way down, she embraces them
like lost orphans on their way home.

She has no time to fix her hair.
It is unruly, uncensored,
like an unattended vegetable garden.
Her eyes are a bottomless liquid well of black ink
that spills into volumes, libraries, and many life-times.

The tragedy of her impoverished childhood,
victimized by politics,
forced her into the confines of her creative mind,
wallpapered with images.
Words were endured before they were delivered.
They matured slowly,
like whimsical children in a delirious dance
without choreography.

Their incessant motion eventually is pacified
when transformed into the page
where they don't dare to lie to her,
for she knows every twist of their craftiness.
Instead, they reap delayed compassion.

On the black-and-white photo on page one,
the author's mouth is closed in a defiant pout.
Why speak?
There is no need to utter a word. She can write.
Some things are better left unsaid,
like the subtlety of abuse at an innocent age,
that others seem to hear, but do not understand
unless they've been there.
The nature of pain at a cellular level.

Her words come to my rescue,
with forceful, involuntary hiccups of inspiration
on every page.

They save me from the consuming madness
of seeking purple hearts and yellow jackets.
Her sensitive phrases bandage my wounds,
make me smile sometimes,
and make me bundle my own human story
into new paragraphs.

While I studied medicine, my stacks of books provided the solid steps of a ladder. Eventually it would be tall enough to help me climb over the wall and see another side. It was a magic imaginary ladder, assembled quietly during nights of study in the library or in the dining room of my landlady, Mrs. D. She would keep my fire burning with buckets of black coal neatly placed in the small opening of the fireplace.

Sometimes I would take one step of study home and line it up against the family fortress. To my parents it appeared exemplary. They were curious about the contents, the anatomy of a rabbit's heart, frog legs, and stems of tulips. I felt proud to open the illustrated pages of any atlas of anatomy. I showed off with the honeycomb structure of a pharmaceutical compound that could rewire the brain.

Reading became a habit that would stay with me for life, once I had stepped outside our living room. It was only when I experienced life outside our gate that I discovered a soul sickness within my family still trapped inside. I devoured books that were outside my grasp within my family boundaries. It was the cumulative story and the strength and hope of those addicted to substances or to habitual judgment, prejudice, and negativity.

My addiction to books might qualify as life-altering. My own list includes such classic stories as *The Old Man and the Sea*, *Of Human Bondage*, and *The Chess Game*. It could be any story that sheds light on the universal human struggle of man against man, man against nature, or man against himself. I am equally selective with my friends as I am with my books. I bond with those who offer life experiences to be shared and those who challenge me to grow.

As an author it behooves me to examine my own writing in the context of obvious or more subtle conclusions. At the end of my story I would like to step back and find a purposeful progression.

My shy and timid childhood may be considered a non-verbal phase of my life. I frequently hid under and inside the kitchen sink cabinet to avoid the shrieking buzz of the vacuum cleaner or my father's boisterous voice that heralded trouble when he came home from the office. Then I did not know how to speak up.

During my training as anesthesiologist and later as a professional I first found my voice as a fervent advocate for my patients from behind my mask and the ether screen. As for myself, it was only when I endured prolonged periods of chronic pain that I was eventually forced to speak up for my needs.

It has taken six decades to transition from the silence of written words to humming along with the music of my remaining life. Books bridged the gap. Books were my many teachers.

Revolving Door

The revolving door groaned as I stepped lightly into the sunshine. All morning this vertical wheel had propelled a large volume of patients into the lobby of the Mecca of Medicine, including myself. I didn't seem to mind spending a few hours at the hospital as a patient on my day off. I wove my way through groups of doctors engaged in anonymous case discussions, adorned with white coats and stethoscopes, and thought to myself, "I understand what you are talking about; I am one of you." I skirted around scared patients in wheelchairs and their entourage of family and friends. They had brought them along for moral support as they fought their way through traffic. I understood their pain, fear, and suffering better than their healthy relatives. I felt a strong pull to slip into my usual role to become any patient's best advocate. I almost forgot why I had made an appointment this morning at my own doctor's office.

There was nothing seriously wrong with me. It was just my old familiar occupational back injury. I had developed it somewhere along my career by lifting the dead weight of anesthetized patients. It could have happened when I held the weight of a head with my left hand while I placed a routine endotracheal tube with my right hand. Or maybe the disc snapped out of place while I bent over to comfort someone softly with words meant only for their ears.

This morning I was determined to look for a new solution, a fresh approach to the chronic nerve root pain, which darted down the back of my leg. It had been classified as chronic and degenerative. There was scar tissue from the original surgical intervention, twenty years ago. But now it woke me up at night and made the long hours of standing in the OR increasingly difficult. Sometimes it threw me off balance. I did not like being distracted by my own physical discomfort. While I centered my attention on a patient, I wanted to feel grounded and steady on my feet.

I arrived early for my appointment. The young woman across from me wore olive corduroy slacks with a warm fleece jacket that did not match in color but matched in comfort. Fashion was not her priority. A blue cotton bandana disguised her scanty hair from either a recent course in chemotherapy or a craniotomy. She spelled out her diagnosis of cranial osteosarcoma to the woman next to her, who filled out a questionnaire. I was privileged to understand the term and knew what it involved. I could imagine the initial shock of the diagnosis that had probably turned her life upside down. I recalled the statistical odds of survival of such an aggressive tumor. I had witnessed the technical difficulty of removing such a lesion surgically. It could invade an area near the brain stem. This is our vital center for the autonomous function of respiration and the rhythm of our heartbeat, which beats sixty times a minute for our entire life. I knew all about the retching nausea that goes hand in hand with chemotherapy and have the name and the cost of the best drug to treat it at the tip of my tongue. I knew about the questions that might invade her sleep more than the tumor itself and crowd the brain with fear and hopelessness. By now I felt ridiculous sitting across from her with my tingling leg and foot. I was wasting the doctor's time. There were so many patients with life-threatening conditions.

I had to remind myself that I had a day off. Perhaps I was also wasting my own precious time, a rare day to smell the first fragrance of spring in the park. I could stumble upon the thrill of drifting into small shops in my navy blue sweater and coming out with a bag and a bargain, perhaps in mint green. It was a chance to lighten up or take a risk outside the confines of medicine. Compassion for others came easy. It was always comfortable, familiar, and natural. Finding joy elsewhere sometimes took a willful decision to switch gears.

A Yoga Class

A simple place, a safe and sacred space.
Shoes waiting patiently on a rack by the door
for their respective owners, going nowhere at this time.

Earth-colored floor cornered by dimmed walls.
Framing the window,
a transparent gauze draped loosely
over a strong branch of birch,
gently curved like my spine.
Two white candles, flicker silently.

Mostly women, from all walks of life and all ages.
Quietly spreading their cotton blankets,
as they prepare for their own silent prayer.
Still there is a whisper,
until the teacher rings silence with a chime.

Shifting into position,
A quick transition into slow motion.
Sitting on cushions of folded legs,
palms open, resting on knees.
They come into stillness, leaving today outside.

Crown of the head lifted,
sinking my "Sitzbones" into the floor.
Elongating the spine,
I become taller with each breath I take.
The ceiling does not exist anymore,
neither the floor beneath me.
I become a tree, linked between heaven and earth,
Fearlessly trusting and firmly rooted.
I declare myself vulnerable but feel safe from all harm.
I prepare with new willingness to stretch beyond limits,
until the pain in my knee has stopped shouting.

Content, without wanting, nothing to do.
The time I chased all week, suddenly surrounds me,

embraces me with eternity.
"Shoulds" and "Woulds" have no voice,
while I focus on refining my posture.

Chapter Four

The Cost of Duty

Weariness invades your spirit.
Gravity begins falling inside you,
Dragging down every bone.

The tide you never valued has gone out.
And you are marooned on unsure ground.

John O'Donohue[8]

Total Knee Replacement Surgery

First Encounter

At the pinnacle of my career I worked at one of the most prestigious orthopedic hospitals in the country. Patients, including professional athletes, flew in from all over the world to consult with the most brilliant surgeons that the specialty of orthopedics had to offer.

It was a time in my career where my acquired technical skills and experience in clinical judgment were perfectly linked to confidently confront the most challenging cases. These included lengthy revisions of failed hip replacements, with massive blood loss, and insertion of spinal Harrington rods to permanently correct scoliosis, an extreme curvature of the thoracic spine. The latter required a brief but critical intra-operative "wake-up" of the anesthetized patients in a prone position who, in order to establish that the spinal cord was intact, were asked to move his or her feet with their backs wide open.

It always surprised me how unperturbed these world-renowned surgeons appeared to be in the OR. They knew better than I that once their amazing carpentry was done, an equally competent team of support staff would rehabilitate any patient back on his or her feet.

---

8   From TO BLESS THE SPACE BETWEEN US: A BOOK OF BLESSINGS by John O'Donohue. For One Who Is Exhausted p125 © 2008 by John O'Donohue. Used by permission of Doubleday, a division of Random, House,Inc.

There I was a frequent eyewitness to total knee replacements, a relatively new procedure in the mid-seventies. I was glad that my responsibility did not require me to prop up the dead weight leg once the patient was anesthetized. This sustained physical exertion was usually delegated to the most junior member of the surgical team.

I was separated from the surgical field by a heavy sterile green sheet that was suspended vertically between two IV poles, one on either side of the OR table. This procedure had replaced the old metal ether screen and provided a more extensive barrier. The head of the patient, usually intubated and wrapped with warm blankets with eyes taped shut, was mine. The rest of the body belonged to the surgeons.

The drape was a visible dividing line of an invisible but dynamic tug of war for the best outcome. As long as the patient's vital signs remained within safe parameters and the patient did not move in response to a painful stimulus, team members on both sides of the drape worked happily side by side. Patient movement, however, was considered a basic blunder, as was a surgeon who severed an artery inadvertently. Both were potentially hazardous if they occurred at the wrong time or the wrong place.

At any time I could peek across the green cloth to keep a close watch on how the case was progressing. I was most interested in the long skin incision that extended across the kneecap in one vertical downward sweep. I just wanted to be certain that the patient was adequately anesthetized and did not react to the razor-sharp edge of the scalpel. Although the steady pulse rate did not indicate that he or she was in any distress, I was taught to always look at the patient and not rely entirely on monitors.

Tiny beads of pale serous fluid that looked more like sweat than blood hugged the separated edges of the skin. By design, it was not really a bloody procedure, since the arterial blood flow was intentionally restricted by a very heavy tourniquet around the upper thigh. Its pressure was calibrated and maintained by a square box on my side of the screen.

Still, it was an unsettling operation to observe. It required a noisy saw to cut across the femur and the tibia to prepare the surfaces of both connecting bones for the insertion of the new metal joint.

While I felt grateful that I could guarantee a deep sleep for my patients to spare them this raw experience, I also feared for their wake-up once the surgeon wrapped up the new knee with a neat white dressing. I could only imagine the pain once I brought them back to consciousness. Post-operative suffering was not a popular topic amongst the surgeons. It was rarely discussed. The procedure was carried out with unquestionable confidence that each patient would rise to the occasion and tolerate whatever effort and stoic endurance was expected of them.

Brief but intense patient contact had always been a unique feature of my chosen specialty. While I sometimes regretted this short exposure to individual patients, this was one of the circumstances when I was relieved to have less post-operative responsibility than my surgical colleagues. When I visited patients with joint replacements the next morning, I usually found them still asleep from heavy doses of narcotics throughout the night. They were still unaware of the lengthy and strenuous rehabilitation process that lay ahead. At that time, a knee replacement appeared crude and cruel.

Never did I suspect that one day I would end up on the OR table myself for such an invasive joint replacement. Just the thought of it kept me running up and down hills, stairs, or the long hallway of the OR. I bent like a pretzel as best I could in a yoga class for years. "Just stay active and thin," I told myself, "and this will never happen to you."

Then came the day when OR life was interrupted by a breakdown of my weight-bearing capacity. Having bent and flexed for a lifetime to accommodate others, one of my worn-out knees mandated my crawl out of the OR, only to return as a patient. I wondered if twenty years later the same procedure had become less of a challenge for the patient. It took a total knee replacement to experience long-term disability, so different from the recovery from anesthesia, usually measured in hours.

A Dire Decision

There was no distinct memorable incident that led to the first surgical repair of a torn meniscus of my right knee. The injury was classified as "wear and tear," which was slightly more acceptable than "degenerative" at the age of forty-five. Since I was not a serious athlete, I could only conclude that the "wear and tear" was a consequence of fast tracking in the OR for the past twenty years. It was at least a possible contributing factor.

Within a few years of a second repair and several courses of injections, the persistent pain in my right knee progressively limited most of my normal activities. I could not even get on the floor with my husband's grandchildren or pet the neighbor's dog. My exercise routine of walks, swimming, and yoga were all frozen into ice packs around my knee while I drove to work. Some initial denial finally melted, and the date for my own partial knee replacement had been set for the middle of December.

There is a certain group of patients we sometimes refer to as "pain in the neck" patients. They know too much, often have their own agenda, and never fit neatly into the limited lines of pre-printed forms. They usually arrive late, having had breakfast on the way, despite written instructions not to. More often than not, they use up excessive and valuable time with cumbersome details irrelevant to the procedure.

I took pride in being the perfect patient. I was well informed and answered all health-related questions to the point, with replies that were easy to document. I didn't go off on a tangent. Never did I want to fall into the "pain in the neck" category. But long before my surgery, I had already broken all the rules of surgical etiquette.

Three weeks before the surgery, I was symptom-free for a few days and was able to walk a mile without much discomfort. I took it upon myself to cancel the surgery, only to be back in pain a week later. It was not possible to reschedule me for another month.

I sadly realized that I had already become a "pain in the neck" before my surgeon raised his scalpel to my skin. I had managed to inconvenience everyone, most of all myself. Now I had to endure the throbbing pain while I tried to smile through the holiday gatherings of friends and family. The surgical coordinator begrudgingly started all over with the paperwork, this time at a different hospital. There was no OR time available at the same renowned orthopedic hospital where I worked and witnessed joint replacements so many years ago.

Now I was to meet my surgeon at a different hospital. It also had a fine reputation and was well endowed by a wealthy community. It was mostly known for its excellent obstetrical care, which was hardly my concern. Usually I am not superstitiously inclined. I know that any surgical specialty is grounded in hard-core scientific knowledge, as well as technical skill and experience. Therefore I raised no objection. At the same time, it felt as if I had been steered to a restaurant table that was too noisy, too drafty, or simply outside my comfort zone, and I sat down without waiting for another. There was no other window of opportunity that matched the surgical schedule with my own work schedule. With good reason, I signed the informed consent.

Blood Donation

I was required to donate two pints of my own blood prior to surgery. These were to be banked for up to three weeks in case I needed them or else would be discarded.

I considered this more of an inconvenience than a likely necessity and reluctantly gave up precious time on my day off. But I knew that it was in my best interest to show up without a grudge.

The hospital lobby appeared like a frantic beehive. As soon as I took the elevator to the fourth floor, it became very quiet. The transfusion center was located adjacent to the sleep lab, where patients with sleep apnea snored through the dawn. The same floor was also shared with a separate unit for chemotherapy. It was a field of medicine I had little experience with, except to sort out the complexity of the chemo agents that might interact with our anesthetic drugs.

The young lab technician expected my arrival with great professional enthusiasm to puncture my arm. First I was amazed at her computer skills. She hardly looked at the keyboard while she took in the vital demographics, which included my religious preference. It was easier to answer "Catholic" than to explain my personal belief system that had evolved over decades of life experiences. Since I was raised Catholic, this was hardly a lie and would be of no clinical consequence.

This question was not raised when I gave blood as a medical student during my first visit to the United States. I wanted to see everything I had read about in *National Geographic* since I was fourteen years old: the Rocky Mountains, the desert, and the Golden Gate Bridge. A visit to my grandmother's sister, who had settled on the outskirts of San Francisco after her escape from Hungary, was enough reason to climb onto the Greyhound bus at 42nd Street in New York City. The northern route across the country took seventy-two hours coast to coast. Only when it was pitch dark did I close my eyes to catch a few hours of sleep. I did not read anything but the broad U.S. map that stretched across two seats, all marked and tattered from refolding it a hundred times along the way.

I imagined what it would be like to live in the smallest of towns where the only visible sign of business was an old rusty gas pump next to a small store that sold Gatorade, hard-boiled eggs, and beef jerky. We had stopped there to refuel and stretch our legs. All the same, having traveled on the bus for seventy-two hours, I discovered that my feet were so swollen that I could barely get my shoes back on.

After a hearty welcome at my aunt's house, I wanted to venture out on my own to sightsee and shop. My travel allowance had dwindled quickly. A call for volunteers in the local newspaper had caught my interest. For the donation of a unit of blood, one could earn twenty dollars. That seemed like a fortune to me and well worth the effort. Of course, I did not tell my aunt about my plan. Once on the trolley, I found the Red Cross Center in an obscure part of town. When I reached the center, I was less sure that this was a good idea. There was a long line of disheveled people, thin and emaciated, who probably needed the money for food, cigarettes, and alcohol. One of my ulterior motives was to lose some weight, and I calculated that a unit of blood would drop at least one pound off the scale.

Since I had come so far, I decided to see the project through. I subjected myself to the routine questions of hepatitis or other recent infectious diseases. My blood count was adequate. After donating the blood, I was rewarded with a crisp twenty-dollar bill and a cool glass of orange juice. I don't remember how I spent the money, but I pretended that I had had a good time when I returned in time for dinner at my aunt's house. She would have been horrified if she knew of my whereabouts.

This morning, thirty-seven years later, I was the only patient in the transfusion lab. A large window overlooked a garden with picnic tables turned upside down for the winter. Oprah smiled encouragement from the morning show on TV. Propped up in a comfortable lounge chair, I felt like a passenger who traveled first class compared to my experience in San Francisco, which was more like sitting on the floor of a cargo plane.

I marveled at the improved sterile technique and the hot pink self-adhesive bandage around my elbow, applied with careful instructions not to lift anything for the rest of the day. The entire process was strictly conducted according to a routine protocol, no matter who came through the door—patient or physician, it made no difference.

No doubt, the procedure of blood donation had come a long way, as had I. Instead of the trolley, I looked forward to driving my own car to our own home and resuming my uninterrupted healthy lifestyle.

While the dark venous blood trickled into the receiving bag, I felt grateful that I did not have to come for chemotherapy next door instead. Of course, one never knows. Doctors are not exempt from cancer. I imagined what it would be like to be confronted with a terminal malignancy. I realized that I would approach it like any other challenge in my life. I would show up on time, dress as best I could, ask for help, and engage with small talk in the healthy lives of my caretakers. I would take away with me their smiles, gratitude for their dedicated service, and some kind of personal lesson that would help me at least get through the day with renewed hope.

I also realized that over a the span of my career, my priorities had shifted from obsessing about twenty dollars and a few unwanted pounds to a deep gratitude for the simplicity of a healthy day.

Angst

It was predictable that my mobility would be severely restricted for the next few weeks, maybe months. It seemed reasonable to take the day off to prepare myself physically and mentally. I set the alarm extra early to make the most of my last day of freedom before my operation.

During a short walk with my husband, my knee felt especially irritated. The sharp pain had been as persistent as the yellow light in my car that indicated that the required maintenance was past its mileage. It reminded me constantly that repair was necessary and that to cancel surgery again was not an option.

It was helpful to stay busy during the day to keep the common pre-operative anxiety contained so it did not unnerve me. I thought having boosted the confidence of so many patients pre-operatively would exempt me from the same. Instead, I found it extremely unsettling to have my structured routine disrupted. Whenever the fear of the unknown caught up with me, I would tell myself the same rhetoric that I tell my patients. "You are in good hands, and you've come to the right place. Let us take care of you, and everything will be fine." How empty these words rang all of a sudden, when I was trying to be my own doctor. They had even less impact than when I was trying to reassure an anxious patient during his or her pre-op visit. I realized that my speech was at best a friendly distraction, void of any unarticulated, yet ever-present risk that accompanied any surgical procedure.

It was almost a well-rehearsed lie, cushioned with a smile and a squeeze of my hand, as I would often usher a patient back to the waiting room and place his or her medical paper trail in the rack. Sometimes I felt that I abandoned a very tense pre-op patient into his or her own world of doubts too quickly as I hurried to pick up the next chart. The OR had already called for the next patient.

The next day would challenge my own trust in the state-of-the-art orthopedic ingenuity and the skill of my surgeon who had kept me going since I first tore a meniscus in my knee, many years ago.

I would also have to trust an anesthesiologist I had never met. I calculated that he would administer a routine anesthetic to me. I considered myself basically a low-risk patient. Since my profession was mentioned in my chart, I was concerned that he might feel tense putting a colleague to sleep who knew what can happen on the other side of consciousness. I was afraid he might do something unusual to do me a favor. The less we dwelled on our mutual specialty, the better the chances for an ordinary, routine case. Besides, I had no influence over his ability to detach from the circumstances. This time my job would be limited to lying back and relaxing.

Next I began to fret over the allotted day of the week and the slot of time. Nobody liked to start a major surgical procedure on a Friday afternoon. I imagined that the focus of my caretakers had already shifted into weekend gear. It would probably be the last case of the week for my surgical team. Saturday plans would already be in motion, the family, the gym, or some traveling, maybe the start of a vacation.

It had been my experience that on the last day of work before a planned vacation I needed to become more focused and vigilant to compensate for a subtle mental drift that began to roll in like a bank of fog. There was a slight psychological disconnect that occurred before the physical separation from the workstation.

In a matter of hours I would have to find a way to let go of my fear of not being in charge, or else be dragged to the OR. Any residual doubts needed to be left at home, along with my jewelry. I was told to come as I was— "just bring the body." That meant no fancy, stylish clothes, just something practical that would roll up easily in a plastic bag called "patient's belongings." It also meant following instructions to the letter and not making up my own rules. It meant keeping my clear liquid intake within the required boundaries of time and not cheating with a cup of Jell-O that I could rationalize as clear liquid, solidified.

I could see it was an exercise in surrender. I began to think about my caretakers instead of myself, hoping that they would also benefit from our serendipitous encounter. All I could do was to present myself naked and quietly in the narrow space of my stretcher with a spirit of gratitude for their service, even while asleep. Quite often I could sense the vibes from my patients even while under anesthesia.

Either I felt peaceful in their presence, or I would be aware of their unsettled anxieties.

Finally I made a decision to expect a good outcome, just like any other day, when I escorted my patients from conscious to unconscious and back without bending an eyelash out of place.

Admission

The bright hospital lobby was not unlike the gate at an airport. The large glass panels all around still connected me with the world outside, while inside a remote unknown destination stirred up a strange flutter. Angular chairs with sleek chrome armrests were a good match for the contemporary, minimal look of Asian simplicity, but were most uncomfortable.

At the registration desk the receptionist with long, brassy hair and long earlobes from the weight of earrings the size of chandeliers handed us the next round disc from a stack of pagers. Her long red nails matched a circular row of red blinking lights that she demonstrated. They would flash when my time was up. The scattered piles of exhausted magazines did not pique my interest, and neither did I bring a book, my usual habit of occupying any unpredictable gap of waiting time.

My husband, who avoids hospitals if he possibly can, retreated to the children's playroom. There he found a long, carpeted bench close to the floor. It was tucked in underneath a dormer-like ceiling, next to a faux window lit up by a yellow transparency. I encouraged him to stretch out, for I could see he was tired. He had helped me with my pre-op appointments and listened patiently to the daily status report of my knee for quite a few weeks now.

I placed my husband's knapsack under his head with my small travel pillow. In less than two minutes, he fell asleep like a child, without the benefit of my anesthesia. However, I was quite content having someone to watch over while asleep, ready to alert him in case any children might come and claim their rightful territory. None did. It was a familiar, comfortable role for me to slip into. As long as I was in a hospital and monitoring someone else sleeping, I could still fool myself into considering it a normal day. I could hardly imagine and still denied any other reason for being here. But then the beeper flashed and it was time to undress in the pre-op cubicle.

I wanted to hold my own hand. I was used to my husband's correct demeanor. He was almost never demonstrative with his affection for me in public places. He did brush my hair away from my forehead over and over and gave my hand a little squeeze of encouragement. There was nothing left to say. We both had unquestionable faith in the surgeon who showed up at the side of my stretcher, appearing as fresh at 2:00 PM as if it was his first morning case. His blue scrubs were starched as crisp as his white coat in the office. He did not seem hungry, anxious, or tired. He explained that he would determine the most appropriate surgical solution after another thorough examination of my knee while I was asleep. I trusted his judgment without another thought.

My anesthesiologist, hands in pocket, strolled by shortly after the IV had been started. He had heard through the office that I was a colleague from the other side of town. I did not want to burden him with shoptalk. I knew there was a lot to prepare in limited time and did not want to interrupt his concentration to complete his set-up. He offered me a new technique, a supplemental nerve block to reduce the anticipated post-op pain. This made good sense to me. Besides, I was prepared to let him do whatever he considered best for me. After all, this was our job.

It was time for some intravenous sedation and time for my husband to leave. He could not help me any further and had seen enough of the reality show.

I thought about how to find a better way to acknowledge future patients of mine, stuck inside the floppy sleeves of an untied hospital Johnny. How to restore their dignity ever so briefly, as they breathed in and out their own lifetime of experiences and struggles, their pride of their accomplishments, be it a mother or a politician. But I ran out of consciousness.

Recall

The brief exchange of pleasantries with my anesthesiologist was followed by a long lapse of consciousness. Everything around me faded into a blur as I was wrapped into a cloud of unfathomable fog.

I did not even know that I was the recipient of the hypnotic drugs pushed at the other end of the intravenous line, which I pick up each day to induce profound anesthesia for any surgical invasion. It is the lifeline between any anesthesiologist and any patient.

The first recall after surgery was opening my eyes in a large hospital bed. It seemed to occupy most of the footprint of a small private room with a window that overlooked the brick wall of the adjacent hospital wing. The overcast winter sky was as cold and colorless as my skin. I was told that I had lost three pints of blood, which made me sick to my stomach all over again. The frequent dosing of narcotics left me weak and nauseous for two or three days. Besides my husband, the only company I could appreciate was the big white bouquet of hydrangeas that looked like oversized snowballs with a touch of green, just like me.

My surgeon told me that he replaced the total knee instead of the partial compartment as he had hoped. The arthritis was too far advanced to salvage the joint. I felt like I had delivered a girl instead of a boy as expected. The skin incision was seven inches long, divided neatly in equal parts of twenty-eight stitches marked with every promise to heal. I remember the intense pain around the clock despite heavy narcotics, while I tried to drift back to sleep as much as I could.

The end of surgery is the beginning of a different phase of recovery for each patient. For some it may constitute a far more invasive psychological incision in his or her life than ever anticipated. While the physical recovery depends largely on the seriousness of the pathology, the mental recovery depends more on the motivation and resourcefulness of each patient. I brought every ingredient in the equation of the healing process: knowledge, willingness to work through the pain, and a fierce ambition to get back on my feet rapidly.

I was discharged with a neat artist's rendering of an anatomical conception of a knee joint. Nowhere in the brochure did it mention the persistent nature of the pain and nausea that kept me in a small heap of self-pity and misery between the fluffy pillows, while my spirit kept sinking. It took almost a week for the muscle fibers to reconnect with the brain just to activate a normal knee bend and regain some sense of control.

On the eleventh night I ran out of pillows and ideas of how to position myself. After a day of exhausting and painful exercises, I was ready for a good night's sleep. But to find a bearable position of comfort, despite the prescribed narcotic, took some ingenuity. All my collective experiences from different stages of my medical training floated like fluffy clouds above my bed and seemed within reach.

I thankfully realized how much I had learned from observing the nurses in various hospitals. Nurses knew best how to make a newly operated patient more comfortable, without written doctor's orders. A rolled towel placed under the ankle to lift the heel, a folded pillow to support a tired back were props I could assemble without help.

I even remembered the old semicircular metal cages with chipped paint from medical school in Ireland. They were placed in a longitudinal fashion over an ulcerated leg in diabetic patients to keep the sheets off the wounds so they would not prevent the healing process. There are no metal cages in my house. Instead I rigged up the square pink plastic travel bucket that was handed to me at discharge from the hospital for the ride home in case of a bout of nausea. Tilted on its side, it created a perfect window to wriggle my toes without the burden of the massive comforter.

I had already used all the pillows in the room to elevate the good leg and the bad leg at different levels but needed something to support my aching back, usually dismissed by me as a minor nuisance. I wedged a rolled blanket against my right side and found that it served simultaneously as an armrest for an irritated nerve of my skinny elbow. Everything bothered me, for I was merely exhausted.

This set-up reminded me of a yoga class called restorative yoga. While the instructor walked around with various props, blankets, bolsters, and lavender-scented eye-bags to accommodate everyone, half the class had fallen asleep. I could still hear the teacher's throaty voice that dropped a few decibels while she dimmed the lights. Her

Gabriele F. Roden MD

description of weightlessness and total support washed over me then and now and transported me quietly to a state of bliss. Alas, after fifteen minutes this was interrupted by the false urgency of a urinary tract infection, probably acquired during my hospital stay when I was catheterized for three days.

Everything had to be dismantled for the sake of a scant dribble. Back in bed, I started all over again but needed less time for the complete set-up. I was glad that my husband, who happened to be out of town for a few days, was not there to witness my pathetic assembly. I could occupy the entire king size bed all by myself with a radio, telephone, books, writing tools, ice packs, and pillows.

My return to work, estimated at three months after surgery, seemed as far as a walk on the moon. I was the best post-op patient I could be, but I had no idea that the restoration to full function unfortunately was not my path and was to become a long-term battle.

Omission of a Tribute to My Knee

Each morning it was still hard to believe that I went to sleep and woke up three hours later with my knee joint replaced by an ingenious piece of hardware.

I never took a moment to say goodbye to the old one. After fifty-nine years of loyal service, it would have been more considerate to at least say, "Thank you." It would have been fitting to dismiss my worn-out joint with some degree of dignity or a simple embrace for all it had done for me.

Joints are meant to run with kites and jump into lakes. I can't remember when I gave away my old wooden skis but recall my pride once I mastered my first ski slalom turns with a smooth rhythm and graduated from the beginner's snow plow for good. My knee joint swiveled effortlessly from side to side to plant tulips and daffodils. On the beach, the same joint dangled my foot in midair to draw initials in the sand and then planted it to pick up perfectly heart-shaped stones, the ones my mother liked.

In the hospital I had often run up or down the flights of stairs, two steps at once, to arrive at a code blue in time to resuscitate a patient. I didn't notice that my knee had become frozen and stiff standing next to the patients' stretchers for so many years. Ironically, this occurred at the recommended OR temperature of seventy degrees Fahrenheit.

We had a good life together despite me taking my knee's performance for granted. I never thought about my knee until the persistent pain disrupted my lifestyle. Too bad I ignored it until it landed in a pathological bucket.

Post-op Visit

For my first post-operative appointment I was ready to take a long-legged stride into my surgeon's office, upright and confident despite the crutches. I could not wait to proudly show off the hard-earned range of motion of my new joint. With the help of an equally committed physical therapist to get results, we had broken down the early scar tissue with tears of determination. Together we established both early goals, a knee bend of ninety degrees and a straight leg on extension.

A friend drove me to the office through snow and ice. As I tried to move from the backseat of the car, one wrong move seized me with a sudden zigzag of such sharp pain that it threw me helplessly back against the seat. I moaned a continuous sequence of ouches like rosary beads. The knee was locked and immobilized in a state of shock. My first thought was a major dislocation, which would land me back in the hospital. After a few minutes I was able to hobble to the office with my good leg and crutches, where I sank into the first available chair. I was acutely aware that my sobs and winces disrupted other patients who waited their turn. While they flipped through magazines, they glanced at me across the top of the page, curious to find out what had gone wrong. I could not reassure anybody with my moans. As much as I tried to control my vocal reaction to the pain, it only deteriorated when I was told by a well-meaning member of the office staff that I was having an anxiety attack. I regained my composure when the burly office manager, big as a bear, appeared with the largest ice pack I had ever seen. He lifted me into a wheelchair and whisked me away from the waiting room to the examining room to see the doctor.

I felt a sad sight, a helpless bundle dressed in black from head to toe, who meant to look smart. Now my usual smile was reduced to a distorted white grimace with a locked knee underneath my floppy pant leg.

My doctor entered, chart clutched under his left elbow, as stiff and unflappable as his freshly starched, brilliant white coat. I could understand the "white coat syndrome," which would raise the blood pressure of many patients. I was aware that his white shirt matched his starched, stiff coat perfectly. His choice of a geometric tie in blues and pinks dictated immediate orderly control and confidence. He seemed pleased with the report card of my physical therapist and the work we had done, even though I had lost my ability to demonstrate any progress in the parking lot.

He reassured me that no harm was done. It was a temporary muscle spasm partially triggered by a twist of the leg, but more so by the stress and fatigue of the relentless exercises of the past two weeks.

I was discharged with more pain medication and orders for rest and ice packs. My list of questions I had neatly written out at home on a piece of paper stayed in my coat pocket, crumpled and forgotten with the damp balls of tissues.

I was wheeled back to the car with more instructions to calm down. Although I had hoped for compassion and empathy from my doctor, I realized that within the constraint of his schedule, his cool composure was probably the best reset button to arrest my raw panic and my hurt pride.

While driving home I saluted the bare oaks that shivered in their nakedness despite the frosty sunshine. All along the highway, they determinedly held their ground. Then I didn't know that the winter around my knee, with ice packs by the dozen, would never end.

A Major Inconvenience

Two-and-a-half years later I still find myself on the fence as to the conclusions about my knee replacement.

I have worn out several flexible braces while I wait for the new hardware to function as expected. The surrounding skin still feels warm to the touch, a sure clinical sign of inflammation doing its best to heal. By now a possible second knee replacement has come up for discussion, as X-rays and operative reports are shuffled and faxed between various orthopedic consultants. Together we navigate a verdict and time for a reluctant surgical revision that looms over me, while others tell me to "live with it." By most experts, I am considered too young and too active for a second procedure that assures fewer guarantees than the first one. Joint replacements do not come with extended warranties.

It is at best a mental exercise to ask retrospectively what could have made the difference. Was I as good a patient advocate for myself as I am for my patients? As a professional on the other side of the ether screen, I do not render all the power to those who hold the scalpel three inches above the intact skin. But as a patient, I did. Of course, I was asleep. I was already "asleep" during my pre-op visit with physical therapy where I was coached how to go up and down the stairs with my new knee. Up with the good leg, "Heaven up," and down with the bad, "Hell down."

I received instructions as if the operative plan was a total knee replacement from the start, while my surgeon had recommended a partial replacement of the medial compartment only.

In fact, everyone but me seemed to indicate that I might have a total knee replacement. Were they privileged to new information that had escaped me between the busy phone signals at the office of the surgical co-coordinator? When I questioned the pre-op physical therapist about the planned the procedure, I was told, "The PT is all the same."

Maybe during the blood donation it should have dawned on me

that a replacement might be a reality, instead of taking a trip back memory lane back to when I gave my first unit of blood as a medical student. A gnawing premonition about a possible misunderstanding on my part about the planned procedure was confirmed when I talked with my surgeon. We agreed that the final fate for my knee would be decided while I was under anesthesia. My husband recalled this conversation better than I did, since to me, as I curled into a ball to keep warm on the stretcher, it was all a blur with or without sedation on board.

Time will tell how it all plays out. However, the magnitude of the hardship and the inconvenience was beyond my imagination.

I claim to have always cared for my patients diligently, with attention to all their needs during their acute physiological derangement while under anesthesia. It is a significant limitation of my specialty that I bear no responsibility for how the post-op course will alter the daily lives of my patients, their hobbies, and their families. "Not my job" sums up a sad lack of interest and engagement, with an abrupt disconnect in the doctor/patient relationship once the vital signs have stabilized in the recovery room. Like many anesthesiologists, I turn my back and walk away. However, since my surgery, my peripheral vision takes in a larger sweep. I now care more deeply about the outcome and the lives of my patients after their discharge. I try to make my interest known in the pre-op interview, to find out as much as time allows about their lives before they signed in the morning of their surgery.

I have found a new approach: I now embrace any patient with all his or her disabilities and do not just evaluate another airway to maintain for the duration of the anesthetic. I truly care about the morbidly obese patient by suggesting a fresh start with a healthier nutritional regimen in a more supportive environment. I would go to any length to come up with one practical recommendation that might improve the patient's quality of life. I know where to find Med-Alert bracelets, better walking shoes, and firmer pillows for stiff necks. I make post-op phone calls to find out about some patients' transition back home and am happy to meet their families. If called for, I arrange referrals to other specialists who may render a useful second opinion. I also encourage patients to become better advocates in their own medical encounters.

On a busy day with seventeen ORs and supervising up to three nurse anesthetists, with a total caseload of up to twenty-five cases, my colleagues and I remind each other in the locker room to put on our roller skates. On days like these I often wanted to use a pedometer to give myself permission to skip my daily compulsory walk at the end of the day. But since this gadget measures more self-pity rather than useful information, it never made it to my belted scrub pants, where it would only distract from my task. However, these marathon days did eliminate my evening walks in favor of more ice packs around the knee. Any busy workday turned into an ordeal for me. Stop-and-go traffic in a fifty-mile commute during rush hour made me stiff and sore by the time I reached home.

For me this lingering anguish was a life-altering smack in the face that required major adjustment. Although the pain was not severe enough to distract me from my work, a constant ache and swelling remained a fact of life. Ongoing physical therapy for two years connected me with other patients with similar post-operative difficulties. I became best buddies with a retired airline pilot as we teased each other about yet another imperfect brace, bandage, or purple pillow between the knees. Instead of my role as advice-giving physician, I gladly offer my friendship to others who have lost the function of a joint once taken for granted. I can now relate to having my joy of beach walks restricted by soft moguls of sand, standing on one leg, like a pink flamingo, at cocktail parties, and once since my surgery, having needed a wheelchair for transatlantic travel.

This new physical limitation took me for a ride through the entire spectrum of a grieving process and sometimes challenged my residual capacity to meet the physical demands as a doctor. My own long-term yet unresolved healing process forced me to reduce my workload and open windows for a more holistic encounter with my patients. An unforgiving, tightly packed schedule that measures medical care by the minute cannot be part of my routine anymore.

This procedure affected every fiber of my fabric, from my bank account to the bedroom. Letting go of my clothes on admission was child's play compared to the surrender of the office key along with my ID card at a major teaching hospital.

If I had to decide again about a weight-bearing joint replacement, I would seek at least three independent opinions, perhaps live with it longer, ask more questions, and do more research on the subject. I would not rush to get it over with, only to return to work as soon as I could walk without crutches, so as to not inconvenience my colleagues. I believe that whatever lesson we didn't learn the first time will present itself again for better management. Next time I will participate more responsibly in my own care.

I am grateful for not being confronted with a life-threatening illness and for having retrieved my purpose as anesthesiologist in a new environment. Other than the pesky knee, I bounce through any given day at work with less stress and more joy, with the hope of healing eventually.

Chapter Five

Elusive Retirement

For Retirement

… You stand on the shore of new invitation
To open your life to what is left undone;
Let your heart enjoy a different rhythm
When drawn to the wonder of other horizons.

Have the courage for a new approach of time;
Allow it to slow down until you find freedom
To draw alongside the mystery you hold
And befriend your own beauty of soul …

John O'Donohue[9]

The End of the Tunnel

It was a long winter to recuperate from this major knee surgery. At no time in my career as anesthesiologist at a renowned Boston teaching hospital had I been I forced to take such an extended leave of absence from my work. It was my husband's idea that I might benefit from a change of scenery and climate in Florida. I raised no objection.

While in Florida I was drawn to visit a local hospital to investigate volunteer opportunities for the approaching time frame of my retirement. I considered retirement more readily since my surgery.

My husband came along for the ride. However, the closest medical facility, less than two miles away, was no ordinary community hospital. Instead it was a rehabilitation clinic for marine life and an endangered species of loggerhead turtles known as *Caretta caretta*.

Most of the turtle patients were rescued by the Coast Guard after they were found either stranded on the beach or tangled in fishing nets. Sometimes they were spotted floating in a lagoon. Injured or

---

9   From TO BLESS THE SPACE BETWEEN US: A BOOK OF BLESSINGS by John O'Donohue p167 © 2008 by John O'Donohue. Used by permission of Doubleday, a division of Random House,,Inc.

disabled turtles were admitted to the marine hospital for various reasons.

The ward consisted of large, round tubs, eight feet in diameter, which provided a private space for each patient, well marked with their individual name and history. I encountered Pete, who had sustained a left eye injury and some soft tissue damage from a power boat. After a few months of daily attention and care, he was well on the mend. Belle was found on the barrier fishing net near a power plant. She had fishing line wrapped around her right front and rear flippers. The front flipper was very swollen with damage to the bone, which was treated with antibiotics.

The majority of disabled turtles seemed to stay for months rather than weeks to heal and regain their strength. Besides generous feeds of squid, they received antibiotics and vitamins and iron for anemia.

I quietly approved of their treatments by this highly motivated, knowledgeable team of veterinarian volunteers. It was obvious that these dedicated caretakers had established a meaningful patient-doctor relationship with each turtle.

The turtles, while some had arrived in a state of shock, by now appeared trusting and peaceful. Their slow motion and the curious peek of their heads above the water surface indicated no distress.

During our visit we were informed that next Saturday Cruiser would be discharged and released back into the ocean at noon. Cruiser had been found and rescued five months ago, when he was floating sluggishly in the Indian River lagoon. An MRI revealed large amounts of free air in his body cavity, which compressed his lungs and viscera. It also caused a buoyancy problem. Some air was removed surgically, and with time the rest was absorbed. His discharge from the clinic was an event I did not want to miss.

At our arrival a large crowd had already gathered to bid Cruiser farewell, with lots of excited children and flashing cameras. Cruiser, the star of the day, had already been lifted out of his own tub onto a large, wooden pedestal. While he was thoroughly hosed down and scrubbed with a large, stiff brush, a foul, rotten stench was taken lightly by most. I learned that it may have been caused by stress-induced flatulence.

Since trapped intestinal air was part of Cruiser's admission diagnosis and had caused the large animal to float instead of allowing him to submerge to a typical depth of 1,000 feet, I became concerned that he might not be ready for discharge. But an experienced staff member reassured me of his readiness.

Cruiser flapped his front flippers wildly in midair. They resembled soggy leather sponges. I hoped that it was a sign of eagerness for the transit back to his normal habitat. Definitely he was excited.

Cruiser's vital statistics needed to be recorded in a ledger, along with his tag identification number. A computer chip had been inserted into his shoulder two weeks earlier, while preparing him for his release. This was accomplished in another large, square plastic bin, where he ducked quietly while a caring hand stroked his head to comfort him. His shell measured roughly five feet by three feet, and he weighed in at 135 pounds. A loud moan of empathy was offered by all as he was turned on his back, feet in the air, for a final inspection and a scrub of his firm belly.

He was then lifted gently by four men onto a faded canvas gurney, all four flippers hanging over the edge, and was belted in securely so he would not fall off during the bumpy ride to the beach.

A special tunnel had been built just for that purpose from the hospital underneath route A1A, emerging onto the soft sand. It was high enough for all spectators to march upright and ahead of Cruiser. The hot white sand and blue sky at the end of the dark tunnel appeared as a brilliant crystal at the viewer of a kaleidoscope.

It took great discipline to organize all adults and children, well over two hundred of them, to form an aisle between two lines from the edge of the water to the tunnel with enough space in between for the passage of our loggerhead hero. While children darted back and forth between their friends and parents for photo-shoots, the ocean quietly lapped its gentle waves into the sand as an invitation for Cruiser's homecoming.

Finally Cruiser appeared, high and dry on his gurney at the opening of the tunnel. He bumped down along the beach and was encouraged with a cacophony of claps and cheers, like an Olympic champion.

Within ten yards of the water's edge, the gurney was lowered to a few inches from the ground. The belts were untied. Almost instantly Cruiser sensed his freedom and his safety. With a heavy waddle, he disembarked form the gurney onto the warm sand.

The waves wanted to lick his feet, but he was still outside their reach. He did not hesitate to march more quickly in their direction with great determination that overcame the heaving of his heavy body. Step by step he reached the edge. Front flippers wet, he easily propelled the rest of his body into the water. He was a natural, home at last. He never looked back, just swam toward the horizon.

The shadow of his shell still glistened in the water like an upside down boat. Once or twice his yellow head surfaced like a submarine periscope and bopped a last good-bye to all of us, before it submerged for good to find his own friends and family. He disappeared from our witness stand with great purpose into his own world of turtle existence.

I too got lost in my own ocean of tears of joy. I suddenly knew that I also would get back on my feet and regain my strength. This day I could see the end of the tunnel.

As I stood at its edge and looked at the short distance of beach to the water, it reminded me that my planned retirement was only nine months away. I trusted that I too would be carried safely to the edge of my freedom when I stepped into a larger world than my life as a physician at the hospital.

My dream of spending time in Italy and learning the language more fluently could become a reality. At home, in my husband's art studio, there are vacant easels and unpainted canvases. There are rainbows of watercolors for me to dip a brush in and rekindle my creative fire that has been smoldering underneath the surgical drapes, soon to be lifted for good.

Nine months, a natural gestation period for the child of mine that was never delivered. The seed of playful creativity has been planted and now has nine months to germinate. My inner child will have a voice at last. It will let out a loud, sustained cry of joy once born into a world not restricted by the tight and unyielding belt of an operating room schedule. Like the turtle, I will find my way, awkwardly at first, then rapidly gaining momentum, into a new world of freedom, where I can stretch body and mind until I feel complete.

Thoughts on Retirement

The recent addition of brown rice to the menu of the Thai restaurant around the corner from the hospital moved this friendly eatery rapidly to the top of the list of my favorites.

Last night the waiter was attentive beyond what I might normally expect. Most likely, his sympathetic demeanor was elicited by the white patch over my left eye, glued to my forehead with sticky tape. I had a stubborn sty removed by one of my surgeon colleagues. It had grown to the size of a peppercorn inside my lower eyelid and would not budge with hot compresses and antibiotic ointment. To me it was a minor inconvenience. To the waiter, and to the world as I crossed the street, it translated into injury, pain, and being blind, if only temporarily.

The eye patch was a big white lie. While it effectively raised others' concern, I knew what was patched up. Over the years I had studied enough oriental medicine to recognize that any lesion of the eye is connected to the liver meridian, which becomes symptomatic with unreleased anger. Any acute infection, in Chinese medicine, is also considered a physical outburst of anger. I concluded that an infection near the eye represented some inner turmoil that had no place to go outside my friendly shell.

Whenever I thought about retiring, there were too many angles and far-reaching consequences to fit neatly on a balance sheet. Although I made hundreds of clinical decisions, sometimes in a split second, I was not so sure-footed in making huge decisions about my life.

The choice to retire from a career in medicine cannot be contained on one page and may not be a choice at all. It cannot be abrupt. Being a doctor has been a part of me for decades, and I would never want to lose my sharp clinical edge. I will always continue to look disease straight in the eye and challenge it. While standing in line anywhere, I will offer a prayer for the gentleman who carries an extra hundred pounds on his body to find the willingness to give up the empty comfort calories. I would love to show the chronic smokers who wheeze and cough their way to the oxygen tank a picture of a smoker's lung. I have seen this sticky black sponge inside their chests. Most of all, I would want to find a place where I could still hold patients' hands and talk them through their anxiety before surgery, so that they might go to sleep peacefully.

I did not become a physician overnight or the day I received my diploma. I became a physician when I was fourteen years old, while I read about Albert Schweitzer's mission in the African forest of Lambarene. "Reverence for life" was his mantra. It is an innate urge to help those who suffer.

For me anesthesia was a good specialty because I observed early that patients or friends don't take my suggestions readily. Family rarely does. Anesthesia gave me the power to make things happen by altering consciousness in an instant, beyond self-will, moods, lack of discipline, or habits.

There were times during my early adolescence when I was disarmed and lured into embraces that made me cringe. My anger was timid, blind, and speechless. Then I could not argue with a beguiling opponent who crossed personal boundaries under the premise that foul play was for my own good and would not harm me. Anesthesia gave me total control over others without uttering a word. Albert Schweitzer said, "I wanted to be a doctor that I might be able to work without talk."

In a strange way I considered the unique privilege of being in command of the situation delayed compensation for so many times in my adolescence when I was not. Control can come in many forms. I lived within its entire spectrum. Once reclaimed in my profession, I was not ready to give it up again with turning in my locker key and my ID card at the hospital.

Anesthesia is an odd specialty. An uninformed bystander may easily think that we are not really doctors. Sometimes even nurses or surgeons just call us, "Hey, anesthesia!" Unlike any other specialty, there is a beginning and an end to any interaction with the patient and any therapeutic intervention.

Anesthesia is also a contained specialty. Each day I entered the hospital, I brought the willingness to share any patient's emotional load for the day, not always part of my job description. My own complicated sense of duty readily picked up any burden, while genuine compassion finished the job.

Most patients arrived with all kinds of baggage. Besides their fears and anxiety about their surgery, they brought their pocketbooks filled with long lists of illegible, hand-scribbled medicines. There were pill boxes of colored capsules that I could not identify just by looking at them and eyeglasses for eyes that were too teary to read any informed consents, even with the glasses. They brought lumpy scars from previous surgeries, so long ago that they forgot which organ was removed. They brought excess weight they had gained because they could not handle their family feuds, injustices, and personal losses.

At least for the duration of their stay, I helped carry their various loads until they woke up again. As soon as I signed off their vital signs as stable in the recovery room, I handed it all back to them. Often I seemed to collapse on the train into a ball of fatigue from the collective burden of the day. I was relieved that I could walk away from it.

Sometimes I wonder how I would cope with the puzzles of my own life that waited patiently for me at home, while I cheerfully went to work. There are phone numbers of distant relatives with shattered lives who have divorced and moved to China. My own mother, in a nursing home in Germany, has not heard a word from me for months, while I hide behind the certainty that she will not remember. I trust that the nurses will brush her hair each day and will continue to feed her pureed carrots to keep her alive a bit longer. I have already said my goodbyes year after year. There are children and grandchildren of my husband's family who need support. It is time soon to return home and care for my family with the same compassion I have had for my patients. There will be no discharge at the end of the day.

It would not be easy to give up a purposeful schedule and being needed to fill OR 5 in the morning, where colleagues, surgeons, and patients expect me to be ready for an uneventful day. I was afraid to give it up for a wastepaper basket filled with paper balls of tossed-out ideas that will never make it to a publisher.

I often dreamed of being home with plenty of time to pursue my personal interests. I would dust off the piano and try again some simple sonatas marked *adagio*, not *allegro*. I would cook a perfect pot of brown rice without it sticking to the bottom of the pot from too much heat and hurry pushing me out the door for work. I would slow everything down a bit and talk to my clay turtle that sits quietly on my windowsill to remind me not to be in such a rush all the time.

Rice

Three bowls of brown rice is all I need on any given day.
To survive, to slow down,
to reflect with gratitude for all that I have.

A tiny, modest morsel, barely larger than a grain of sand.
Packed with starchy goodness.
Full of wisdom.
Having traveled from other continents for many centuries,
it quietly fulfills its purpose at its unknown destination.
It soothes starvation all over the world.
More capable than politicians.
A neutral world diplomat.

Feeds the poor and the famous alike
without asking questions.
Those malnourished being poor by fate,
but also the rich, malnourished by excess.
Tossed in midair to feed birds
Showers newly-weds.
Single-minded.
Never loses sight of its purpose.
Always ready to provide undefined comfort.
Not swaying body or mind to either extreme,
allowing both to return to their center.
The perfect balance between Yin and Yang.
Always amenable to give until it is consumed.

Content to be a grain in a multitude,
and contribute to the whole.

My holistic approach to a healthy lifestyle reaches well beyond recreational poetry. I once learned from a Reiki master that troubled knees are indicative of a change or herald a life transition. Why do I always find underlying messages to my symptoms that are disturbing in their relentless honesty? Years of informal study of alternative and oriental medicine pay off if I care to listen. I argue that one more operation on one more joint will be a rational bargain to extend endurance at work. However, my cumulative injuries and various inconvenient symptoms generate a new voice that does not escape my ears and my attention. At first I didn't like the idea of being replaceable any more than having my knee joint replaced. It has dutifully carried me throughout my time of service at the hospitals. I have stood firmly, like a planted tree, at the heads of thousands of patients as they transitioned into unconsciousness like the soft fall of a pinecone. I wanted to continue my watch. I try to get comfortable with the idea that my creaky knees might actually be a nudge to consider retirement.

My opinion and the strength of my clinical experience still matters at work, but I have observed that my effectivenss is sometimes less than I would like it to be. It bothers me that I needed assistance with three intubations in the past month. While the patients get heavier and more unmanageable with rampant obesity, I seem less strong physically. My perceived lack of physical strength to manage some enormous patients saps my professional confidence. My usual way to compensate is to take on more of the less complex cases, to still contribute my fair share of work.

My left-brain has been well trained to draw up a convincing list of reasons to justify an extension of my work. What could be more meaningful than a continuous life of service to patients? Isn't that why I am here on this earth? There are so many aspects of my job I still love. I find it challenging, entertaining, and rewarding to engage in relationships with nurses, patients, and colleagues. Opportunities to be inspired sometimes occur in odd places. During a coffee break one of our nurses proudly told us that her twelve-year-old daughter had collected $800 from bottles. She donated the entire sum to a breast cancer charity.

Incidentally, I would also miss my scrubs. To me they represent a practical garb somewhere between the nostalgic and romantic idea of being dressed in my grandmother's lace or the habit of a nun, who lives a quiet life of structure and discipline. Anesthesia is a specialty of rituals and discipline. The scrubs taught me not to focus on appearance but on the work in front of me. At the end of the day, stepping back into my own life is as easy as stepping out of the scrubs and tossing them in the laundry hamper.

Retirement is within my grasp, and yet I hesitate to let go and give up the mission that has been my life and my reason to get up early every morning for so many years. Some days I find evidence all day long that the patients give me more than I give them. An older man gives me an encouraging wink of his eyes while I explain to him that the intravenous might sting for a moment. "Just go ahead, do what you need to do," he says while I reach across his chest to put one more sticky monitor lead below his ribcage. It is a silent contract of mutual trust that supersedes lengthy explanations.

During the last stretch of my anesthesia career, I know that I will leave my specialty more advanced and safer than I found it thirty-five years ago. Technology has not stood still but has marched forward steadily and quietly behind the scenes of everyday surgery. The many journals I have disregarded because of their statistical and mathematical complexities have found their way into our syringes and monitors to deliver faster and safer anesthesia.

The biggest adjustment to being home would be giving up being in charge. At work, while I deal with patients and my support staff I am used to speaking from authority and having the last word. Not that I would be inclined to ever abuse that privilege, but I am used to expecting compliance without much argument. Usually my preferences are followed through, and I am not used to anyone doing the opposite. At home there is no order giving. I feel offended when my well-intentioned suggestions are ignored. I find myself in an instant attack mode instead of gentle and forgiving. I am just not good at compromise because there can be none at work. Sometimes I assume that I won't be heard at home. As a child I was not encouraged to voice much of an opinion , therefore all I can do is bark when I feel stepped on. I have to find a new, gentle way to convey my goals and personal preferences without pointing the finger.

I have not been so visible or talkative lately, needing more quiet time while I eat my tuna in the corner of my office by the large window. The grand view of the old historic section of town has gradually been erased by the new sixteen-story guest tower of a new luxury hotel. Its unique site and construction in close proximity to the world's best medical campus were anything but ordinary and had been the talk of the town for some time now.

It was a bold and mesmerizing concept to convert the old massive granite jail into a four-star hotel. The ninety-foot central rotunda and cupola built in 1851 will give way to a lobby "jail" bar with preserved remnants of jail cells and oversized, arched windows. It is of historic interest to me that this city jail was built just six years after the first administration of ether anesthesia in 1846 under the rotunda of the ether dome, footsteps away from the prison. Both events lend themselves as a curious topic over dinner at the casual second-floor restaurant.

For so many years I felt captive to the confines of the OR and the dictates of a tight schedule. While I walked alongside the long brick wall of the menacing granite prison adjacent to the hospital, I could hardly distinguish which side of the wall I was on. No matter how often I told myself that I was not an inmate, the moment I walked into the main entrance of the hospital, I often felt like one during the short-term incarceration in my cell for the day. Unlike the prisoners whose only visitors were family, attorneys, and a chaplain, my cell was visited by patients, colleagues, nurses, and famous surgeons.

I felt obliged, physically and mentally, to leave my own life, my agenda, and my idea of pleasure at the doorstep. I forgot that I could have it all back again when I left for home at the end of the day.

Over the years I had become attached to the old city jail, knowing that my prison thoughts were a fictitious fantasy I indulged in by my own choice. The last jailbirds had been moved to a new facility on Memorial Day weekend in 1990. What remains, they didn't know. Moving in slow circles inside the hardcore granite walls, they didn't know the green trees that lined the bank along the river, where runners ran freely, and the restful water where sailboats fluttered with the whim of the winds.

During the past two years I have witnessed the historic prison fall victim to its massive demolition process and reconstruction as the new luxury hotel. The historic façade has indeed been integrated by brilliant architects into the guest complex with banquet and conference facilities.

At first I was sadly sentimental to see the old walls tumble and crumble into a pile of rubble. But all of a sudden I saw it as an omen of a new liberty from all forms of job-related restrictions in my life, real or imagined. There was a great sense of freedom that overcame me, and a joy that I have served my duty faithfully but that my days of duty are coming to an end. The fallen, dusty granite was evidence of the end right before my own eyes. It was built to last a lifetime but has outlived its usefulness.

Rocks to Remember

Five medium-sized rocks sat on the railing of my deck. Silently they stood in line as a natural calendar that would end the day I would retire. The last working day of each month, I pitched one into the pond that abuts our backyard.

Each time I sank one, I felt lighter. I was amazed how effortlessly I unleashed each rock, compared to how much energy it took at work to get to the next one. The weight of patients still anesthetized, waiting to wake up, was gravely lopsided compared to the stony lump in the palm of my hand.

As I curled my fingers around the last one, I chose its path of flight with great precision. I wanted to see ripples in the water and believe that the ripples of my presence in our department would outlast those of the rock. The splash had become a personal rite of separation from my experiences that sometimes owned me.

While I would be glad to be done with my obligations at the bimonthly infectious committee meeting, some bright spots of my practice would be irreplaceable.

I would miss the well-deserved satisfaction of dropping onto a thin, stiff mattress with the squeaky rubber lining underneath the sheet. It was clean and was mine for the remaining night. I had earned it. Sometimes I was so tired that I fell asleep naturally, as quickly as my patients with a bolus of propofol.

I would miss a sense of pride going to the neonatal intensive care unit (NICU) of the adjacent hospital. After an extremely strenuous day in the OR, it had been my duty to see three infants in the NICU. It was a time-consuming assignment, as it entailed going to another building in order to prepare the parents and do some cumbersome paperwork for their surgery the following day.

It took time to comprehend the complexity of treatments amongst a maze of monitors and a seriously dedicated staff. The large unit with twelve patient cubicles was kept dark, not unlike the air traffic control center I had visited when I aspired to be a pilot. I imagined the low light level was to resemble the darkness of the womb, when in fact it is a deliberate therapeutic measure to decrease any external stimulation. My eyes and my brain needed to adjust to the rhythm of the monitors that displayed alarming heart rates—at least, much faster than most adult patients under my care. Yet they fell within the physiological range of premature or gravely ill infants. Oxygen levels were often dangerously marginal.

Unless I identified myself quickly as a prospective anesthesiologist for one of their patients scheduled for complex airway surgery at our facility, I was considered a lost foreign body. It took persistence to find the right chart and the right patient amongst this flurry of activity. It took diplomacy to lure away the nurse in charge of the patient, who had her hands full administering drugs, giving reports, and changing diapers. I needed her intimate knowledge of the patient to fill the gaps between hastily written chart entries and updated information in the computer with special access codes.

Each patient's chart was loaded. It contained the patient's history from the time of conception, complex test results, and the current regimen of medications. While I tried to extrapolate the salient features of the history relevant to the anesthesia care, there were large chunks of information I could not decipher. Page after page was filled with extensive notes from various consultants or tired residents who liked to use acronyms I had never seen before. Sometimes the premature infants weighed less than their charts.

The baby I saw the previous night weighed over ten pounds, a heavyweight amongst the tiny ones. His head was disproportionately large compared to the rest of his body, due to a cranial bone deformity. He had a very round, smiley face that appeared overinflated. I could not help joining the nurses in making a big and loving fuss about him to let him know how special he was. Anthony was luckier than he could comprehend, while he smiled happily at our efforts to wiggle his toes.

Anthony was the offspring of a teenage alcoholic mother who had given him up for adoption. Unfortunately, this baby boy was born with a tiny airway. It measured 2mm in diameter, about the size of a toothpick.

When he cried, the struggle for air became dangerous and severely compromised the oxygen supply to enter his lungs. Something more definitive needed to be done. Anthony was scheduled for a tracheostomy the next day by a brilliant young surgeon, who appeared perfectly comfortable and confident with the most complicated airways in infants. While he assembled his team, they seemed to be quickly running out of air and options.

Anthony's first foster parents, very young themselves, could not adapt to the intense medical efforts that had to be made to help him survive. Instead, a physician directly involved with his acute care took a courageous step and dramatically raised the bar for a more fortunate outcome. She and her husband adopted the baby.

I would have liked to have met this highly motivated physician in person. I wanted to tell her how much I admired her heroic effort. She had left to go home and was not present when I examined Anthony. Unknown to her, the ripples of her spirited decision uplifted me with renewed hope that the world of medicine I entered for humanitarian reasons was still alive and well. One woman's choice was a gift of inspiration for others. It rendered a memory I would file under "remarkable" to remind me that the search for opportunities to heal broken bodies and souls could continue for a lifetime.

Yes, these special moments I would miss.

I would not miss, however, the world of medicine where the focus on patient care has become blurred by an ever-growing, relentless administrative drive to improve the bottom line.

A once-handsome bonus at Christmas in appreciation of many hours of self-sacrifice beyond the call of duty had melted into a box of chocolates for a few years now. Older colleagues complained about keeping up with a new record of thirty cataracts a day and became resentful when nobody had time to relieve them for lunch. Some of my younger colleagues lost their manners in their competitive rivalry for tenure or their quiet disappointment over toppled salaries while they tried to raise a family in an environment with most expensive real estate.

These were my thoughts as I was driving home a few days later. After a tedious commute, I happily turned the last corner toward our house at the end of the cul-de-sac. I could hardly believe my eyes. The ragged edge of grass at the turn-around was neatly covered with white gravel. On top of it sat five massive, round boulders, which we had requested from the landscaper crew more than two years ago. The idea was to prevent the snowplow from damaging the lawn.

In over two years nobody had considered the boulders a high priority. But I could instantly recognize their significance. Sometimes I had wondered if the pond would ever dry out enough to retrieve my memories embedded in the rocks I had tossed.

These giant boulders would serve me well as perfect memory

banks for those medical highlights of my career I would never want to throw away into the pond.

Departure Sentiments

The time had come for a long lull of not having to be responsible for the lives of others. Over the span of decades of my career, patients had grown sicker, more obese, and more demanding of skills that had not even been invented when I started my practice. It was hard enough to admit to myself that it was time to retire. It was harder to break the news to our department chief. He was already challenged to provide adequate coverage for the OR with an unremitting shortage of anesthesiologists. I felt as disloyal when I left home at the age of twenty-four for a new world halfway across the earth, for my own adventure in unexplored territory.

I remember when I stood at the top of the roll-away staircase of the airplane, from where I waved good-bye to my parents. I remember my wheat-colored linen dress with blue strawberries, cut on the bias, which had a slimming effect. Since it was sleeveless, I covered myself with a light summer coat across my shoulders to hide my fat upper arms. They were only to get fatter when I found the pizza vendors on either side of the Staten Island ferry in New York. At that time it cost a nickel for the boat ride across the sound, from where I would wave to the Statue of Liberty. A slice of pizza on departure and on arrival was a quarter each.

Now thirty-six years later, leaving the operating room felt like walking out on my family all over again. The large umbrella of the academic institution had felt safe and protective for a long time. Stepping out and away from it seemed like a bold and drastic move. What I feared most was that by handing in my hospital identification card I would also lose a part of my identity as a longstanding member of an extraordinary team. At times my work-related "family" could be as dysfunctional as any family that one lives with for many years, long enough to share the crises and the tragedy besides weddings, babies, and birthdays. But together we had survived more sad and tragic moments than I could have endured by myself.

Sometimes I could not imagine giving up this large slice of life, with its delicious blend of ingredients all melted together in the heat of the operating room. However, at times my various joints felt as worn out as those of our two wobbly office chairs that threatened to collapse under the weight of exasperated and exhausted colleagues.

We all needed an overhaul, as did our small anesthesia office. It was the hub for the entire anesthesia staff, the place where we started and ended our day. All eyes repeatedly scanned the huge magnetic board attached to an entire wall. Patients, their proposed surgery, and anesthetists were slated in chronological order with magnets in different colors.

This strategic and dynamic schedule board was a source of an incessant flow of opinions about the unrealistic surgical block time that was overbooked again and how Mary ended up with yet another MAC (Monitored Anesthesia Care) room. Any attempt to meddle behind the back of the schedule runner stirred up an instant fury. The rise and fall of predicted outcome of events throughout the day was not unlike the stock market.

Staff members breezed through this crammed office many times a day to drop off the paperwork of finished cases. At the same time they would note their next assignment and pick up a piece of equipment or a piece of juicy gossip. Sometimes all you could find was a tired colleague, slouched in the broken chair, who answered with a growl.

Typed schedules, current as well as outdated ones, were scattered on top of the old gray metal desk. Both hands were needed to open the drawers with a jolt. There were never any pens to be found, just useless pencils with broken tips, a few rubber bands, and some paper clips that I bent open to relieve the tension.

When I interviewed fifteen years ago, I was led to this inner sanctum to meet my prospective colleagues. Even then I could hardly believe the antiquity of the collection of the two old desks and the old white vertical metal cabinet with the dinged doors, which resembled remnants from the army. Two cork bulletin boards were cluttered with faded protocols held up with pushpins but turned at such an angle that you had to drop your head on one shoulder to read them. The only addition since then has been a computer.

How strange to feel the same pang of selfishness mixed with a sense of excitement that propelled me into the next phase of my life. I had not ventured into a new territory or a different lifestyle for over thirty years. But now the urge for a change felt like a big lump that had to be coughed up.

The day of my announcement I waited for my chief to finish his case in the mid-afternoon. I paced back and forth between his room and the anesthesia desk like a cat on the prowl. Although I was ready for my pounce, I had changed my line many times before he finally came out. On his way to his office on the upper floor, I simply said, "Chris, I need to retire from this job."

"No," he replied while he kept walking. "Why can't you just work two days a week?" I explained why it was much more complicated.

After the long version about my knee, my husband, and a long commute, my request was received with respect and dignity. My chief made a gentleman's counter-offer, which would allow me to phase out by still working per diem throughout the following year if I desired to do so. I could hardly believe that I deserved such a privilege and walked out of the office taller and not slighted professionally. I wanted to hurry back to the OR to finish my assigned cases. I pulled my mask back over my face. No one could see the transition of my status that had taken place in five minutes, the duration of one cycle of blood pressure readings. And yet for me everything had changed.

But I did not feel finished or diminished. Instead I felt ready to start an equally fulfilling life. I was surprised that my usual afternoon slump was replaced with a new surge of energy, which carried me for the rest of the day.

It took a few days before both our department chairman and I realized that maybe our good working relationship did not have to end so abruptly. Maybe the sudden severance could be softened somehow. My hospital privileges still existed on paper until September. The imminent renewal of the malpractice insurance was to be paid by the department. The chairman offered to switch my status to "per diem," which meant that I could still work occasionally as needed. There would be a predictable staff shortage during the summer. It was foreseeable that I would spend the summer at our home in New England. I would gladly oblige to fill in the vacation gaps for the department. There was no need for a final good-bye to my friends and colleagues.

Epilogue

When I completed this manuscript, I was amazed how heavy it felt cradled in my arm. I realized that it contained the entire load that was burdensome for so many years of my life. The physical act of placing it down on the dining room table felt liberating. I became aware that I was different now, lighter than when I started writing this book.

I remembered that during my residency at Yale, my fellow residents and I were so immersed in our training program that occasionally we encouraged each other to snap out of it by asking the question: "Is there a life after Yale?" Although the end of my story called for a reflective pause, I took a deep breath to remind myself that I still existed outside these pages and that my life goes on beyond my documented past.

When I formulated my initial thoughts, I was still in the grips of my childhood memories and a tight schedule in the OR. Both were a continuum of a relentless demand for perfection. Both were unforgiving. Silently I played along for decades with the same gracious countenance as my mother.

When my father passed on, he took away his yardstick that measured my ongoing progress, but by then it felt as if it was implanted in my spine. Obviously, at work it was necessary to administer the prescribed amount of an anesthetic according to the patient's needs. However, gauging all my activities, even at home, had become a way of life.

I often wonder if my rigid lifestyle was a precursor to the

development of the progressive joint disease that I wrote about. Despite the knee replacement, the diffuse nature of my joint disease forced me to embrace a new lifestyle. My husband and I moved to a sunny seaside town in Florida, where I can at least outrun a turtle.

The warmer climate and slower pace beckoned me to pursue other, more leisurely activities. I signed up for calligraphy and poetry at the local high school. While we explored our new neighborhood, I was struck by the stylish architectural design of a complex building still under construction. What could it possibly turn out to be?

It was barely a month after I relinquished my tenure at the hospital that the huge green sign at this new building stated its purpose. It flashed at me like a green light. A new eye-care center with a state-of-the-art surgical suite was being built within a five-mile radius of our recently acquired Florida home. I found it intriguing that the land for this new campus was purchased a decade ago.

I had read about synchronicity. Now it jumped right at me and shook me by my shoulders. The more I found out about this surgical facility, the more I was fascinated by its intention. I even knew some of the faculty members from national specialty conferences.

When I read about the goals of this task force, I felt newly inspired and wanted to be part of this team.

> *We strongly believe that creating a beautiful environment filled with natural light, intimate waiting rooms for patient privacy, and elegant furnishings is equally important as the latest technology in our desire to provide exceptional service to our patients and an ideal work environment for faculty and staff.*

I was easily won over to be recruited for a part-time faculty position at this first-rate academic institution. This opportunity would allow me to practice within an exclusive niche of my expertise in anesthesia for ophthalmology.

Except for my first job after I had completed my training, this was the only OR that had windows. Then I took note of the seasons' turn by the color of the treetops. It was thirty years ago. I didn't realize the value of staying connected to the outside world.

Besides looking out on sun-drenched beds of begonias, I took in a larger picture. This luscious view made me feel alive. It allowed me to catch my breath long enough to recognize instantly that this is where I belonged. Standing here filled me with a purpose and a privilege that I have rarely encountered along the way.

Suddenly something invisible tugged at the sleeve of my scrubs. From there it started buzzing around my head like an unwanted fly. It was a disturbing question that upset my new-found bliss. Could it be that I was in all the wrong places for most of my life? This misgiving,- I would figure out later, not now. I needed to return to my patients.

Back at home, the open question of perhaps having been in all the wrong places for most of my life begged me to look at my journey. Having completed the book, there was something still unfinished. This last void pulled me back to the beginning. For some reason I returned in my mind to the puzzle of my wobbly start inside my grandmother's one-room apartment. There, like revisiting an old photo album, I searched all the nooks and crannies to find something undiscovered, perhaps a missing link. Instead I found a road sign outside that had stood the test of time.

I remember the blue-and-white street sign perched high above the lilac bushes that lined the last bend of Paul Ehrlich Strasse. Whenever I later visited my grandmother, I felt an intuitive respect for Paul Ehrlich. He remained a rather distant figure to me but was renowned to have my grandmother's street named after him. It had been told to me as a child that Paul Ehrlich was a famous medical researcher. He collaborated with Robert Koch, who was awarded the Nobel Prize in 1905 for his work on tuberculosis. Now I wondered what other contributions he might have made to medicine. Further research on Paul Ehrlich was just a few clicks away in my own library.

There I discovered that Paul Ehrlich's medical thesis was on the subject of "Sauerstoff Beduerfniss des Organismus"(The Need of the Organism for Oxygen). He was appointed Public Health Officer at Frankfurt University in 1899. In 1887 he had received the *Tiedemann* prize of the Senckenberg Nature Research Society, in the Senckenberg Allee, where my second childhood home was located. In 1908 Paul Ehrlich also won the Nobel Prize. I find it remarkable that my childhood home was located in the Senckenberg Allee. Until now I had dismissed Senckenberg with the memory of the massive dinosaur in the museum of natural history across the street. But now my curiosity was piqued. Again I searched for any relevant historic notes on Johann Christian Senckenberg (1707–1772). He also was a German medical doctor and philanthropist. While he intended to write his first dissertation on the subject of melancholy, he promoted the medicinal healing attributes of lilies of the valley, my mother's favorite flowers. Just burying her nose in a delicate bunch made her smile. They matched her teeth in shape and their pearly white color.

Dr. Senckenberg lost two wives in childbirth, his third wife to cancer. He also lost all his children from the first two marriages. As a widower, he donated most of his funds to the medical offices in Frankfurt, as well to as the development of patient care and improved educational facilities for doctors. He was also the founder of the Frankfurt University library and the Frankfurt Civic Hospital. Tragically, he did not witness its completion, as he took a deadly fall from a scaffold of the cupola.

Both historic figures had been remote scientists. Today these two professors take on a retrospective role as two mentors who are dear to me, while I imagine that unknowingly to all of us, they may have grandfathered me into my journey in medicine. They suddenly have come to life as witnesses of my first destined steps toward the medical world. They contribute to my conviction that every station along my path was perfect.

More recently I received a distinct nod from the universe that affirmed my present sense of purpose and belonging. A frail elderly gentleman arrived at our clinic for his cataract surgery. I noticed his nicely tailored blue shirt. Besides my job of numbing his eye with local anesthesia, it is common practice to supplement this technique with IV sedation. I thought he would fare better without the latter, since he had suffered a slight stroke. Instead I chose to just hold his hand throughout this short procedure to reassure him of my presence. Surgery went smoothly. Shortly after we returned to the recovery room, his wife graciously informed me that I would receive a sizable donation for the charity of my choice.

A rush of disbelief and gratitude flooded me all at once. Such a gift was totally unexpected and as grand as winning the lottery. While I struggled for words and to keep my composure, its purpose became clear very quickly. Here was an opportunity to contribute to Dr. Vicky Guzman's outreach program in El Salvador in addition to giving anesthesia during our one-week mission. On this day my professional knowledge of sophisticated techniques and drugs paled when compared to the ripple effect of a simple act of kindness. Thanks to the generosity of this gentleman, our quiet interaction could materialize into shoes for the "Barefoot Angels" and steer them away from the smoldering dump. My heart skipped and jumped all the way home, knowing that I could serve as an instrument for the greater good of those less fortunate than I.

Adorno said, "For a man who no longer has a homeland, writing becomes a place to live."[10] Writing my story has taught me to know where I belong and, more importantly, where I don't belong anymore. Just yesterday, while filling in temporarily at my former hospital, I had a grave reminder of the moments of terror that within seconds can annihilate years of an uneventful anesthesia practice. The sudden inability to ventilate a patient with oxygen for pathological reasons hit hard and drove home that even though the patient survived, my career is dead. It was the final jolt to walk away from it still intact.

I found a way to phase out my career in a gentler and less risky professional setting. There, arm in arm with my patients, I can walk out of the clinic with my sunglasses and a smile. Leisurely, I wait on a bench, with a bag of books, for my husband to take me home.

---

10 *Minima Moralia.* Reflections from Damaged Life, p87. (First published in German in 1951.) London (NLB).

Disclaimer

Chronological childhood events are told as I remember them from my own experience, my siblings' experience, and my parents' stories around the fireplace. Family and friends described agreed to be mentioned by their first names.

For my career-related vignettes, while they are true in content, I chose to change patient names and other characteristics to protect individual identity.

As previously stated, I am deeply grateful to all family members, patients, friends, and colleagues who have shaped and contributed to my life lessons.

Timeline

December 3, 1889 ; My grandmother, Marie-Louise d'Harnoncourt, born in Ecka, Hungary

December 11, 1906; My father, Albert Julius Troll, born in Frankfurt, Germany

May 1, 1923; My mother, Felicitas Marianne Von Carstenn, born in Austria

August 13, 1940; Albert & Felicitas Troll, married in Frankfurt, Germany

October 16, 1943; My brother, Sven Axel Troll , born in Linz, Austria

April 18, 1944; Senckenberg residence bombed

April 1945; End of World War II

June 14, 1946; Gabriele Felicitas Troll , born in Frankfurt, Germany

November 8, 1947; Baptized-Godparents aunt Alice & Hans Priegnitz, Stuttgart, Germany

1947; Moved to temporary housing in Mitteldick/ Frankfurt

1948; Returned to Senckenberg Avenue home

April 21, 1952; March 25 1956 - Bonifatius Grundschule, Elementary School/ Frankfurt

May 5, 1955; First Communion confirmation

April 11, 1956; Comenced Bettina High School in Frankfurt

April 6, 1959 - My sister "Cita" Felicitas Mariella, born in Lugano, Switzerland

March 1963; Left Bettina High School to relocate to Ireland

May 1963; Family relocated to Dungarvan Ireland

January 3, 1966; My grandmother " Omi" died

Summer 1969; First visit to United States as medical student, Staten Island Hospital

June 26, 1970; Graduated University College Cork Medical School, Ireland

July 1970; Began internship St. Vincent Hospital, Worcester, Massachusetts

July 1971; Anesthesia Residency, Yale University, Connecticut

July 1973; Appointed Chief Resident, Yale New Haven Hospital

August 1975; Recruited by Harrington Memorial Hospital, Southbridge, Massachusetts

October 1980; First back surgery

October 1984; Our father passed away in Ireland

October 1985; Six months sabbatical in Germany, relocated Mom to Frankfurt

April 1986; Returned to United States for new job at Ophthalmic Surgicenter, Boston, Massachusetts

July 1986; Met my husband, Robert Roden

September 1989-Married to Robert Roden

August 1992; Staff anesthesiologist at Massachusetts Eye & Ear Infirmary, Boston

May 1999; Mom moved to Nursing Home in Bad Wimpfen, Germany

June 2003; Repeat back surgery

January 2006; Total knee surgery

January 2007 Moved to Juno Beach, Florida, new job at Bascom Palmer Eye Institute

September 30, 2007; Our mother passed away in Germany

My brother Axel, my sister Cita, and me, September 2007.
Bad Wimpfen, Germany